British Black and Asian Shakespeareans

RELATED TITLES

Julius Caesar and Me: Exploring Shakespeare's African Play
Paterson Joseph
978-1-3500-1118-2

Adrian Lester and Lolita Chakrabarti: A Working Diary
Adrian Lester and Lolita Chakrabarti
978-1-3500-9277-8

Shakespeare and Postcolonial Theory
Jyotsna G. Singh
978-1-4081-8554-4

British Black and Asian Shakespeareans

Integrating Shakespeare, 1966–2018

Jami Rogers

THE ARDEN SHAKESPEARE
LONDON • NEW YORK • OXFORD • NEW DELHI • SYDNEY

THE ARDEN SHAKESPEARE
Bloomsbury Publishing Plc
50 Bedford Square, London, WC1B 3DP, UK
1385 Broadway, New York, NY 10018, USA
29 Earlsfort Terrace, Dublin 2, Ireland

BLOOMSBURY, THE ARDEN SHAKESPEARE and the Arden Shakespeare
logo are trademarks of Bloomsbury Publishing Plc

First published in Great Britain 2022

Copyright © Jami Rogers, 2022

Jami Rogers has asserted her right under the Copyright, Designs and Patents Act, 1988, to be identified as the author of this work.

For legal purposes the Acknowledgements on pp. x–xi constitute an extension of this copyright page.

Cover image: Julius Caesar, 2009: Noma Dumezweni as Calpurnia.
Photo by Ellie Kurttz © RSC

All rights reserved. No part of this publication may be reproduced or transmitted in any form or by any means, electronic or mechanical, including photocopying, recording, or any information storage or retrieval system, without prior permission in writing from the publishers.

Bloomsbury Publishing Plc does not have any control over, or responsibility for, any third-party websites referred to or in this book. All internet addresses given in this book were correct at the time of going to press. The author and publisher regret any inconvenience caused if addresses have changed or sites have ceased to exist, but can accept no responsibility for any such changes.

A catalogue record for this book is available from the British Library.

A catalog record for this book is available from the Library of Congress.

ISBN: HB: 978-1-3501-1292-6
PB: 978-1-3501-1488-3
ePDF: 978-1-3501-1294-0
eBook: 978-1-3501-1293-3

Typeset by Integra Software Services Pvt. Ltd.

To find out more about our authors and books visit www.bloomsbury.com and sign up for our newsletters.

CONTENTS

List of figures viii
List of tables ix
Acknowledgements x
Notes xii
Abbreviations xiii

Introduction: Forgotten Shakespeareans 1
    Shakespearean pioneers, 1866–1947 7
    Shakespearean pioneers, 1950–1965 13

1 'Difficult to justify this casting without sounding racist': breakthroughs and stereotypes, 1966–1972 19
    Macbeth, Royal Court, 1966 24
    The Tempest, Mermaid Theatre, 1970 27
    The Black Macbeth, Roundhouse Theatre, London, 1972 31
    'Difficult to justify this casting without sounding racist' 33

2 'Why weren't we auditioned?': the 'Black canon' and the battle for Othello 37
    'Why weren't we auditioned?' 39
    Reclaiming Othello 42

3 From 'suitable roles' to leads, 1980–1987 49
    'Black roles' at the RSC 53
    Macbeth, Young Vic, 1984 54
    Leading roles, 1984 55
    Rosaline, RSC, 1984 58
    'Othello was an Arab', RSC, 1985 61
    Emergence of a new 'Black canon' 63
    RSC 1986 65
    'They're nurturing you' 68

Antony, Contact Theatre, 1987 70
Isabella, RSC, 1987 71
Julius Caesar, Bristol Old Vic, 1987 75

4 Owning Shakespeare – Temba, Talawa and Tara Arts, 1988–1994 79

Romeo and Juliet, Temba, 1988 81
Antony and Cleopatra, Talawa, 1991 82
Troilus and Cressida, Tara Arts, 1993 85
King Lear, Talawa, 1994 87

5 Cracking the glass ceiling, 1988–1996 93

'You can't have a West Indian actor playing a Welsh poet…' 95
… But West Indian opera singers can speak the verse? 97
Troilus 98
Young lovers 101
Rosalind 102
Portia 106
The Shakespearean glass ceiling, 1988–1996 109
'Are we saying we're white people?' 112
'That wouldn't have happened here' 115
Birmingham Repertory Theatre, 1993–1996 116

6 'Monarchs to Behold': 1997–2003 121

'I belong here' 124
Othello, National Theatre, 1997 126
Women of colour: pushing against the glass ceiling, 1998–1999 127
RSC, 1999 131
Troilus and Cressida, National Theatre, 1999 134
Identity and colourblind casting 136
Adrian Lester, Hamlet, 2000 138
David Oyelowo, Henry VI, 2000 142
Romeo and Juliet, Mu-Lan, 2001 144
Adrian Lester, Henry V, 2003 146
The peak of progress? 148

7 Progress postponed, 2004–2011 151

'There's a few more parts we could play, you know' 153
Tragic heroes and the Shakespearean glass ceiling, 2004–2011 155

Cross-cultural casting 157
'I think I need you to do an accent' 159
Maids and prostitutes, stereotyping Lucetta and Bianca 163
A new dawn 167

8 Shakespeare from multiculturalism to Brexit, 2012–2018 171

Julius Caesar and *Much Ado About Nothing*, RSC, 2012 173
Othello 178
Joseph Marcell, King Lear, Shakespeare's Globe, 2013 182
Shakespeare's histories, 2013–2015 185
Paapa Essiedu, Hamlet, RSC, 2016 189
'It was a lack of faith' 195
Black Theatre Live's *Hamlet* and Talawa's *King Lear*, 2016 197
Alfred Enoch, Edgar, *King Lear*, Talawa, 2016 200
Women of colour in Shakespeare, 2016–2018 201
Josette Simon, Cleopatra, RSC, 2017 205
'They never asked me' 207
Sheila Atim, Emilia, *Othello*, Shakespeare's Globe, 2018 208
Troilus and Cressida, RSC, 2018 210
Coda – 2019 … and beyond? 213

References 217
Index 223

FIGURES

1 Abraham Sofaer (Claudius) and Dorothy Greene (Gertrude) in *Hamlet*. Old Vic Theatre, London, 1935. Photo by © Hulton-Deutsch Collection/CORBIS/Corbis via Getty Images 9
2 Jumoke Debayo, Femi Euba and Zakes Mokae as the Witches in *Macbeth*. Royal Court Theatre, London, 1966. Photo by Central Press/Hulton Archive/Getty Images 26
3 Rudolph Walker as Othello. *Othello*, Young Vic Theatre, London, 1984. Photo by Donald Cooper/Photostage 44
4 Joseph Marcell as Othello. *Othello*, Lyric Theatre, Hammersmith, London, 1984. Photo by Donald Cooper/Photostage 45
5 Josette Simon as Rosaline. *Love's Labour's Lost*, Royal Shakespeare Company, Stratford-upon-Avon, 1984. Photo by Donald Cooper/Photostage 59
6 Ben Thomas (Lear) and Mona Hammond (Fool). *King Lear*, Talawa Theatre Company, 1994. Photo by Donald Cooper/Alamy Stock Photo 89
7 Adrian Lester (Rosalind) and Patrick Toomey (Orlando). *As You Like It*, Cheek By Jowl, 1994. Photo by John Haynes 106
8 Michael Wildman (Margarelon), Dhobi Oparei (Hector), Chu Omambala (Paris), Oscar James (Priam), Vernon Douglas (Helenus), Peter de Jersey (Troilus), Mark Springer (Deiphobus). *Troilus and Cressida*, National Theatre, 1999. Photo by Donald Cooper/Photostage 135
9 Kulvinder Ghir as Feste. *Twelfth Night*, Albery Theatre, London, 2004. Photo by Photoshot/Getty Images 162
10 Paapa Essiedu (Hamlet) and Natalie Simpson (Ophelia). *Hamlet*, Royal Shakespeare Company, Stratford-upon-Avon, 2016. Photo by Donald Cooper/Alamy Stock Photo 194

TABLES

1. African-Caribbeans cast in *Julius Caesar* by the RSC, 1968–1983 54
2. Performers of colour playing one of the three largest parts in Shakespeare plays, 1984 56
3. Parts in which actors of African-Caribbean or south Asian heritage were cast three or more times, 1980–1987 64
4. Performers of colour in the Royal Shakespeare Theatre, 1986 66
5. Performers of colour in the Swan Theatre (X), 1986 67
6. Performers of colour in the Royal Shakespeare Theatre, 1990 98
7. First casting of actors of colour as young male lovers 102
8. Total roles played by people of colour by play, 1988–1996 109
9. *Twelfth Night* characters by number of times cast 110
10. Roles most and least frequently played by performers of colour, 1988–1996 111
11. Performers of colour in National Theatre Shakespeare productions, 1963–1992 113
12. Number of times performers of colour played male title roles in Shakespeare in Britain, 1966–1999 139
13. Plays ranked by total number of roles played by performers of colour 152
14. Integrated vs all-white productions in the 1990s and 2000s 152
15. Total leading roles cast, by genre, 1988–2011 153
16. Patrick Robinson's roles in *Macbeth*, 1986–2018 154
17. Roles ranked by total times played by performers of colour in Britain, 1966–2011 156
18. First casting of a performer of colour in the six largest roles of *Richard II* 169
19. Performers of colour appearing in the 'Shipwreck Trilogy', Royal Shakespeare Theatre, 2012 174
20. Title roles played in British productions, by actor 184

ACKNOWLEDGEMENTS

This book would not exist without Tony Howard who hired me as Research Assistant on the AHRC-funded Multicultural Shakespeare project at the University of Warwick and then allowed me free rein to create the British Black and Asian Shakespeare Performance Database. Without Tony and his vision to create a resource documenting the contributions of practitioners of colour, and his support of my continuing access to the Database and the resources at Warwick, there would, quite simply, be no *British Black and Asian Shakespeareans* in print. Susan Brock and Steve Ranford were also instrumental in helping build this Database from the ground up and whose help throughout was invaluable.

This book is about practitioners and their work. None of this would have been possible without their generous donations of time and recollections of both the Shakespearean parts they have played and their experiences in the industry: Akintayo Akinbode, Sheila Atim, Rakie Ayola, Nicholas Bailey, Paul Bazely, Lolita Chakrabarti, Sam Dastor, Noma Dumezweni, Alfred Enoch, Paapa Essiedu, Ray Fearon, Jamie Garven, Kulvinder Ghir, Marcus Griffiths, Amber James, Paterson Joseph, Iqbal Khan, Martina Laird, Adrian Lester, Daniel York Loh, Wyllie Longmore, Joseph Marcell, Patrick Miller, Tanya Moodie, Lucian Msamati, Cyril Nri, Theo Ogundipe, Patrick Robinson, Leon Rubin, Lucy Sheen, Josette Simon, Natalie Simpson, Julie Spencer, David Thacker, Ben Thomas, Cathy Tyson, Jatinder Verma, Rudolph Walker, Graham Watts, David Yip, Ashley Zhangazha.

My parents, Jim and Roxanne, who have suffered my addiction to Shakespeare for decades.

Thanks also to Hugh Quarshie, who graciously answered fact-checking queries about his career; Raad Rawi for his background information about the Duke's Playhouse, Lancaster repertory in the 1970s; Edward Bennett for introducing me to Iqbal Khan; Melody Brown for the loan of a foot pedal, which made the interview transcription easier; Kevin Fitzmaurice for his insight into the production process for Iqbal Khan's *Much Ado About Nothing*; Tina Price at Tina Price Consultants; Mary Davies for helping me acquire material during the lockdown; Jeanmarie Bishop for sharing her recollections about Zakes Mokae; Stuart Hampton-Reeves and Paul Prescott for supplying much-needed volumes in the middle of the global pandemic when all the libraries were shut; the Shakespeare Institute Library's Kate Welch for helping to check references while the library has been closed to visitors; Andrew French for identifying everyone in the *Troilus and Cressida* photo; David Thacker, Margot Leicester, Jan Pick for helping with the cost of photographs for this book; Tony Howard and David Taylor for their invaluable diligent notes on numerous drafts of this manuscript; Mary Stewart Burgher for her stellar copyediting.

The encouragement and support of friends and colleagues have kept this project on track: Jen Baker, Liz Barry, John Byrne, Paul Chahidi, Nigel Clauzel, Anna Coombs, James Cooney, Imogen Cooper, James Corrigan, Mumba Dodwell, Emma Fielding, Katie Forstyth, Kim F. Hall, Margo Hendricks, Kobna Holdbrook-Smith, Andrew Howard, Bella Howard, Ben Howard, Janice Howard, Rebecca Johnson, Steven Kavuma, Debbie Korley, Margot Leicester, Kevin McCurdy, Jodie McNee, Morgan Lloyd Malcolm, Emma Manton, Karen Mapplethorpe, Ken Nwosu, Chinonyerem Odimba, Jan Pick, Erin Quill, Sarah Rappaport, Sule Rimi, Colin Ryan, Adam Smethurst, John Stempin, Katy Stephens, Stephanie Street, Elizabeth Thacker, Paddy Toomey, Harry Waller, Lydia Wanstall, Aly Woodhouse, Karen Woodhouse, Danny Lee Wynter.

Special thanks to the Society for Theatre Research for a grant to help with research and interview expenses.

NOTES

Unless otherwise indicated, interviews quoted in this volume are with the author. (Interviews with Alby James and Bill Alexander were with Tony Howard for the Multicultural Shakespeare project oral archive.) The interviews included in each chapter are listed below:

Introduction: Rakie Ayola, Lolita Chakrabarti, Adrian Lester, Wyllie Longmore, Joseph Marcell.

Chapter One: Jeanmarie Bishop, Wyllie Longmore, Cyril Nri, Lucy Sheen, Rudolph Walker.

Chapter Two: Joseph Marcell, David Thacker, Rudolph Walker, David Yip.

Chapter Three: Paterson Joseph, Daniel York Loh, Wyllie Longmore, Joseph Marcell, Cyril Nri, Patrick Robinson, Leon Rubin, Lucy Sheen, Josette Simon, David Thacker, Cathy Tyson, Rudolph Walker, Graham Watts, David Yip.

Chapter Four: Lolita Chakrabarti, Kulvinder Ghir, Alby James, Cyril Nri, Ben Thomas, Jatinder Verma.

Chapter Five: Bill Alexander, Rakie Ayola, Paul Bazely, Jamie Garven, Paterson Joseph, Adrian Lester, Joseph Marcell, Patrick Miller, Cyril Nri, Patrick Robinson, Julie Spencer, David Thacker, Rudolph Walker.

Chapter Six: Bill Alexander, Rakie Ayola, Nicholas Bailey, Paul Bazely, Sam Dastor, Noma Dumezweni, Ray Fearon, Paterson Joseph, Adrian Lester, Daniel York Loh, Josette Simon, Cathy Tyson.

Chapter Seven: Paul Bazely, Kulvinder Ghir, Martina Laird, Cyril Nri, Patrick Robinson, Ashley Zhangazha.

Chapter Eight: Akintayo Akinbode, Sheila Atim, Rakie Ayola, Alfred Enoch, Paapa Essiedu, Marcus Griffiths, Amber James, Iqbal Khan, Martina Laird, Adrian Lester, Joseph Marcell, Patrick Miller, Tanya Moodie, Lucian Msamati, Cyril Nri, Theo Ogundipe, Josette Simon, Natalie Simpson, Julie Spencer, Rudolph Walker, Ashley Zhangazha.

The capitalization of Black has not been retroactively applied when referencing works that were printed before style guides were revised.

ABBREVIATIONS

AP	The Associated Press
BEP	*Bristol Evening Post*
BOVTS	Bristol Old Vic Theatre School
BP	*Birmingham Post*
CL	*Country Life*
DM	*Daily Mail*
DT	*Daily Telegraph*
ES	*Evening Standard*
FT	*Financial Times*
Guardian	*The Guardian*
ILN	*Illustrated London News*
NT	National Theatre
NYT	National Youth Theatre
NYTimes	*New York Times*
RADA	Royal Academy of Dramatic Art
RP	Received Pronunciation
RSC	Royal Shakespeare Company
RST	Royal Shakespeare Theatre
TSTT	*The Stage and Television Today*
SMT	Shakespeare Memorial Theatre
ST	*Sunday Telegraph*
STimes	*Sunday Times*
Times	*The Times*
ToI	*Times of India*

Introduction: Forgotten Shakespeareans

The history of the integration of Shakespeare in Britain begins with an African-American émigré, Ira Aldridge. Born in 1807 in New York, and unable to pursue an acting career in America, Aldridge left for England while still a teenager. He made his British stage debut as Othello in 1825 at the Royalty Theatre in London's East End. Between 1825 and 1848 Aldridge toured the country with a repertory that mixed Shakespeare with what would later come to be called 'Black parts', characters specified as African-Caribbean. One of Aldridge's recurring 'Black parts' was Oroonoko, an African prince forced into slavery in an adaptation of Aphra Behn's novella of the same name.

Having started his career playing 'Black parts', Aldridge increasingly challenged the status quo, performing what were, by default, considered 'white parts'. In 1831 Aldridge tested out four new roles in Hull, Yorkshire, all of which were white characters: 'Italian and Scottish Robin Hoods, a Russian count, and a Greek wild man' (Lindfors 2011: 204). Aldridge also expanded his Shakespearean repertory after 1833, playing Shylock, Macbeth and Richard III while touring in Ireland (Lindfors 2011: 287). Notably, Aldridge also played many of his Shakespearean triumphs in whiteface. He eventually added King Lear to his credits and revived *Titus Andronicus* for the first time in 128 years, 'which [Aldridge] arranged to have blended with a melodrama specially written for him… so he could play Aaron the Moor as a hero rather than a villain' (Lindfors 1999: 349).

Aldridge's brief spell as manager of The Coventry Theatre is a little-known aspect of his career. Arriving in the Midlands town in January 1828, his talent won over its sceptical inhabitants. There he 'received more favourable attention in the press than anywhere else he had performed' during his first years as a professional actor (Lindfors 2011: 132). The Coventry Theatre had been badly run and, seizing the chance to remain in a city that had given him a warm welcome, Ira Aldridge took over as its actor-manager for a short season. Although Aldridge's tenure at the Coventry lasted only a few months, its importance should not be underestimated. Aldridge was the first person of African descent known to have taken charge of a theatre building in Britain and it would be 190 years before there was a second (Kwame Kwei-Armah at London's Young Vic).

This book traces the history of those who followed Aldridge and whose contributions to British Shakespeare have largely gone unacknowledged. The remainder of this chapter first offers an overview of Aldridge's legacy before chronicling the pioneering performers of colour working between 1866 and 1965 who came after him. The remaining eight chapters, organized chronologically, chart the history of integrated casting since 1966 through the experiences of actors who have followed in the footsteps of those first pioneers and the changing contexts in which they worked. The foundation of this history was the creation of the British Black and Asian Shakespeare Performance Database, an open access digital humanities resource that has identified over a thousand practitioners of African-Caribbean, south Asian and east Asian heritage who have been involved in 1,300 professional productions of Shakespeare in Britain since 1930.

This book also hinges on interviews with nearly forty practitioners of colour, forming an oral history of integrated casting. Their experiences are presented alongside casting data from the British Black and Asian Shakespeare Performance Database which, when combined, present a picture of an industry that continues to marginalize people of colour. The interview material also gives space for practitioners from African-Caribbean, south Asian and east Asian heritages to discuss the roles they have played, providing their perspectives on the playwright that binds them together: William Shakespeare. This aspect of the book is invaluable, as performers of colour continue to be marginalized by theatre historians, including in recent volumes by Stanley Wells (*Great Shakespearean Actors*) and Barbara Roisman Cooper (*Great Britons of Stage and Screen*). Out of twenty-two performers, Cooper's volume includes twenty-one white actors with Ben Kingsley the only actor of colour included; only Ira Aldridge features in Wells' book. Similarly, out of seventy-four contributors to the influential six-volume Cambridge University Press *Players of Shakespeare* series, Adrian Lester and Ben Kingsley are the lone minority ethnic voices discussing their playing of a Shakespearean character. These editorial decisions have contributed to the eradication of African-Caribbean, south Asian and east Asian performers from the historical record, maintaining the status quo fiction that 'great' Shakespearean actors are white. This volume seeks to redress that balance.

This history is also the story of racism in Britain, as seen through the prism of Shakespearean production. The database contains a feature that counts the number of times a performer of colour has been cast in a Shakespeare role, displayed in descending order (see Rogers 2021a for more on the database). It is the tool that shows most succinctly where the disparity and inequality is located for performers of colour on the British Shakespearean stage. When the British Black and Asian Shakespeare Database was officially unveiled to the public at the Tricycle Theatre (now the Kiln) in Kilburn, north London in January 2016, performers reflected on what the identification of a glass ceiling through casting data meant. As Paterson Joseph told *The Stage*, 'Anecdotally, we've talked about it, but seeing it in that official way is a reassurance that we're not imagining our ghettoisation into the more minor roles' (14 January 2016).

Ira Aldridge stands as a beacon for many of the performers whose work features in this book. The unearthing of both his acting career and his status as the first Black theatre manager has been invaluable for people of colour, as Rakie Ayola explains:

> I think Ira Aldridge's legacy is hugely important because it gives us someone to hold on to. We have someone we can refer to who was very visible at the time. And that's massively important and it means that, when talking to younger actors, he is a name we can put in the conversation. And not just actors. I was talking to some girls at Manor Girls School, it's a comprehensive. It was Black History Month and behind me was a screen of faces coming up, people through time. And I started my speech by saying, 'Here's somebody whose name isn't up there, whose face isn't up there. I understand why, but let me tell you about [Ira Aldridge].' And when you tell his story to a bunch of fifteen-, sixteen-, seventeen-year-olds, their eyes light up when you say what he did and where he did it and when he did it. And you repeat that, 'Let me just tell you when this was happening.' And they go, 'Really?' And I say, 'Yeah.'

Wyllie Longmore, who emigrated from Jamaica in 1961, remembers when he arrived in Britain:

> Nobody had ever heard of [Ira Aldridge] and when I used to mention him to people when I was teaching (and every time I encountered

a Black actor), I used to say, 'You should know this person. He is your forebear. He is the beginning in this country for you.' [The response would be:] 'Who's Ira Aldridge?'

One of the few memorials to Aldridge in Britain was a bronze plaque bearing the African-American actor's name. It was once attached to the back of a seat in the auditorium of the Shakespeare Memorial Theatre in Stratford-upon-Avon, where he played Othello in April 1851.[1] It was one of thirty-three similar plaques honouring great Shakespeareans including Richard Burbage, David Garrick, Edmund Kean, William Charles Macready, Sir Henry Irving and Ellen Terry: all were white performers.

In his history of African-Americans in New York City, *Black Manhattan*, James Weldon Johnson briefly recounts his involvement in fundraising for that plaque:

> In December 1928, at the request of the committees organized for the purpose of rebuilding the Shakespeare Memorial Theatre at Stratford-on-Avon [*sic*], I undertook to plan the raising of one thousand dollars by coloured people in the United States for the endowment of an Ira Aldridge Memorial Chair in the theatre. A committee was formed and the money promptly raised and forwarded through the American Shakespeare Foundation to the Shakespeare Memorial Fund in England.
>
> ((1930): 86–7)

That Ira Aldridge's legacy was left to African-Americans poses questions about his erasure from British history. As the British actor of St Lucian heritage Joseph Marcell observes, the reasons are not complicated:

> Well, he's a Black man in a white society, so he has to fade out. There's no future. I think if he were in a Black society, it might be different. But yes, once his powers had waned, there was really no interest in him. But he did achieve quite a lot. And that's really the thing we have to face.

Marcell first discovered Aldridge 'when I was 18 years old at a library in Nunhead in Peckham. And was astonished. And I kept it all the way through my formative years.' Marcell, like James Weldon Johnson, is one of the many people who have kept Ira Aldridge's legacy alive.

Marcell was a founder member of Paines Plough theatre company, where he developed professional partnerships with both the white playwright David Pownall and the white director John Adams. At Paines Plough in

---

[1] The Royal Shakespeare Theatre auditorium was rebuilt and reconfigured, reopening in 2010. I have been unable to trace the current whereabouts of the Ira Aldridge plaque.

the mid-1970s, Pownall wrote plays with key roles for Marcell, including *Motorcar* and *Richard III, Part Two*. Marcell takes up the story:

> Then [Pownall] asked me: Did I have any ideas of Black heroes that I would like a play about? I suggested Ira. He'd never heard of him. We got in touch with the Arts Council and [one of Aldridge's first biographers] Herbert Marshall (Mildred Stock was dead by then), so we spent a lot of time with Herbert Marshall and we worked on [the play].

The result of this collaboration was *Black Star*, written by David Pownall, directed by John Adams, staged at the Octagon Theatre, Bolton in 1987 and starring Marcell as Ira Aldridge. As the *Manchester Evening News* describes it, the play was 'set in Russian-occupied Poland in 1865 and takes a beady-eyed look at politics as well as the problems of being a Black actor in a white society' (5 March 1987). The parallels between Aldridge's career and those of his successors are a running theme in more recent work, as performers of colour continued to honour Aldridge and keep his legacy alive.

A quarter of a century later, Wyllie Longmore took to the stage in a one-man show, *Speak of Me as I Am: A Conversation with Ira Aldridge*. Longmore developed the piece with playwright Maureen Lawrence, taking it on a small-scale tour around Britain in 2011 and again in 2013. Longmore elaborates:

> I did it here [at the Royal Exchange, Manchester] a couple of times and then I toured it around, as far as Tara Arts in London. And the basic premise is: I have this lectern, I'm standing at the lectern and Ira and I speak. I was looking at it again the other day, because Maureen and I had a conversation about it, and I was thinking: *So much has happened.* When I was speaking to Ira, all my difficulties about being an actor in this country came out. All my difficulties about playing Shakespeare and who can play Shakespeare and who is Shakespeare for and who dares to speak Shakespeare. All of that came out because through my whole career I've had to deal with that.

'It's a meditation on how things have changed – and how they haven't at all', the actor told Kevin Bourke (Creativetourist.com, 4 April 2013).

Lolita Chakrabarti's 2012 play, *Red Velvet*, begins and ends with Ira Aldridge in his dressing room in Lødz, Poland shortly before his death in 1867. In the final scene, Aldridge sits at the mirror putting on make-up in preparation to play King Lear. As the stage direction says, 'He dips his sponge into the [make-up] pot and starts to white up his face' (2012: 94). The complexities of Ira Aldridge whiting up to perform Shakespeare are articulated by Adrian Lester, who played him in the original production at London's Tricycle Theatre:

For me, it is a redressing of an imbalance, an act of saying, 'Fuck you! I will play these roles the same way you play others.' Many people saw it as an admission of defeat in some way. For them it was, 'I need to do this otherwise I won't be accepted'. Both views are real. Which is it? Ira plays Shylock the way white actors played Othello. In my mind he should have been able to play Shylock without whiting up, but the audience wouldn't have accepted that. The more ignorant the audience, the more narrowminded. The more limited their ability to accept any point of view except their own.

Neither Chakrabarti nor Lester had heard of Ira Aldridge until 1998, nearly a decade after they had both left RADA. Chakrabarti recalls:

Adrian did a reading about Ira Aldridge at the Brighton Theatre Festival. It was excerpts from the 1958 biography. Adrian came back and said to me, 'Have you heard of this guy?' And I knew nothing. Neither of us knew anything him about him. I'd been writing for a couple of years and I thought: This sounds interesting. So I started to follow the trail.

Chakrabarti's play centres on Aldridge's appearance as Othello at Covent Garden in 1833, a moment of professional triumph that ran squarely into British racism. The events depicted are a century-and-a-half old, but the play's language embodies twenty-first-century realities for performers of colour. The actress and writer of south Asian heritage felt a personal connection with Aldridge that spanned two centuries. Chakrabarti explains:

At the time, I was just following my instinct: his story held me and I needed to write it. I told a million different versions of this story over the years because there's so many versions, in one life. In retrospect I was trying to tell some of my own story through him because I intrinsically understood his journey: he was an actor of colour in a white society where people didn't want him. And that's how it sometimes felt in 1990 when I came out of RADA, where people were thinking, 'We're not quite sure what to do with you.' I'm not at all suggesting that my journey was anywhere near like his, but I definitely identified with him. When you read his reviews in Russia, it is clear that this was a man driven by creative excellence. It's not colour; it is creative excellence. I often wonder how did he have the vision to think beyond the limitations of society? When I was younger, I was cast as a non-English speaking Asian character on a TV show. I felt constrained by the limitation of that vision from the writer, director and producer but when you are cast in a role and you accept it, you have to play what is written.

This history of the integration of British Shakespeare is the story of that transcendence of performers of colour over society's limitations, which continue to operate well into the twenty-first century. Personal triumphs are mixed with the collective constraints of an industry riddled with stereotyping and institutional racism. This is also the story of the pioneers, from Ira Aldridge to performers of colour in the twenty-first century, who continue to break the Shakespearean colour bar.

Shakespearean pioneers, 1866–1947

Samuel Morgan Smith was the second performer of African descent known to have carved out a career in Britain, working as an itinerant actor for sixteeen years. Born in Philadelphia, Pennsylvania in 1832, he travelled to England in 1866 with his wife and infant son. Within a week of his arrival, Smith had taken over the management of the Theatre Royal in Gravesend in Kent. Billed as a 'coloured tragedian from the United States', Smith first tackled Othello and within three weeks also added Hamlet, Macbeth, Richard III and Shylock in *The Merchant of Venice*, the latter role drawing praise in the press from as far afield as London. Smith's venture in Gravesend was short lived and the theatre closed in June, but he had rapidly made his mark and secured positive comparisons with Ira Aldridge (Lindfors 2018: 47–57). The publicity Smith garnered at the Theatre Royal enabled him to launch his career and, two weeks after leaving Gravesend, Smith became the second performer of African descent to play Othello in London at the Olympic Theatre, where he also briefly played Shylock and Hamlet. Smith's Hamlet was deemed a major success in Belfast in 1867, the year Ira Aldridge died in Poland (Lindfors 2018: 104–5).

Smith intermittently maintained his career for a decade, interspersing theatrical engagements with drawing room entertainments. In 1878 he decided to focus on the latter and his traditional theatrical career effectively ended, although excerpts from Shakespeare's plays remained in his repertoire. Smith succumbed to pneumonia in Sheffield in 1882 at the age of forty-nine and such was his theatrical standing that newspapers in both Britain and America published his obituary. The *Morning Post* wrote that he had been 'little known in London, but popular in the provinces' (Lindfors 2018: 239). Another half century passed before the third performer of colour appeared in professional Shakespeare in Britain, Paul Robeson. Robeson was one of only three performers of colour known to have appeared in a Shakespeare production in Britain between 1930 and 1947, along with Abraham Sofaer and Robert Adams.

Paul Robeson had initially intended to practise law, but racial prejudice forced an unintended career change. Robeson's early success came in a brace of Eugene O'Neill plays: *All God's Chillun Got Wings* and *The Emperor Jones*. His major break came in 1924 when he played the lead in the world premiere of *Chillun* with the Provincetown Players, located at the tip of Massachusetts' Cape Cod. Eugene O'Neill subsequently chose Robeson to play Brutus Jones in the London production of *The Emperor Jones* in 1925. Robeson returned to the West End in 1928 to play a part with which he would become indelibly associated, Joe in *Show Boat*. The Rodgers and Hammerstein musical was a resounding success and proved the catalyst for Robeson's first foray as Othello, a role that, as his biographer notes, 'had long been in the back of Robeson's mind that he would someday like to play' (Duberman 1989: 122).

Paul Robeson's first Othello, at the Savoy Theatre in London in 1930, marked a major step towards an integrated British Shakespeare. The white producer Maurice Browne directed the production and ineffectually played Robeson's Iago, while the white actress Peggy Ashcroft was cast as Desdemona. In preparation for the role, Robeson took elocution lessons from Ira Aldridge's daughter Amanda, who passed down to him the earrings her father had worn as Othello the previous century (Duberman 1989: 91).

Robeson was a sensation as Othello, partly because of the novelty of an African-Caribbean in the role. The *Daily Express* somewhat gleefully noted, 'He will not require any make-up to appear as the Moor' (7 May 1930) and a *Sunday Express* headline referred to him as 'Robeson, a Coal-Black Othello' (18 May 1930). Almost all the reviews were, as Tony Howard observes, 'notoriously tainted by last-gasp Imperial racism. They presented Robeson's Othello as a primitive' (2010: 97). One nugget in the press coverage, however, stands as a monument to the unfulfilled potential of not just Robeson, but of many who followed him.

'Paul Robeson would like to play Hamlet', was the headline of the same *Daily Express* article that observed he would not have to black up to play Othello. Robeson had actually said that he did not aspire to Hamlet, but harboured ambitions to tackle other Shakespearean tragic leads: '[Othello] is my first Shakespeare play. I hope some time to act Macbeth and Shylock and finally King Lear, but not Hamlet' (7 May 1930). That Robeson's only Shakespeare role was Othello says volumes about the thwarted ambitions of classical actors of colour to this day. Even eighty years on from Robeson's Othello, no performer of colour has played that particular line of parts, although Abraham Sofaer came closest.

Born in Rangoon, Burma in 1896, Abraham Sofaer was an actor of Burmese-Jewish heritage whose career lasted more than six decades and spanned two continents. He made his theatrical debut with a walk-on part in *The Merchant of Venice* at the Palace Theatre in Newark-on-Trent in 1921 for the Charles Doran Shakespeare company, whose members included the white Shakespeareans Ralph Richardson and Donald Wolfit. Abraham Sofaer spent the 1930s working in radio for the BBC and on the West End stage, building an enviable Shakespearean résumé that few performers of colour have since been allowed to match.

Abraham Sofaer's Shakespearean CV rivalled that of his white contemporaries, playing Bolingbroke in *Richard II*, the title role in *Henry IV*,

FIGURE 1 *Abraham Sofaer (Claudius) and Dorothy Greene (Gertrude) in* Hamlet. *Old Vic Theatre, London, 1935. Photo by © Hulton-Deutsch Collection/CORBIS/ Corbis via Getty Images.*

Claudius in *Hamlet*, Leontes in *Winter's Tale*, Berowne in *Love's Labour's Lost*, Malvolio in *Twelfth Night*, Don Pedro in *Much Ado* and Othello in the 1930s and 1940s for the pre-eminent directors of the day, including Tyrone Guthrie and Michael Macowan.

Sofaer's work garnered praise from the critics, including the notoriously acerbic James Agate, who found Soafer's Bolingbroke 'a rich, resonant, and finely controlled performance; here is the man who is master not only of England but of himself' (*STimes* 15 October 1934). Sofaer was a Shakespearean pioneer in the sense that his portrayals were the first time many of Shakespeare's leading roles were played by a performer of colour. In some cases, like Berowne in *Love's Labour's Lost* and as King Henry IV, Sofaer still remains the only performer from African-Caribbean, south Asian or east Asian heritage to play the roles professionally in Britain. With other leading roles, it would be decades after Sofaer's pioneering firsts that another performer of colour would be cast. For example, Sofaer played Bolingbroke in 1934 but it was not until 2019, when Sarah Niles played Bolingbroke in *Richard II* at Shakespeare's Globe, that a second performer of colour would take the part. The lack of representation following Sofaer's career is indicative of the continued exclusion of performers of colour from leading roles in the Shakespearean canon.[2]

At the height of his classical career, Sofaer had a level of celebrity that found him participating in a fundraising evening for the National Theatre Appeal in 1935 alongside white performers such as Gwen Ffrangcon-Davies, Godfrey Tearle and Sybil Thorndike. In 1949, Sofaer was chosen as principal guest at a champagne reception celebrating twenty-one years of *Spotlight*. He had appeared in every edition of the casting directory since its first and attended the reception, along with other established actors, 'to drink the champagne they have helped to buy [with their subscription fees]', quipped the *Daily Mail* (9 March 1949).

In 1936, the British playwright and novelist Charles Morgan, who also served as *The New York Times*' drama critic for nearly two decades, praised Sofaer's classical acting talent:

> [Abraham Sofaer] speaks verse as no other English actor – not excepting Gielgud – can speak it, so using its music to clarify its meaning that, under his control, even the language of [Berowne] in *Love's Labour's Lost* comes to the audience with unfading lucidity.

In the same article Morgan identified the inequalities of an industry growing increasingly discriminatory, observing that Abraham Sofaer:

> has never held the place he deserves among the leaders of his profession. The reason is his appearance, which, though handsome, is so pronouncedly Oriental as to limit the range of his parts... though he has played with success in pieces of all kinds, he is chiefly known, as far as leading roles are concerned, as a Shakespearean actor. The reason is the simple one that, while Shakespeare created Shylock and Othello and even Iago, who may be cast as an Oriental, if you please, modern playwrights, unless they want an Oriental villain for a thriller, generally write for Occidental leads.
>
> (*NYTimes*, 12 July 1936)

Abraham Sofaer's range of parts also included two of Shakespeare's tragic heroes: Othello and King Lear. The former he played at the Old Vic in 1935, but that performance seems to have fallen short of expectation. Ironically,

---

[2] This history of integrated casting of Shakespeare in Britain gives increasing importance to the definition of a leading role as it moves forward in time. Using the statistics in the *RSC Complete Works*, this book designates leading roles as those listed in that volume as the three largest parts in each of Shakespeare's plays.

Sofaer played Iago in another production of *Othello* at the Shakespeare Memorial Theatre in Stratford-upon-Avon in 1943, about which J. C. Trewin observed:

> Mr. Abraham Sofaer's Iago is beautifully spoken, but this demi-devil of the Renaissance, his mind as swift to villainy as his hand to the sword-hilt, could hardly have been mistaken for Othello's 'man… of honesty and trust.' It would be happier, perhaps, if the parts [of Iago and Baliol Holloway's Othello] were exchanged.
>
> (*Observer* 25 April 1943)

Played in the same season as his Iago, Sofaer's King Lear was one of his finest performances, in which Trewin felt 'he can show his true quality':

> Unlike many Lears, he waxes as the tragedy mounts; his later pathos is better than his early passion…. The meeting with Gloucester, the recognition of Cordelia, the tenderness of "We two will sing like birds i' the cage," the last fading into death – these passages are movingly and subtly done. Not every inch a Lear, but a performance of rare accomplishment.
>
> (*Observer* 23 May 1943)

Sofaer's performance made such an impression on Trewin that the critic continued to sing its praises well into the 1980s.

Despite its obvious quality, Sofaer's King Lear has all but vanished from the annals of theatrical history. Sally Beauman's comprehensive history of Stratford's theatre, *The Royal Shakespeare Company: A History of Ten Decades* does not mention it nor the actor himself. Jonathan Croall's only reference to Abraham Sofaer in *Performing King Lear: Gielgud to Russell Beale* is as an atmospheric wartime aside that pairs the production with Donald Wolfit's in London and notes that their directors 'offered fast-paced, heavily cut versions, designed to enable audiences to catch their last trains home in the blackout' (2015: 7). After the Second World War, the open doors that had given Sofaer access to a wide variety of Shakespeare's roles closed behind him as a Shakespearean colour bar rapidly appeared. Few of his fellow south Asians would tread in his footsteps until the beginning of the twenty-first century.

The third Shakespearean of colour in this period, Robert Adams, was, as Stephen Bourne notes, 'once Britain's leading black actor but, like many black achievers in British history, he is now forgotten' (2001: 72). Born in what was then British Guiana (now Guyana), Adams trained originally as a teacher. He arrived in Britain in the 1920s and at first could find only low-paid work. A sports promoter encouraged Adams to try professional wrestling, and he eventually became the heavyweight champion of the British Empire. Adams moved into the fledgling film industry in the mid-1930s, sustaining a career on stage and screen into the 1950s. Adams was also an early antiracist activist, working with Dr Harold Moody as a founder member of the League of Coloured Peoples in 1931 and establishing the Negro Arts Theatre toward the end of the Second World War (Bourne 2001: 72–6).

By the early 1940s Robert Adams had gained sufficient stature as an actor to be considered for the role of Othello for the Old Vic, mostly likely Tyrone Guthrie's 1942 production. His experience presaged that of many African-Caribbeans who followed him, as he recounted to *Film Reel Review*:

> Everything was apparently satisfactory, then suddenly a continental was given the chance to do it. While he brought a much needed virility to the part, his lack of knowledge of English was obviously a drawback, his power was alright but his inflections were ludicrous. Yet what was the explanation for rejecting me? I was told that I had not sufficient Shakespearian technique.
>
> (qtd in Bourne 2001: 75)

Adams would have been the fourth man of African descent to play Othello in London, after Aldridge, Smith and Robeson, had Guthrie not chosen the Czech actor Frederick Valk instead.

Although passed over for Othello, Robert Adams has the distinction of being the first African-Caribbean performer to play a Shakespeare role on television in Britain. In 1947 he appeared as the Prince of Morocco in the BBC's production of *The Merchant of Venice*, which starred Abraham Sofaer as Shylock. In the early days of television, programmes were broadcast live and therefore had much in common with theatre performances. Whether from illness or the stress of the live broadcast in what was likely a hot studio on 1 July 1947, Adams was unable to finish the performance. Both *The Times* and the *Manchester Guardian* reported the incident the next day, with the latter providing the most complete account:

> Mr. Adams had started his opening speech to Portia, played by Margaretta Scott, when he hesitated and then stopped. The voice of the prompter was audible giving him his cue, but Mr. Adams suddenly crumpled and fell out of the viewers' sight. At the end of the play the announcer explained that Mr. Adams fainted, but had later fully recovered and gone home. The "casket scene," in which the Duke [sic] of Morocco should have reappeared was not given.
>
> (*Manchester Guardian* 2 July 1947)

Scott, who described Adams as 'a splendid black actor' recalls she was 'left saying "Help, ho! The Prince!" and so on' as he lay in front of her. In live television, she said, 'There were always surprises' (qtd in Bourne 2001: 67).

Shakespearean pioneers, 1950–1965

The foundation of what is now called integrated casting was laid in the years between 1950 and 1965. During this period, the casting of performers of colour was largely limited to the appearance of African-Caribbeans as servants along with a handful of performers as Othello, including Gordon Heath and Errol John. Gordon Heath had landed the role of Brett Charles, a decorated African-American war hero who returns to his home town in the American South after fighting in Europe, in Arnaud d'Usseau and James Gow's *Deep Are the Roots* for its Broadway debut in 1945. The production made its way across the Atlantic in 1947 for a run at Wyndham's Theatre in London, with Heath again in the lead.

After his success in the West End, Gordon Heath was hired to play Othello by the white theatre critic and writer Kenneth Tynan. Gordon Heath had experience with Shakespeare in America prior to coming to Britain, playing Hamlet at the Hampstead Institute in Virginia in a 1945 production by African-American scholar and practitioner Owen Dodson. Errol Hill praised Heath's performance: 'This Hamlet was a haughty and passionate prince. He spoke Shakespeare's verse beautifully but could also be emotionally explosive when the occasion required' (1984: 131).

Heath was the first actor of African heritage to play Othello in Britain since Robeson, twenty years before. Tynan's production toured to mining towns in the north of England and Wales, in what the programme describes as 'a joint arrangement between the Arts Council of Great Britain and the Miners' Welfare Commission'. Reviews of Heath's Othello in the local papers were largely positive, with the *South Wales Echo* describing his performance as 'a well-planned, impressive and often moving performance' (21 November 1950), while the *Western Mail* declared, 'Gordon Heath acted Othello's tragic role brilliantly' (20 November 1950).

By the 1950s the Shakespearean colour bar was becoming increasingly apparent, as men and women of colour arrived to follow their dreams. One was the actor, playwright and historian Errol Hill who, in 1949, became the first Trinidadian to win a British Council scholarship to RADA. The catalogue of injustices he faced as an aspiring actor of colour in Britain included whiting-up to play parts at RADA and racist comments from the school's principal, who, as Hill recalls, thought he was 'from darkest Africa and thought my cultivated English accent was a remarkable achievement'; Hill had spoken English all his life (1984: xx).

Two observations in Hill's reflections on England in the early 1950s demonstrate the nearly unscalable mountain that performers of colour faced as aspiring classical actors in Britain. First, Hill noted that, 'In my three years of playgoing in Britain I never saw a black actor in Shakespeare' (1984: xx). The second involves his fellow Trinidadian, Errol John, who also attended RADA in the early 1950s. Errol Hill praised John's acting skills effusively, saying that seeing him perform 'only confirmed my opinion that he was an actor of tremendous potential and I predicted a great career for him in the classical theater. That has not happened. He is black' (xxi).

Errol John is perhaps best remembered in Britain for his 1958 play, *Moon on a Rainbow Shawl*, which he wrote as an antidote to the lack of opportunities afforded performers of colour in Britain. Although classically trained, John's only professional work in British Shakespeare was one season at the Old Vic in 1962–1963 appearing in *Merchant of Venice*, *Measure for Measure* and *Othello*. In fact, Errol John was a late addition to the company, having been cast as Othello as a replacement for a white, Danish actor, Mogens Wieth, who had died of a heart attack shortly before rehearsals began (*The Stage* 11 October 1962). In his first Old Vic role, John received praise for his performance as the Prince of Morocco, with the *Daily Mail* observing that, with the part, the actor 'stakes out his claim [for Othello]' (18 October 1962).[3]

Critics laced their reception of Errol John's Othello, however, with the subtle language of exclusion. Arts journalism often serves to maintain the status quo, apparently threatened by John's takeover of the title role of Shakespeare's tragedy from a deceased white actor. The *Tatler* critic, Pat Wallace, observed John was 'a fine West Indian actor but not yet of the stature for this tremendous part' (13 February 1963). J. C. Trewin for *The Illustrated London News* was blunter, claiming 'The nobility of the Othello music is lost: the verse is chopped up like parsley on a board' (16 February 1963). Bernard Levin of the *Daily Mail*, having first called Caspar Wrede's *Othello* 'a disastrous production', had similar views, but more explicitly claimed that the Trinidadian did not belong in Shakespeare's play:

> Now [the Old Vic has] fallen into the even deeper error which holds that because Othello is a black man he ought to be played by one, and engaged the West Indian actor, Mr. Errol John, because he is the right colour. But so, I must point out, is an Englishman with burnt cork on or a very heavily sunburnt Chinaman or a Lithuanian Jew before an audience wearing dark glasses.... What counts in an Othello is not the colour of his skin but the quality of his acting and of his verse speaking. And on these counts, particularly the second, Mr. John does not even begin to be an adequate Othello.
>
> (31 January 1963)

The hostility with which the press greeted Errol John's Othello was a by-product of the growing animosity to immigration from Britain's former colonies. In later decades, criticisms about 'verse speaking' became part of

---

[3] Mogens Wieth was originally cast as both Othello and Antonio in *The Merchant of Venice*. The white actor Esmond Knight was due to play the Prince of Morocco in the latter. After Wieth's death, Esmond Knight took over as Antonio and Errol John was brought in to play Othello, the Prince of Morocco and Barnadine in *Measure for Measure*.

an arsenal that white reviewers used in protest at the growing presence of performers of colour in Shakespeare productions.

Perhaps the unlikeliest of the mid-century Shakespearean pioneers, Cy Grant was born in British Guiana in 1919. He joined the Royal Air Force in 1941 and was shot down over the Netherlands in 1943, spending the next two years as a prisoner of war. Returning to Britain, he qualified as a barrister but, like Paul Robeson before him, the racism of the legal profession dictated a career change to entertainment.

Cy Grant first encountered Shakespeare early in his career, when he auditioned for Laurence Olivier's 1951 double bill of Shakespeare and George Bernard Shaw. Grant played two parts in Shakespeare's *Antony and Cleopatra*: a Nubian Messenger and an Attendant on Cleopatra. As performers of colour were almost entirely excluded from the national playwright at that time, this was both a remarkable achievement and an early indication of persistent stereotyping of African-Caribbeans as servants. Like many fledgling actors, however, Cy Grant found the experience of spear-carrying invaluable in learning his craft. An illuminating anecdote of Grant's Shakespearean debut in *Antony and Cleopatra* also speaks to the continuing denial of racism in Britain. Grant recalls that Laurence Olivier suggested to him that he not travel to New York with the productions when they transferred to Broadway at the end of 1951. The reason given was Olivier's concern that Grant would experience racism in America. Cy Grant rebutted Olivier's argument with, 'Come on, Larry, this country is just as racist as America.' Olivier relented and Grant made his Broadway debut (qtd in Pines 1992: 45).

Two productions – Tony Richardson's *Pericles* and John Hale's *Comedy of Errors* – became early examples of cultural appropriation used to manufacture opportunities for performers of colour in Shakespeare. In 1958 Edric Connor became the second African-Caribbean to perform Shakespeare in Stratford-upon-Avon, after Ira Aldridge's Othello over a century earlier. Connor played Gower in *Pericles* for the white director Tony Richardson at the Shakespeare Memorial Theatre. Richardson had originally invited Paul Robeson to play the part, having 'reconceived' it to be 'a tale of endurance sung by Robeson' (Howard 2010: 103). Robeson had been unable to take up the part because the United States government had, in retaliation for his political activism, confiscated Robeson's passport in 1950, not returning it until 1959. Rather than cancelling the production, Richardson kept the concept and hired Edric Connor as the African-American's replacement, for what would be Connor's only Shakespeare role.

Cy Grant's trip to America with Olivier's company proved a decisive turning point in his career. While there he discovered the popularity of West Indian calypso; upon his return to England, he bought a guitar and began working in cabaret (*Leicester Evening Mail* 8 April 1960). Calypso brought Cy Grant fame, particularly through the light entertainment programme, *Tonight*, in which the news of the day was transformed into calypso songs performed by Grant. It was his fame as a calypso singer that led to Grant's second Shakespeare production at the Bristol Old Vic in 1960. Grant was cast as an extra-textual Ballad Singer in John Hale's production of *Comedy of Errors* with calypso music its star attraction, at least for *The Stage*:

> One felt that a suitable finale might have been for Mr. Grant to have led dancers, actors and audience triumphantly out of the theatre to weave through the Bristol streets in Conga formation. Whatever the purists may have to say about it, the production makes a rollicking end-of-season entertainment.
>
> (7 July 1960)

As popular as it was, the director had used Grant's heritage – and musical fame and talent – to provide the entertainment, but did not allow him to speak Shakespeare's text. Without Cy Grant uttering a line of blank verse, the calypso *Comedy* was also cultural appropriation as exclusion. Hale's production was the first in a long line of cross-cultural productions that included performers of colour, but depicted them as foreign and therefore not British.

The final Shakespeare role of Cy Grant's career was Othello at the Phoenix Theatre in Leicester in 1965. The production was not well received, partly because Laurence Olivier's interpretation was fresh in reviewers' minds. 'Anyone who does not have Olivier's genius would do well not to try and achieve his style', wrote the *Guardian*'s Gareth Lloyd Evans. 'Cy Grant has, with a seeming eye on the master, played Othello at the Phoenix, Leicester, not wisely and not well' (21 October 1965). As with Errol John's Othello two years previously, Evans' major objection to Grant was one that remained in currency for another thirty years: a claim he could not speak the verse.

What follows is the history of the integration of British Shakespeare since 1966, which is also the struggle to refute claims like those levelled at Cy Grant and Errol John. As the entertainment industry does not exist in a vacuum, it is worth noting that the changes to British Shakespeare mirror the country's evolution on matters of race. The backdrop to this book are events that have shaped Britain, beginning with the introduction of the irascibly racist character of Alf Garnett on the BBC in 1966 and Enoch Powell's overtly racist anti-immigration 'rivers of blood' speech in 1968. As the 1960s waned into the 1970s, the National Front and related neo-Nazi organizations targeted people of colour by methods that ranged from firebombing houses to throwing banana peels onto football pitches as the national game became more inclusive of African-Caribbean players.

This history of integrated casting also spans the 1981 inner city uprisings, the 1993 murder of teenager Stephen Lawrence by a gang of white, racist youths and the 1999 release of the Macpherson Report, which brought the term 'institutional racism' into the national lexicon. Through all of this, running from chapters 2 to 6 in this volume, there were advances, sometimes incremental, in the integrated casting of British Shakespeare. The decade after September 11, 2001 saw an increase in anti-immigrant rhetoric and a simultaneous decline in the diversity of British Shakespeare (chapter 7). The London 2012 Olympic Games were shrouded in multicultural unity and chapter 8 begins with two productions that were part of that summer's Cultural Olympiad, running in tandem with the Games: the RSC's staging of *Julius Caesar* and *Much Ado About Nothing* with casts comprised solely of African-Caribbean and south Asian descent, respectively. Chapter 8 spans the most recent period of British history, from the embracing of multiculturalism during the Olympic Games through to Brexit, which has also fostered a national backlash against diversity. As Stuart Hall presciently observed, 'There has been change – but racism just as deeply persists [in Britain]' (1999: 192). As the country goes, so does British Shakespeare.

1

'Difficult to justify this casting without sounding racist': breakthroughs and stereotypes, 1966–1972

When the British Parliament passed the Race Relations Act of 1965, it was the first piece of legislation to directly address racial discrimination in Britain. While it was relatively toothless – civil, rather than criminal law – and excluded employment and housing, it was an acknowledgement that postwar immigration was changing Britain. While there is no direct correlation between this legislation and classical theatre, notable castings followed in the wake of that ground-breaking legislation. In 1966, four performers of colour were cast in British professional Shakespeare productions: one in *Othello* (Rudolph Walker as Othello) at the Malvern Festival Theatre and three in *Macbeth* (Zakes Mokae, Femi Euba and Jumoke Debayo as the Weird Sisters, more commonly known as the Witches) at the Royal Court in London. All four were immigrants: from Trinidad (Walker), South Africa (Mokae) and Nigeria (Euba and Debayo); all but one (Debayo) were male. Four performers of colour appearing in Shakespeare in the course of a single year was also a British theatrical record.

The role of Othello serves as a benchmark to which we will return throughout these pages, an illustration of the slow integration of classical theatre in Britain. As we saw in the opening chapter, despite a handful of exceptions after 1930, the norm in 1966 remained a white actor blacking up to play Othello. Perhaps no performance of the role was more culturally significant in Britain than Laurence Olivier's in 1964. Its reach remains extensive, as the production was filmed and released as a commercial venture in 1966 and is still available for purchase.

Olivier spent two and a half hours each night on his make-up, shifting his skin tone from 'Brighton white' to 'Caribbean black' (Holden 1988: 378), covering himself from top to toe in various hues of brown and black, donning a black curly wig and lowering his voice by an octave. As biographer Anthony Holden notes, Olivier's 'lifelong obsession with make-up reached its apogee' with *Othello* (1988: 378). Holden links Olivier's 'Black man' directly to recent Caribbean immigration into Britain, noting the actor 'would look and talk and walk like a negro – yes, a contemporary negro, of the kind now commonplace (if only recently) on the streets of London', who were living and working on the South Bank 'on the edge of the black ghettoes developing in the south of the capital' (378). Olivier justified going to these extraordinary lengths to change his physical appearance by stating, 'I had to *be* black. I had to feel black down to my soul. I had to look out from a black man's world' (Olivier 1986: 106). Of course, a white man covered in thick, ebony make-up (which prevented him from kissing his Desdemona, lest it rub off on her) had no way to 'be black'. Instead, Olivier presented his audience with, as Ayanna Thompson says, 'a full-on racial impersonation' (2016: 82).

As Colin Chambers shows, blackface minstrelsy 'became central to the performance of Otherness in Britain, rising with the abolition of slavery' (2011: 52) and it continued well into the twentieth century. *The Black and White Minstrel Show* debuted on the BBC in 1958 and ran for twenty years, its final episode broadcast in 1978, well over a decade after Olivier's *Othello*. An episode of ITV's popular 1990s series *Jeeves and Wooster*, with Stephen Fry and Hugh Laurie, featured characters – including Laurie's Bertie Wooster – made up as blackface minstrels. The programme's US co-producers could not air the episode, as American audiences were arguably more attuned to the blatant racism.

The practice of blacking up was so ingrained in British culture that even Olivier's wife, Joan Plowright, considered it when playing Portia in Jonathan Miller's 1970 production of *The Merchant of Venice* (*Guardian* 7 October 1974):

> At one stage, we had the idea she might black up when she goes to Venice: it would at least have made plausible the fact that her husband never recognises her and it would have given a certain point to the Duke's 'Came you from old Bellario.' I could also have imitated Larry as Othello. But in the end, perhaps wisely, we dropped the idea.

Black men in Britain who aspired to be professional actors in the 1960s faced a very different reality from that of the white men who casually blacked up to play Othello. As Rudolph Walker recalls, 'What I faced as a young actor in this country is that Shakespeare – and especially the leading role in

Shakespeare – wasn't meant for us, as Black actors'. The data in the British Black and Asian Shakespeare Performance Database corroborate Walker's statement. Performers of colour filled few roles, leading or otherwise, in Shakespeare productions before the early 1980s, even after the influx of immigrant talent after the Second World War.

The exclusion of actors of colour from Shakespeare was symptomatic of an attitude within the wider British entertainment industry. A 1950s-era BBC internal audit claimed that people of colour were represented in television drama, but only when a programme contained what decision makers called 'suitable roles' (Newton 2011: 106–7). The term is itself opaque, but what was most often meant were parts specifying a character's ethnicity, as with The Boy in Shelagh Delaney's 1958 play *A Taste of Honey*. The almost complete exclusion of performers of colour, driven by a perceived lack of 'suitable roles', marked the period when this story starts.

Like many of his contemporaries, Wyllie Longmore emigrated to Britain from Jamaica in the early 1960s. Having come across a prospectus for what was then the Rose Bruford College of Speech and Drama and aware of the precedent of previous students, such as fellow Jamaicans Yvonne Brewster and Trevor Rhone, Longmore arrived in London in 1961 intending to train as an actor. He eventually obtained a grant from Ealing council and enrolled in Rose Bruford's dual teacher–actor training course in 1965. Longmore's experiences at drama school help to paint a picture of an industry struggling with inclusion. 'It shocked me greatly when I discovered there were so few Black people at the college. In fact, one in every year practically', Longmore recalls of his time there.

Two key points from Longmore's years at Rose Bruford are indicative of prevalent industry practice: the expectation around accent and the ways in which Longmore himself was cast. Although a plethora of regional and international accents is now heard on contemporary British stages, as late as the 1980s actors had to suppress their natural accents in favour of Received Pronunciation (RP), the standard British dialect. Longmore found practical as well as professional reasons to succeed at the elocution lessons Bruford offered: 'If you didn't get rid of your accent and you came from overseas, your diploma said "overseas student", which meant that you probably couldn't teach here, couldn't work here.' In other words, students were expected to assimilate, to sound British by changing their way of speaking. This was particularly important in the acting profession, where any difference was carefully neutralized. As Lucy Sheen explains, in the 1980s drama schools were still 'pounding' regional dialects 'out of you' because:

> you had to speak in a particular way. The only way – especially for classical theatre – you could do that was to sound like a bad imitation of John Gielgud or Ralph Richardson or Laurence Olivier. RP was the language of the classics, particularly Shakespeare. So any kind of regional differences, any regional colour, was smacked out of you.

What was true when Sheen was entering the profession was exponentially more so in the 1960s when Longmore attended Rose Bruford. White actors, from both Longmore's generation and those acting in the early twentieth century, provide countless anecdotes about having to adapt their natural speaking voices. Performers such as Laurence Olivier and Alec Guinness did not, however, have to contend with the prejudice meted out to Wyllie Longmore and Rudolph Walker because of the colour of their skin.

While training at Rose Bruford, Longmore quickly discovered the struggles he would face in the profession in terms of how he was cast. He recalls, 'I was playing Colonel Fitzwilliam in *Pride and Prejudice* and I was the only Black boy in my year and so of course I had to play whatever the syllabus was.' Just as Ira Aldridge played roles like King Lear in whiteface, Longmore was required to white up to play Colonel Fitzwilliam. There were also few roles for him in Shakespeare during his training and never full productions, only Prospero in the opening scene of *The Tempest* and one scene as Bardolph in Shakespeare's history plays: 'I was never given any work in *Othello* and so I left college after three years with only that smattering of Shakespeare.'

For all its faults, Rose Bruford was more enlightened in casting Longmore than the wider profession at the time. He remembers, 'When I left, there was hardly any work for Black people. I graduated in 1968 and I came up here [Manchester] to audition at the Library Theatre for *A Taste of Honey*. That's where I was heading, really, that's the sort of role.' Longmore was not interested in playing servants and the other marginalized roles given to Black performers. Lacking acting opportunities and having a family to support, Longmore used his educational training at Rose Bruford to begin teaching at drama schools, first at Rose Bruford and then LAMDA, East 15 and Webber Douglas, before eventually joining the drama department at the University of Manchester. Longmore nevertheless returned to acting in the early 1980s and made history by being the first performer of colour to play a succession of Shakespearean roles in both Manchester and London, including Mark Antony in *Antony and Cleopatra*.

The prevailing atmosphere in the late 1960s meant that actors of colour had limited opportunities to develop careers in mainstream theatre, film and television. This makes Rudolph Walker's early and largely unknown success in Shakespeare more remarkable, especially as he recounts that Shakespeare had been 'alien to me as a youngster growing up in Trinidad'. Walker arrived in England in 1960, the year before Longmore, having been encouraged to emigrate by his fellow Trinidadian pioneer, Errol John. Walker had planned to go to America, but John convinced him that the training was better in England (*Guardian* 22 October 2001). Walker spent his first few years in England working with amateur dramatic groups such as the Mountview Theatre Club and attending evening classes. Walker had his first experience acting Shakespeare in 1963, when an amateur company decided to stage

Othello and asked him to play the lead. This fortuitously provided Walker with what he calls a 'working knowledge' of the play, which allowed him 'that little extra luxury to do a little exploration' when he first came to play the part professionally.

In 1965, Walker found himself in a recurring role in a BBC television drama about a fictional Second Division football club, *United!* Immigration was gradually changing all aspects of British life, a trend that was reflected, on rare occasions, on television. First Division football clubs had engaged Black footballers as early as 1909, when Tottenham Hotspur fielded Walter Tull. By the end of the 1960s, a number of other clubs had hired their first Black footballers, including Portsmouth and Everton. The BBC's *United!* had incorporated this growing trend into its scripts, which meant that there was a 'suitable role' for an actor of African-Caribbean heritage. As Walker recalls, after he had filmed several episodes of *United!*:

> this offer came through to go to Malvern Festival Theatre to play Othello. I had a choice then of continuing in the television series because there was a short gap [in filming *United!*] and they were thinking of making my character a running character. I remember the executive producer saying 'If you take that job, the chances are that you might not get back into the series.' I thought: *You know what? The opportunity to play Othello professionally, I have more to gain by doing that.* I never got back into the series, but that was neither here nor there.

Rudolph Walker's casting as Othello in 1966 at the Malvern Festival Theatre went against the prevailing climate. The director, John Ridley, had contacted Walker directly about the opportunity, leaving his agent out of the loop. When Walker told her that he was going to be in *Othello*, she asked him, 'Which part are you going to play?' His agent's response shows how ingrained the idea was that African-Caribbean men were not considered for the lead in Shakespeare's tragedy. The reaction of the local paper – which announced Walker's presence in the three-week run with a front-page headline, 'Coloured actor as Othello' (*Malvern Gazette* 10 February 1966) – also reflected the rarity of his casting.

The Malvern Festival Theatre *Othello* with Rudolph Walker received little attention from the national press, making barely a ripple in theatrical history. The *Malvern Gazette* praised Walker's Othello as 'a striking figure, with a fine voice'. There were hints of prejudice in the review as well, as the author felt it necessary to point out that Walker had 'obviously analysed most carefully this character', a comment that contains centuries of stereotypes of African-Caribbeans having inferior intelligence and lacking in work ethic (*Malvern Gazette* 17 February 1966). This comment was mild, however, in comparison to what the national press would write in the 1980s as performers of colour attained leads with larger repertory theatres and the two subsidized national companies.

Director John Ridley was clearly more enlightened than his contemporaries. Walker himself notes:

> It was quite something for Malvern to do it. Certainly that a man of that era invited me to play Othello. It's not to say that I was a name or anything like that. I was just a young actor, sort of struggling, and he located me and said, 'You know, look, I want you to do that'.

Between 1966 and 1972, three other white directors played significant parts in the history of integrating British Shakespeare: William Gaskill, Jonathan Miller and Peter Coe. In *Macbeth* (Royal Court, 1966), *The Tempest* (Mermaid Theatre, London, 1970) and *The Black Macbeth* (Roundhouse Theatre, London, 1972), respectively, these directors cast actors from African-Caribbean heritage in significant roles in the canon.

These three landmark productions begin in earnest our history of a more inclusive Shakespearean landscape in Britain. Collectively all three were innovative while also conforming, consciously or unconsciously, to dominant perceptions of African-Caribbeans in British society. These early examples of integrated Shakespeare set precedents, in both the casting of ethnic-minority performers in Shakespeare roles and the framing of the actors' work. These productions also mark the beginning of a glass ceiling that has been a feature of Shakespearan production for the past fifty years. They demonstrate the ways in which the concept of 'suitable roles' was adapted to the Shakespearean medium.

Macbeth, Royal Court, 1966

On the surface, London's Royal Court Theatre is an unlikely venue to provide a seminal moment in the history of integrating Shakespeare. The Court's policy, according to former Literary Manager Graham Whybrow, was to 'conscientiously search for new voices, new playwrights, and new social worlds that hitherto hadn't been seen on the stage' (qtd in Little and MacLaughlin 2007: 20). The importance of this policy cannot be underestimated for Black British theatre history, as some of those new voices were writers of African-Caribbean heritage. In 1958 the company staged Lloyd Reckord's *Flesh to a Tiger*, swiftly followed by the premiere of Errol John's *Moon on a Rainbow Shawl*, which were 'the first in a long line' of work by 'African and West Indian authors and actors' that was 'unequalled by any other British theatre' (Findlater 1981: 46). Along with Lloyd Reckord and Errol John, the Nigerian playwright Wole Soyinka was active with the Royal Court Writers' Group, helmed in the 1950s by William Gaskill.

Wole Soyinka's success as a playwright in the mid-1960s led directly to the first known casting of performers of colour as the Witches in William Gaskill's *Macbeth*, starring Alec Guinness. Soyinka had joined the Royal

Court Writer's Group in 1957 on the strength of a play he had written while a student at the University of Leeds, *The Lion and the Jewel* (Little and MacLaughlin 2007: 59). Gaskill's involvement in nurturing the Writer's Group and his championing of Soyinka's work likely drew him to the Hampstead Theatre in June 1966. At that time, the Ijinle Theatre Company was producing what its publicity called 'a series of African plays' with Soyinka's *The Trials of Brother Jero* staged in a double bill with Athol Fugard's two-hander, *The Blood Knot*.

The casts of both one-act plays at the Hampstead included Fugard's frequent collaborator, Zakes Mokae, playing opposite the actor–writer in *Blood Knot* and the eponymous hero in Soyinka's *Jero*, along with two Nigerians of Yoruba heritage, Femi Euba and Jumoke Debayo. *The Trials of Brother Jero* takes place in Lagos, Nigeria and satirizes the hypocrisy of organized religion. One critic of the Hampstead production described it as a 'full-blooded religious jamboree that outdoes anything in *The Amen Corner*' (*Times* 29 June 1966). William Gaskill would likely have been preparing for the production of *Macbeth* at that time and he records in his memoir that one of the play's perennial problems 'is how to embody the supernatural without diminishing Macbeth's responsibility for his actions' (1988: 76–7). Whether or not the 'religious jamboree' element of *Brother Jero* triggered a parallel immediately, Gaskill notes that he cast Mokae, Euba and Debayo in *Macbeth* because he had 'enormously admired' their work in Soyinka's play at the Hampstead (1988: 78). The trio would become the first in a dubious tradition of actors of colour playing the Witches.[1]

While the three actors were undoubtedly cast on the strength of their work, an ingrained preconception of African culture also lurks not far beneath the surface. Photographs of the Nigerian and South African actors as the Witches show them in wigs of long white hair and sporting beards, even Debayo, who was the sole female of the group. Each Weird Sister had dolls and six hand puppets that they used for the prophecies and to illustrate the 'procession of kings' (*ILN* 28 October 1966). Gaskill's solution to the problem of the supernatural aspect of *Macbeth* clearly drew on the African heritage of his three actors.

Almost all the critics assessed Gaskill's *Macbeth* as an unmitigated disaster. While their objections were not limited to Gaskill's use of three African-Caribbean actors to play the Witches, their response indicated a deep-seated antipathy to performers of colour in mainstream theatre. '[P]lease do not tell us that the Jacobeans saw their Weird Sisters, "fairies or nimphes," just like this', wailed *The Illustrated London News* (28 October 1966) while

---

[1] This was not the first time in the performance history of *Macbeth* that the Witches were coded as other. In *The Politics of Parody*, David Francis Taylor notes that it was standard in the eighteenth century and into the nineteenth century that the Witches were played by male actors who 'specialized in physical comedy' (2018: 108). As comedic figures the Witches stood outside the regular dramatic action.

FIGURE 2 *Jumoke Debayo, Femi Euba and Zakes Mokae as the Witches in* Macbeth. *Royal Court Theatre, London, 1966. Photo by Central Press/Hulton Archive/Getty Images.*

the *Daily Mail*'s Peter Lewis noted that the 'apparitions' had 'simply raised a laugh' (21 October 1966). Critics also gave paternalistic descriptions of the three actors, redolent of imperialist attitudes, including 'kindly coloured folk' (*Guardian* 21 October 1966). Milton Shulman was perhaps the most hostile, his pen dripping with sarcasm as he injected the political debate about immigration into his review: 'With such a sunny climate it is perhaps not surprising that medieval Scotland, unaware of immigration quotas, was populated by amiable coloured folk who seem to have cornered most of the jobs as witches and murders' (*ES* 21 October 1966). Shulman's casual drawing of parallels between immigration and familiar tropes of violence, exoticism and immigrants 'taking jobs' was rooted firmly in British attitudes to race.

The one ingredient missing from these early critiques of the work of ethnic minority performers is overt claims that they were unable to speak the verse. These became a feature of press reaction to performers of African-Caribbean and Asian heritage, but the absence of such comments in 1966 speaks to such actors' rarity on the Shakespearean stage. The situation, however, was beginning to change and a second ground-breaking production in 1970 opened *The Tempest* up to integrated casting.

The Tempest, Mermaid Theatre, 1970

Norman Beaton arrived in Britain from British Guiana (later Guyana) in 1960, the same year as Rudolph Walker and a year before Wyllie Longmore. In British Guiana, Beaton had appeared in an amateur production of Molière's *Le Bourgeois Gentilhomme* and started a musical career. He founded a vocal group called the Four Bees, recorded eight singles, became the Calypso Champion of Guyana and had a number-one hit single in Trinidad and Tobago, all before emigrating to Britain. Beaton continued his career in music upon arrival, playing Liverpool's famous Cavern Club and London's Marquee Club. In 1965 Beaton began working in theatre as a composer and musical director, eventually taking on small acting parts in theatre, radio and television.

Beaton had also developed a lifelong love of Shakespeare, although he had few opportunities to hone his skills professionally. His early classical acting was with the Connaught Theatre in Worthing, where he worked as composer, lyricist and actor in the 1968 season. At Worthing, Beaton took part in a schools tour of an adaptation of Shakespeare's *Richard III*, played Solanio in *The Merchant of Venice* and the title role in an adaption of the same play by Christopher Denys called *Shylock X*. Two years later, Beaton auditioned for Jonathan Miller, presenting a reading of Ariel's 'You are three men of sin' speech (3.3.53–82). Miller offered him Ariel on the spot and told him, 'You're one of the most beautiful readers of verse I have ever heard' (Beaton 1986: 143).

Rudolph Walker worked with Jonathan Miller for the first time the year after playing Othello at Malvern. In 1967 at the Mermaid Theatre in London, Walker played the slave Babo in an adaptation of Herman Melville's novella, *Benito Cereno*, by the American Robert Lowell. Walker's casting was another example of an actor of colour gaining a role because the text specified ethnicity. The difference was that *Benito Cereno* had prominent parallels with the American Civil Rights Movement: for example, Walker's slave successfully mutinied on a slave ship. Robert Lowell explained, 'Melville wrote his story on the eve of the Civil War and it came into his work in an intuitive, clairvoyant way. All kinds of things were in my mind when I wrote the play – the Civil Rights issue most of all' (qtd in Billington 1988: 113).

Rudolph Walker found working with Miller on *Benito Cereno* 'a fantastic experience' and recounts that Miller also had 'a lot of good things to say about working with me – things that I wasn't party to, in that he said it to other people, that got back to me'. Given the overall climate actors of colour endured in the late 1960s, being told either subtly or with overt racism that they did not belong, Miller's glowing recommendation went against established norms. As a measure of Miller's esteem, *Benito Cereno* was the beginning of a rewarding working relationship. Walker explains, 'To crown it all, he invited me to come in and play Caliban' in his production of *The Tempest* in London, once again performing at the Mermaid Theatre.

Jonathan Miller hired a total of five performers of colour for his 1970 production of *The Tempest*. Norman Beaton and Rudolph Walker became the first to play Ariel and Caliban, the second- and third-largest roles in the play. In addition, Miller cast three women of colour as Iris, Ceres and Juno: Miriam Nathaniel, Dorothy Ross and Nell Hall, respectively. Miller's was also the first British professional production of Shakespeare to employ more than three actors of colour.

Miller had become fascinated by Octave Mannoni's anthropological study *Prospero and Caliban: The Psychology of Colonialism*. The key to Miller's exploration of *The Tempest* was his distillation of Mannoni's theory as 'the effect of the paternal white imperial conqueror on an indigenous native population' (Miller 1986: 159). This meant setting the production in the former British colony of Nigeria and having Ariel and Caliban represent two of its tribes: the Ibo and Hausa. As with *Benito Cereno*, Miller harnessed the contemporary within a fictional framework and Rudolph Walker recalls the director's 'twist' on Shakespeare's play was in the 'master and servant element, which was happening within African society. To me that worked.' Prospero was clearly the white master in Miller's *Tempest* and contemporary Nigerian politics mirrored the relationships between servants and master.

At the time of Miller's production, Nigeria had been engaged in a destructive civil war – also known as the Biafran War – since 1967. This conflict involved the three major tribes of Nigeria: the Hausa-Fulani of the north, the Yoruba of the west and the Ibo of the east. Miller chose to focus his postcolonial reading of *The Tempest* on the first and third of these major players in the Biafran War, the Hausa and the Ibo. A contemporaneous *Guardian* piece helps to illustrate the context in which Miller framed his *Tempest*, which described the Ibo as 'strongly Catholic, land-hungry, enterprising and ubiquitous (the "Jews" of Nigeria), but arrogant and ruthless when in power' and defined the Hausa as 'Moslem, backward and feudalistic but accustomed to ruling others with moderation' (*Guardian* 6 December 1969). Historian Michael Gould provides a more nuanced picture (2013: 2), noting that the:

> Northerners [Hausa] had historically failed to embrace western ideologies [equating to 'backward' in the *Guardian* description], continuing to favour their Muslim and Middle Eastern heritage... [and] failed to adapt to western ways.... Because the South [Ibo] had readily absorbed western ideology, its people were only too willing to fill this vacuum. This meant that much of the economic and administrative life of the North was controlled by people from the South.

While the dynamics of postcolonial Nigeria were more complex than these descriptions allow, they afforded Miller a ready parallel for his postcolonial reading of *The Tempest*. The director's concept used these basic outlines of Nigerian society to present a world where 'the Ibo tended to become deft, accomplished, westernized civil servants' and the Hausa 'tended to become totally demoralized and de-tribalized in servitude' (Miller 1986: 160). Miller's *Tempest* used these simplifications to illustrate Ariel as a civil servant (an Ibo) and Caliban as the type of Hausa Miller describes. While the overall concept was new, the interpretation of Caliban and, to a lesser extent, Ariel replicated traditional stereotypes of so-called primitive subservience.

The parallels between Gaskill's casting of the Witches in *Macbeth* and Miller's of Ariel and Caliban in *The Tempest* can be found within the contemporaneous 'suitable roles' framework. Rudolph Walker observes that the only parts available on television for non-white performers in the early 1970s were 'what we call stereotypes of black people – the black person being downtrodden, the black person carrying the spear' (qtd in Pines 1992: 78). In Miller's postcolonial context, Caliban and Ariel were 'downtrodden' and the Witches in *Macbeth* were 'carrying the spear'.

Rudolph Walker was aware of the stereotypes of Caliban and what he describes as the 'half-man, half-monster' presentation of him when played by white actors. Walker and his director were keen to break this tradition; as Walker puts it, 'one of the things that was very important' was that Caliban would be 'all human. There's no question about it, there is nothing demon or nothing animal about him. He was very, very human. I think that is one of the striking things that, for me, was very important in the production. Jonathan didn't want this half-animal and this half human.' For all that the casting of Beaton and Walker fell within the parameters of 'suitable roles', Miller viewed them not as monsters or spirits but as human beings.

After centuries of white conquerors, including the British, dehumanizing African peoples, Miller's was a radical approach. The *Evening Standard*'s

Milton Shulman resisted the production and reduced Ariel and Caliban to servants and collaborators (16 June 1970):

> Ariel, instead of the usual athletic sprite, is a rather sedate, world-weary Haitian butler who goes about his ethereal tasks with a magic whisk and looking for the most part as if his chief concern is overtime. Norman Beaton handles this novel interpretation with the circumspect dignity of an old hand from a domestic agency. The only evidence of Caliban's semi-human proportions is the fact that he wears a soiled, army greatcoat and Rudolph Walker's grumbling creature has the endearing quality of a rasping, grovelling, ingratiating Uncle Tom.

While Beaton later recalled that he had found Shulman's review 'most amusing' (1986: 144), Miller's *Tempest* was uncomfortable viewing for some critics. For the first time a clear Black-and-white racial binary had been staged in Britain through that most sacred of texts, the Shakespeare play.

Despite the carping of critics like Shulman, others praised Beaton and Walker. John Barber in the *Daily Telegraph* found that Ariel and Caliban were 'excellently played by two West Indian actors' (16 June 1970) and Peter Lewis in the *Daily Mail* likewise felt 'the strongest thing in the cast are the black actors – Rudolph Walker's great giggling Caliban and Norman Beaton's elegant native batman of an Ariel' (16 June 1970). The prevalence of the baseless idea that African-Caribbean actors were not 'suitable' for Shakespeare makes the praise for Beaton and Walker all the more remarkable.

The final image of the production obliquely referred to Miller's reading of Mannoni's work through the Nigerian prism, referencing the perceived differences between the Hausa and Ibo: 'Caliban shook his fist at the departing ship as Ariel lifted Prospero's bent staff and began to straighten it: one native rejected western technology, the other sought to appropriate it' (Vaughan and Vaughan 2011: 114). A second type of freedom was born as Beaton and Walker paved the way for performers of colour to play substantial roles in Shakespeare's play. In hiring two actors – Walker and Beaton – who were both African-Caribbean men and immigrants from Trinidad and British Guiana, respectively, Jonathan Miller, in Rudolph Walker's words, did 'something that wasn't done. It wasn't acceptable.' Jonathan Miller was also one of the people, along with David Thacker, who had the most impact on Walker's career. Walker feels that he was 'really, really, blessed with having two of the finest directors very early on in my career', who provided him with opportunities that were systematically denied to actors of colour. Norman Beaton expressed similar praise for Miller in his autobiography, and felt *The Tempest* was one of the highlights of his career: 'it was generally agreed that I had come through this rigorous test with flying colours. *The Tempest* was my first theatrical triumph in London' (1986: 144–5).

The Black Macbeth, Roundhouse Theatre, London, 1972

Peter Coe's *The Black Macbeth* at the Roundhouse in 1972 was the first recorded professional Shakespeare in Britain with an all-Black cast. One reporter noted, 'it is, we are assured [by Coe], not a gimmick but [done] "to put the important witch-craft element in a more credible setting"' (*ST* 9 January 1972). By 'a more credible setting', Coe referred to his transplantation of *Macbeth* from Scotland to Barotseland in Zambia. Alterations to Shakespeare's text were made to accommodate this shift. The Witches became 'ju ju' and the eponymous couple were rechristened Mbeth and Lady Mbeth. Other tweaks to Shakespeare's script erased any doubt that its locale was no longer Scotland, as shown by: 'We hear our bloody cousins are bestowed in Somalia and the Congo' and 'The devil damn thee white thou black-faced loon'. In his *Daily Telegraph* review, John Barber described the energy of the production, with 'masked and be-feathered dervishes in animal skins who dance to jungle-drums and intrude frequently into the action throughout'. Across the board, Barber builds the picture of a *Macbeth* infused with African tribal heritage; this left him dissatisfied because the actors' 'speech-rhythms and intonations are not ours' (24 February 1972).

Peter Coe had assembled a largely untrained cast of African, Caribbean and African-American heritage for *The Black Macbeth*. The actors were untrained in the manner critics would recognize as English stage conventions, epitomized by the technique of white stars such as Laurence Olivier, John Gielgud, Alec Guinness and Peggy Ashcroft. Many of the cast also spoke Shakespeare's verse in their natural accents, or one adopted based on the production's African setting. In the days before Barrie Rutter's Northern Broadsides guided British Shakespeare towards greater inclusion of regional and international accents, critics greeted speaking Shakespeare in anything other than RP with varying degrees of scorn, derision and superiority.

Critics dismissed most of the cast outright, largely on the basis of poor verse speaking, but rewarded two with accolades. Irving Wardle ebulliently praised Jeffery Kissoon's Malcolm (Meru) and Mona Hammond's Lady Mbeth, describing the latter as 'a reading of true passion and originality whose stone-faced exhaustion after the banquet and sleep-walk scene are as good as any I have ever seen'. Seemingly oblivious to the primary reason for his approbation of Hammond and Kissoon, the *Times*' critic continued, 'Both performances, interestingly, are delivered with the fluency of standard British acting' (24 February 1972). Wardle's use of 'interestingly' denotes an element of surprise that these actors could act as well as their white counterparts. This response to the 'fluency' of the verse speaking and the dismissal of the rest of the cast speak to deeply ingrained notions about the ownership of Shakespeare's plays, highlighting the ways in which speech has been used to exclude performers of colour from the classical canon. The African-American actor Paul Robeson had understood the importance of RP to the British theatrical establishment, taking elocution lessons from Amanda Ira Aldridge, Aldridge's daughter, when preparing to play Othello at the Savoy Theatre in 1930, in order to assimilate.

Some critics scrutinized *The Black Macbeth*'s African setting in ways that highlight cultural prejudices that still permeate white British society. First, the perception of the continent as exotic and, to a large extent, primitive is visible in the drums, animal skins and 'ju ju'/witch-doctors in Coe's recreation of Africa. Commenting on these aspects, Frank Marcus noted in the *Sunday Telegraph*, 'The tribal rivalries of ancient Scotland, the witchcraft, and the ghosts (although Banquo's remains surprisingly invisible here) have much in common with African folklore' (27 February 1972). While tribal ceremonies occur in Africa, media coverage partially drives western European and North American *perceptions* of the continent. In a recent *National Geographic* issue on race, the magazine issued a *mea culpa* for its own part in perpetuating these exotic images of Africans and their descendants in the western world (Goldberg 2018):

> … until the 1970s *National Geographic* all but ignored people of color who lived in the United States, rarely acknowledging them beyond laborers or domestic workers. Meanwhile it pictured 'natives' elsewhere as exotics, famously and frequently unclothed, happy hunters, noble savages – every type of cliché.

The use of African rituals within *The Black Macbeth* similarly perpetuated stereotypes of African-Caribbeans.

The portrayal of Malcolm also drew on imagery familiar to the contemporary white English audience. In Coe's production, Malcolm – who inherits his father Duncan's throne after Macbeth's death – was the Shakespearean equivalent of the western-educated African leader: 'The king's son… alone among ebony torsos and heavy fur robes, wears colonial khaki (an Oxbridge graduate perhaps?)' (*Observer* 27 February 1972). This very image of the Oxbridge graduate may have enabled reviewers to praise Kissoon's acting. Along with the 'colonial khaki' that had been seen in numerous films about the British Empire, Frank Marcus's perception of this particular son of a monarch included an image of postcolonial turmoil: 'Mr. Coe finds in his *Black Macbeth* a modern political analogy, namely a transition from feudal barbarism to a new-style military efficiency, represented by Malcolm (played with relaxed assurance by Jeffery Kissoon)' (*ST* 27 February 1972). In using the African setting, both for its tribal and postcolonial semiotics, Coe presented his largely white English audience with simple signifiers that were readily identifiable and simultaneously stereotypical.

'Difficult to justify this casting without sounding racist'

By 1972, the seeds of integrated casting in British classical theatre had been sown. Gaskill's *Macbeth*, Miller's *Tempest* and Coe's *Black Macbeth* were all firsts in providing opportunities to performers of colour. Each of these productions contained breakthrough moments for African-Caribbeans aspiring to classical theatre in the late 1960s and early 1970s. These firsts also had an unforeseen legacy: the Witches, Ariel and Caliban all feature in what I have called elsewhere the 'unofficial black canon' (see Rogers 2013). These roles frequently default to performers of colour who, in the twenty-first century, remain less likely to play Macbeth or Prospero. While these productions created huge opportunities for the actors who played these roles fifty years ago, the parts now inhabit a comfortable status quo beyond which many performers of colour are not allowed to pass.

Such castings also have origins in cultural stereotypes, specifically the exotic or the subservient. The use of African rituals in *The Black Macbeth* reinforced stereotypes of the continent's peoples as exotic or alien to the dominant white culture in which it was being performed. The portrayal of the Weird Sisters as witch-doctors in William Gaskill's *Macbeth* similarly capitalized on the white audience's preconceptions of Africans and their rituals. Gaskill was aware of the problematic nature of his cultural appropriation, writing in his memoir that it 'was difficult to justify this casting without sounding racist. Certainly they handled the supernatural without self-consciousness and in their white wigs they looked like something from the Kabuki' (1988: 78). Similarly, Jonathan Miller's concept for *The Tempest* was steeped in racial stereotypes of the subjugated, framed for the white audience by the Black faces in those roles. Caliban, in particular, has a long history of racial stereotyping, even without an actor of colour portraying the role. Trevor R. Griffiths notes that this has included portrayals of Prospero's 'slave' (1.2.309) as an '"underdeveloped native", ... a Darwinian missing link, and latterly, to some sensitive critics, an oppressed minority' (1983: 160). When the white actor Roger Livesey became the first blacked-up actor to play Caliban in 1934, the line between African heritage and the stock image of the character was explicitly drawn; the dominant white culture saw the so-called savage as synonymous with people of African heritage.

Although these productions capitalized on racial stereotyping, playing in them in the late 1960s and 1970s was also a major achievement. Cyril Nri explains about the role he would inherit from Norman Beaton in Miller's 1988 revival of *The Tempest*, 'Even though Ariel is outside of the central family, he's definitely within the central, intellectual kernel of the piece.' This is a concept that will recur because the act of being involved in the centre of the action – 'the intellectual kernel' – is key to the importance of the journey taken by African-Caribbean, south Asian and east Asian

Shakespeareans from 1966 to 2018. The period between 1966 and 1972 comprised breakthrough years precisely because performers of colour had finally been admitted into the heart of Shakespeare's plays in central, traditionally white roles. The norm at the time, as Norman Beaton noted in his autobiography, was that most work offered to actors of colour consisted of 'the very occasional character part on television or the already stereotyped and hackneyed roles that British playwrights have written into their plays' (1986: 104). Perhaps the real tragedy for this generation of performers was the lack of access to classical theatre, that prestigious corner of the arts that Norman Beaton called 'a closed shop' (*Guardian* 9 February 1979).

The *Guardian* obituary of Zakes Mokae, one of Gaskill's Witches, has a telling description as its subtitle: 'South African actor who helped break the taboos of apartheid' (10 November 2009). While it condenses for its readers the nature of Mokae's contribution to society, it also pigeonholes him into the type of work that dominated his career. Mokae came to Britain with Athol Fugard to stage the latter's play *The Blood Knot*, which tells the story of two brothers in South Africa under apartheid, one Black and one who passes as white. Fugard wrote the part of Zachariah, the visibly Black sibling, for Zakes Mokae and took the part of Morris in the play's premiere in Johannesburg, South Africa in 1960. According to Fugard, that was the first time 'that black and white performers had appeared on the same stage in South Africa', breaking taboos as well as the law under apartheid (*NYTimes* 15 September 2009). Mokae recalled, 'We took *The Blood Knot* to London and it was a success'; he remained in England afterwards to study acting because he knew 'there wouldn't be many roles for me in South Africa' (Solomon 1982: 27).

Mokae never completely escaped the shadow of apartheid and his best-known work was in story-telling about the apartheid experience, winning a Tony award for playing Sam in Fugard's *Master Harold... and the Boys* and appearing in Richard Attenborough's film *Cry Freedom*, among other distinguished work. The injustices and tragedies of South Africa's racial discrimination laced his personal history, including the execution of his 23-year-old brother in 1982. The social justice work he was best known for 'kept him in that place, that dark, sad, awful place where he had to spend so much of his time', his friend Jeanmarie Bishop recalled. She said that he had found it 'such a relief to be out of South Africa' when he arrived in London and he relished 'doing non-activist work' such as Gaskill's *Macbeth*, which had been 'great fun for him'. Bishop also said that Mokae 'was always being offered work, but he wanted to play fun parts. I'm sure he would have loved to have played Macbeth and he would have been brilliant in that part, but in 1961 in London, nobody was going to give him that part.' In his later years, Mokae had intended to do more Shakespeare in Las Vegas with the Nevada Shakespeare Company, which Bishop founded, 'but he had been diagnosed with Alzheimer's by then and it really set in at that time'. Mokae passed away before he could realize his long-held ambition to play more Shakespearean roles.

Norman Beaton likewise had a curtailed Shakespearean career, mostly because of the lack of access for performers of colour in British theatre. Despite his triumph as Ariel, Beaton's next opportunity to perform in a Shakespeare play came eleven years later, as Angelo in a Caribbean-set *Measure for Measure* at the National Theatre in 1981. The role was even more of a breakthrough than *The Tempest* had been; as Beaton puts it, 'I was once again a member of the National Theatre. Now, however, I would be one of the leading actors playing in Shakespeare' (1986: 224). Angelo was to be Beaton's second and final major Shakespearean role, although his ambition had been to play King Lear in Britain.

When Yvonne Brewster cast Norman Beaton as Lear for her 1994 production for Talawa Theatre Company, it seemed he would achieve one of his life's goals. Unfortunately, Beaton became ill shortly before rehearsals began and was replaced by Ben Thomas in the title role; Beaton died in Guyana that December. Brewster's coda to the story is almost unbearable in its sense of lost opportunities for actors of Beaton's generation: 'Norman came with me to see the production before he died. We slipped in at the back and I held his hand. He was weeping – and at the interval, he said, "I can't see the end. This is *my* play. I wanted before I died to do Lear"' (*Guardian* 1 February 2016).

2

'Why weren't we auditioned?': the 'Black canon' and the battle for Othello

In 1967 – the year after Rudolph Walker played Othello in Malvern and Zakes Mokae, Femi Euba and Jumoke Debayo were cast as witches in *Macbeth* – the Royal Shakespeare Company took its first step toward integrated casting.[1] The RSC's intake of young performers that year included four men of colour: one British south Asian (Ben Kingsley), one South African (Alton Kumalo), one Trinidadian (Oscar James) and one Gambian (Louis Mahoney). Their white contemporaries were Helen Mirren, Roger Lloyd Pack, Roger Rees and Jeffery Dench, Dame Judi's brother, all of whom would go on to have long careers in theatre, television and film. Like their white counterparts, the four actors of colour were spear-carriers, playing huntsmen, lords, senators, citizens and soldiers. Only Oscar James had a named part in that first season: Potpan in *Romeo and Juliet*.

As a South African Black man working in Britain's performing arts sector in the 1970s, Alton Kumalo's experience was typical of the era's glass ceiling for actors of colour. Like Zakes Mokae before him, Kumalo had taken refuge in Britain from South Africa's toxic apartheid regime. After he arrived in Britain with the musical *King Kong*, a grant from the British Council enabled him to train at Rose Bruford (*Ottawa Citizen* 11 February 1978). Kumalo subsequently gained experience in television before joining the RSC in 1967, where he remained until 1972.

---

[1] The first performer of colour to be cast in a Shakespeare at the RSC was Zia Mohyeddin, who was to play Romeo for Peter Hall in 1961. Mohyeddin left a week before the opening and was replaced by the white actor Brian Murray.

Alton Kumalo gave a frank assessment of his time at the RSC, recounting he had 'learned a lot' while also discussing its less hospitable side. Kumalo felt 'there was a quiet, unspoken hostility' to him because of his ethnicity:

> For about two years all I ever played there was messengers. I got tired of playing the same roles because they are limiting. If you play a servant, you cannot raise your voice. You never know if your voice can carry or not. So I made a very vocal protest. They argued that Shakespeare did not write black roles and that there weren't many black[s] in England in Elizabethan times. I got some better roles, but the feeling remained there. Directors were always worried about the audience. America is better now, but in England there is still an uneasiness.
>
> (*Ottawa Citizen* 11 February 1978)

Kumalo also recalled that, 'After three years there was a lot of shuffling and a bit of muttering along the lines of "What'll we do next with him" and it was a bit embarrassing when they started thinking "Well, he was a servant at the end of that play last season, maybe he can be a servant in the middle this time"' (V&A Temba collection). A look at the range of parts Alton Kumalo played at the RSC explains his objections.

In 1967 and 1968 Kumalo played a succession of servants, including 'Paris's page' in *Romeo and Juliet* and Lucius in *Julius Caesar*. For an inexperienced actor, Kumalo's RSC trajectory initially followed normal practice, first playing supernumeraries ('Servant', 'Paris' page', 'Senator/Aedile/Citizen/Soldier', 'Townsperson') followed by a small named role in *Julius Caesar* (Lucius). Kumalo's white contemporary, Roger Rees, also played generic parts in 1967 ('Huntsman', 'Unnamed parts'), but in 1968 their paths diverged as Rees climbed the ladder of Shakespearean hierarchy.

As Kumalo was cast almost exclusively as servants, most notably Fabian in *Twelfth Night* and Speed in *Two Gentlemen of Verona*, Roger Rees built a varied Shakespearean résumé. Rees played in comedies, tragedies and, significantly, histories, the genre from which people of colour most often remain excluded. When compared to Kumalo's line of servant parts, Rees' roles show an astounding range: two young romantic male lovers (Fenton in *Merry Wives*, Claudio in *Much Ado*), a hapless nobleman (Roderigo in *Othello*) and a regicide (Exton in *Richard II*). Rees' two lovers are perhaps the most telling, however, as Kumalo was never cast as a romantic Shakespearean character. As we will see in chapter 5, it would be nearly two decades before African-Caribbean men would be viewed as potential romantic material.

Alton Kumalo's typecasting cemented a pattern of African-Caribbean actors playing servants at the RSC. The few African-Caribbean actors hired by the RSC between 1967 and 1983 inhabited not just a type but the same parts, handed down from production to production. The RSC staged four productions of *Julius Caesar* between 1967 and 1983; each included an African-Caribbean performer playing Lucius. In 1981 Joseph

Marcell inherited Valentine's servant Speed in *Two Gentlemen of Verona* from Kumalo, who had played him in the company's previous production in 1969. These parts were the Shakespearean equivalent of 'suitable roles', adhering to the dominant view of African-Caribbeans as inferior and subservient. This narrow view, seemingly held by directors and audiences alike, meant that performers of colour were also consistently excluded from the wider Shakespearean canon, including one of the few characters written as a Black man: Othello.

'Why weren't we auditioned?'

The reclamation of Othello for performers of African-Caribbean heritage began with television. The catalyst was the proposed hiring by the BBC of the African-American actor James Earl Jones for the role in the influential *BBC Television Shakespeare* series. A furore erupted in early 1979 when British Actors' Equity refused to support the African-American's work permit. The standoff between the two organizations lasted two years and concluded with the hiring of a white actor, Anthony Hopkins, to play Othello. The dispute originated from a perfect storm of long-term inequalities in British television, lack of access to professional Shakespeare work for performers of colour and the vagaries of international television finance, then in its infancy.

By the time Cedric Messina, the first producer of *BBC Television Shakespeare*, cast James Earl Jones as Shakespeare's Moor, the African-American had won a Tony and an Emmy, and had been nominated for an Oscar. Unlike his British counterparts, Jones had also been able to gain extensive experience in professional Shakespeare. He had appeared in at least seven plays at Joseph Papp's Public Theater, including supporting roles in *Coriolanus* and *Troilus and Cressida*. Crucially, Jones' professional résumé also included the title roles of four Shakespeare tragedies: Hamlet, Macbeth, King Lear and Othello, playing the latter twice. As late as 2021, no actor of colour in the United Kingdom has played this same line of title parts.

In Britain in 1979, a white actor 'blacking up' to play Othello remained acceptable, amply evidenced by the two national theatre companies' productions, led by white actors: Donald Sinden (RSC 1979) and Paul Scofield (NT 1980). Although British television aired *The Black and White Minstrel Show* until 1978, in America a 'blacked-up' Moor had become unacceptable with the Civil Rights Movement. When the film of Laurence Olivier's *Othello* premiered in US cinemas in 1966, film critic Bosley Crowther expressed astonishment at Olivier's appearance, noting in his review, 'He plays Othello in blackface!' and assessing Olivier's performance as an 'outrageous impression of a theatrical Negro stereotype' (*NYTimes* 2 February 1966). America's move away from 'blacking up' to play Othello was critical because as Peter Plouviez, Equity's General Secretary from 1974 to 1991, recalled, 'The BBC had said that it was obliged to cast a black actor, for without one it could not sell the programme to America' (*Independent* 3 August 1990).

In the official *BBC Television Shakespeare*'s published text of *Othello*, Henry Fenwick begins his account of the production by glossing over the BBC–Equity dispute, noting that producer Cedric Messina's 'plans foundered because British Equity refused permission for the great black American actor, James Earl Jones, to play the title role' (1981: 18). Echoing Fenwick, Lois Potter provides a similar reading in her performance history of *Othello*, noting Cedric Messina 'was prevented [from casting Jones] by the refusal of the British Actors' Equity Union to let a non-British actor play the part' (2002: 154). What Fenwick and Potter portray as a decision to oppose an American actor taking a British performer's job was, in reality, a fight about the inequality and prejudice faced by actors of colour in Britain.

The BBC posed a dubious argument that the casting of James Earl Jones was necessary on the grounds that no Black British actors were capable of playing Othello. Equity's counter-argument was laid out by Peter Plouviez:

> Equity can't honestly say there isn't an actor here who can't play Othello. James Earl Jones would undoubtedly make a splendid Othello, but we are not required to say who would be the perfect Othello. Black actors are not getting the opportunity at home to give them the experience, and some of them were born here.
>
> (*DM* 10 February 1979)

This was not the first time Plouviez and Equity had advocated for better representation for the union's minority ethnic membership.

A 1974 survey into the diversity of British television – then just three terrestrial broadcast channels – commissioned by Equity unveiled stark results. In the week between 26 May and 1 June 1974, 891 artists had appeared on British television. Out of those 891, only forty-five were people of colour – and twelve of those were members of the Harlem Globetrotters exhibition basketball team (Husband 1975: 29). Pared down solely to scripted output, the survey's results clearly show television's culture of exclusion. Only six out of thirty-nine drama programmes scrutinized contained an actor of colour, and none had a person of colour in a leading role (*Guardian* 23 August 1974). Plouviez responded by challenging the broadcasters:

> There is a resistance by the broadcasting authorities to do more than reflect the racial composition of the society. We think they can go on and do a positive service to help it on by simply not casting black people in the lower stratas [*sic*] of society. When there is the part of a Church of England clergyman or bank manager and if there is a black actor available who is capable of sustaining the role, he should not be ignored because the role is not specifically described as a black bank manager.
>
> (*Guardian* 23 August 1974)

With this type of pressure from Equity and a vocal group of African-Caribbean actors protesting their relegation to 'suitable roles', it seems remarkable that Cedric Messina would contemplate casting an African-American to play Othello five years later.

In the 1970s, while Black Britons – and, to a much smaller extent, other minorities – were allowed to play servants, they were not seen in ways that gave them access to Shakespeare's more complex parts. While Roger Rees could play young lovers and patricians at the RSC, Alton Kumalo continued to be viewed as a servant. Kumalo's experience was not unique, and this had very real consequences for actors of colour, who were unable to learn their craft in parity with their white peers, as David Yip's experience demonstrates.

David Yip became the first British east Asian to play a named role in a professional Shakespeare production – Cleopatra's servant Alexas in *Antony and Cleopatra* – at the Young Vic Theatre in 1976. A native of Liverpool, Yip had graduated from E15 Acting School in 1973 and found himself in the Young Vic company three years later. Unique for the era the London fringe theatre, under its founding artistic director Frank Dunlop, was the first to fully represent Britain's multiculturalism in productions of Shakespeare. Between 1974 and 1977 a quartet of performers from African-Caribbean (Cleo Sylvestre and Tony Osoba), south Asian (Darien Angadi) and east Asian (David Yip) heritages – all of whom had been born in Britain – were integrated into the Young Vic Shakespeares. The Young Vic also broke the 'suitable roles' model when casting Yip and his three peers as often as it followed it. For example, Angadi was stereotypically cast as a Witch in *Macbeth*, but he also played Conrade in *Much Ado* (self-described as a 'gentleman'), Sir Eglamour in *Two Gentlemen of Verona* (who Silvia refers to as 'gentleman' and thrice calls 'Sir Eglamour') and Lennox (one of the Scottish thanes in *Macbeth*).

The Young Vic's inclusive practices were more ad hoc than permanent and David Yip says he 'was only ever cast play by play, but I was at the Young Vic for thirteen months'. Crucially Yip also worked his way up from Alexas to Romeo's close friend Benvolio in *Romeo and Juliet* and finished his Young Vic career with the lead role in a children's play, *Tobias and the Angel*. For Yip, the Young Vic 'was a wonderful training ground', as 'partly they were educating you'. Yip equates this experience to professional football, where 'a young kid comes in and starts to play' and, through hard work, progresses into the first team. On-the-job training is as crucial with Shakespeare as football, and, as a performer of colour, Yip recognizes that he has never consistently had it:

> I've never had a season at the RSC or anywhere like that [in order] to have this consistency where you start to learn about how to handle the verse. [You get one job in Shakespeare] then it stops again and I'm talking years, big gaps [between Shakespeare roles]. You're working muscles that haven't been worked for a long time and you're not fully fit.

And that was not me saying, 'I don't want to do Shakespeare'. I never got the offer.

The gaps in his Shakespearean résumé were costly for Yip. Even though he rose through the ranks at the Young Vic, the larger and more complex roles in Shakespeare remained elusive and it would be another ten years before his next Shakespeare part.

In the 1970s performers of colour were consistently unable to build careers like their white peers. David Yip, Alton Kumalo and other contemporaries, such as Norman Beaton and Rudolph Walker, were systematically denied the experience necessary to compete in the marketplace on an equal footing with James Earl Jones, who had not faced the same obstacles in working his way up to leading tragic Shakespearean roles in America.

On the day it was announced that the BBC would indefinitely postpone *Othello* because Equity was not prepared to alter its position, Norman Beaton eloquently laid out the actors' case in the *Guardian*, starting with the industry as a whole. 'For a number of years', he wrote, '"black" (for want of a better name) actors have sat back patiently, or have fumed impotently, while directors and producers overtly ignored their existence.' Beaton's frustration with the overall industry is palpable, but his focus on the exclusion from British classical theatre is particularly poignant. 'Classical theatre', he wrote, 'appears [to be] virtually a closed shop' (*Guardian* 9 February 1979) to performers of colour.

As James Earl Jones remarks in his reflections on playing Othello, 'What happened is that no black actor got to play Othello in the BBC production.... I was happy when I saw the production not to have been involved with it. It was unfulfilled' (2003: 109). The cost for British actors of colour, however, was considerable and they continued to face the status quo of small, mostly stereotypical, parts in Shakespeare without the possibility of advancement. As Rudolph Walker noted at the time, 'I feel insulted, not for myself, but for all black actors. Why weren't we auditioned? James Earl Jones is an actor of the highest calibre but where are the British Joneses to come from if we don't get the chance?' (*DM* 17 February 1979).

Reclaiming Othello

Between 1950 and 1980, five African-Caribbean men played Othello in British professional theatre: Gordon Heath, Paul Robeson, Cy Grant, Errol John and Rudolph Walker. Between Rudolph Walker's first professional Othello in 1966 and the early 1980s, the role remained solely the purview of white actors. Between 1981 and 1984, after the BBC's abortive attempt to cast James Earl Jones, change rapidly occurred. Thomas Baptiste, Doyle Richmond, Rudolph Walker and Joseph Marcell became the first African-Caribbeans to play Othello in Britain since the 1960s. This rapid expansion in the number of Black Othellos easily disproves the BBC's assertion that no actor of colour in Britain was capable of undertaking the role in 1979.

Like Alton Kumalo, Thomas Baptiste was an actor whose name should be firmly established in the annals of British theatre history. Baptiste emigrated from British Guiana (now Guyana) in the 1940s and became an early member of Joan Littlewood's Theatre Workshop. According to contemporaneous press reports, Baptiste was also the one British actor of colour auditioned by the BBC for Othello (*DT* 9 February 1979). Baptiste became the first African-Caribbean to play the role in a mainstream theatre after Equity's dispute with the BBC came to its unsatisfactory conclusion.

Thomas Baptiste had worked at Exeter's Northcott Theatre in 1981, playing Boyet in *Love's Labour's Lost*, which was regarded by one reviewer as 'a very fine character study' (*TSTT* 1 October 1981). That portrayal likely led to Baptiste's return to Exeter in the spring of 1982 for a repertory season with a company of seventeen actors who had each agreed to play two main and two supporting parts. As director Stewart Trotter observed, this 'means you will see Thomas Baptiste as Othello one night – then as the coalman the next! It also means that we will have the highest standard of playing in even the smallest parts' (*Hamlet* programme).

The lone review of Baptiste's Othello was favourable:

> with his deep and resonant voice, [Baptiste] reveals from the opening speeches an inborn dignity of the commanding general, a dignity which will hold firm when confronted by his white Venetian superior and his defence against his marriage to Desdemona. This majestic portrayal contrasted sharply with the inevitable fall of the great soldier which came with his poignant speech 'Farewell tranquil mind'.
>
> (*TSTT* 27 May 1982)

As apparently successful as Baptiste's portrayal of Shakespeare's Moor was, two London productions of *Othello* – with Joseph Marcell and Rudolph Walker – proved to be a watershed in the history of integrated casting in Britain.

By 1984 Joseph Marcell and Rudolph Walker both had extensive professional experience. Marcell had worked at the RSC in the early 1970s, leaving in 1974 to become a founding member of Paines Plough. His television credits included a central role in the BBC's ground-breaking *Empire Road*, the first series to depict multicultural Britain. Marcell had returned to the RSC – playing Puck in *Dream* and Speed in *Two Gentlemen of Verona* – when he was approached by David Porter, then producer of the Lyric Theatre in the west London borough of Hammersmith. As Marcell recalls, Porter's negotiation began with, '"I think it's time that you attack something" – did he say "difficult?" Or "interesting?" – Anyway, it was one of those words.' The producer proposed that Marcell play Othello at the Lyric, Hammersmith. With Marcell's preferred director – Paines Plough's John Adams – unavailable, Porter recommended an emerging white director, Michael Boyd.

Rudolph Walker had also built a formidable résumé after playing Othello and Caliban, including appearances at the Royal Court, Hampstead Theatre and Bristol Old Vic. By 1984 Walker had a profile from television, including *Empire Road* and the popular sitcom *Love Thy Neighbour*. Walker found himself at the Young Vic, tackling Othello once again, because the white director David Thacker opened his tenure as artistic director of the theatre with the play. Crucially, Thacker recognized the overall lack of opportunity for 'actors from ethnic minority groups to play any great roles in wonderful plays' and felt 'it would be insulting to all Black actors, politically completely unacceptable and artistically stupid, ridiculous actually, worthy of ridicule' to cast a white actor as Othello and inappropriate to 'take away from Black actors one of the greatest roles ever written'.

The productions of David Thacker and Michael Boyd were polar opposites in style. Thacker opted for contemporary dress, still comparatively rare, while Boyd chose to stage *Othello* in Renaissance costume. Where Thacker incorporated khaki uniforms, green berets, lounge suits, cocktail dresses, cigarettes, briefcases and whisky decanters, Boyd used 'Tintoretto costumes' and 'swelling Monteverdi' to create a more traditional *milieu* (*Times* 19 September 1984). Thacker's production actively challenged the view of African-Caribbeans in contemporary society, with the press release stating 'the play is an investigation of class, race and power'. In the context of Thatcher's Britain – where class and racial fissures were being opened, not

FIGURE 3 *Rudolph Walker as Othello*. Othello, *Young Vic Theatre, London, 1984. Photo by Donald Cooper/Photostage.*

FIGURE 4 *Joseph Marcell as Othello*. Othello, *Lyric Theatre, Hammersmith, London, 1984. Photo by Donald Cooper/Photostage.*

closed – this assertion proved provocative. By contrast, Michael Boyd's use of an early modern Italian setting framed Marcell's Othello as a man who was the equal of the Venetians, even as they rejected him for his perceived difference.

Signifiers of assimilation were embedded both in Boyd's production and Marcell's performance. The design signalled Othello's equality with the wealthy Venetian nobles through a costume Anthony Masters perceived as 'the finest of all'. The critic continued, providing the astute observation that, even with this attire, Venice 'will never fully accept him' (*Times*

19 September 1984). In addition to the design, Marcell's voice signalled Othello's equality with the Venetians and, crucially, his social class. Michael Coveney described Marcell's Othello as 'not so much as a brooding General' but 'a Sandhurst Silver Sword graduate of good middle-class African background' (*FT* 19 September 1984), indicating that Othello had been integrated into the upper echelons of Venetian society.

John Barber's comment perhaps best illuminates the fine line between playing Othello as a Black man and being an actor of African-Caribbean descent in Britain. The *Daily Telegraph* critic found Marcell's Othello was the 'main interest' of Boyd's production, but other references speak more poignantly to both the grudging acceptance of the actor as an equal and ultimately his exclusion from the elite classical theatre club. Barber's remark that Marcell's 'considerable experience with the Royal Shakespeare Company has taught him much about the speaking of verse and the shaping of a speech' was an accolade that highlights the equality with which Marcell is seemingly regarded. Yet Barber's review also rejected that equality by marking Marcell out as 'a black actor' (*DT* 19 September 1984). Still used well into the twenty-first century, the label was applied, perhaps subconsciously, to illustrate Marcell's inequality with his white peers. Marcell, like Othello, was in equal parts both accepted and rejected, marked out as other and denied the full accolade he undoubtedly deserved.

Where Michael Boyd's production reflected the complexities of assimilation, acceptance and rejection in modern Britain, David Thacker's drew attention to discrimination. The programme included an essay by Richard Wilson titled 'The Empire Strikes Back' with the white academic posing multiple provocations, but one sentence is particularly relevant to the reclamation of the part of Othello for African-Caribbean men: '[Othello] is subversive simply by asking to be accepted.' While Wilson's comment described Othello's place in Venetian society, it applies equally to actors such as Rudolph Walker and Joseph Marcell, who were subverting the previous norm of white actors blacking up as Othello.

The press release for Thacker's production unequivocally challenged the status quo with its headline: 'First Black Othello on London stage for over twenty years.' David Thacker makes clear he 'didn't decide to do the play so that we could say this is the first time a Black actor's played this role for God knows how many years', but the search for ways to promote the production had uncovered uncomfortable facts. Rudolph Walker was already cast when the production team discovered not only that it had been twenty years since the last time an African-Caribbean man had played Othello in London but that Walker would be only the fourth to do so. In major London revivals of *Othello*, only Ira Aldridge (1833), Paul Robeson (1930) and Errol John (1963) had preceded Rudolph Walker, who became 'the fourth in line', as the *Othello* programme notes (Samuel Morgan Smith's London Othello was then unknown).

In 1984 any theatrical institution overtly highlighting racial inequality would have been radical, but for classical theatre it was seismic. The production formed a learning curve for David Thacker, who feels that, in not having previously worked in London and encountering the national critics en masse for the first time, he was unprepared for the way in which:

> programme notes lead reviewers more than anything else. At the time I was innocent of all that, so I think some of the negative reviews were negative because they thought I was hijacking the play to turn it into a political event.

However inadvertent the framing of the Young Vic *Othello*, through the publicity and the programme notes, it had exposed the truth of Norman Beaton's description of British classical theatre as 'a closed shop' to people of colour (*Guardian* 9 February 1979).

For Rudolph Walker, playing Othello was, at least in retrospect, a personal political act, inextricably linked to the treatment of African-Caribbeans in postwar Britain:

> I, as a Black actor/Othello walked on the stage and felt a certain amount of inner power and strength. And as a person – and also an actor – suddenly the carpet was pulled from under you. It's a painful experience.

Rudolph Walker also felt a sense of ownership of Othello, something that had long been denied African-Caribbeans:

> You see productions that are being played by white actors blacked up and you realize that all they were doing was a caricature of a Black man. What was fantastic about David was, he said, 'Look I don't want you to be a Royal Shakespeare Theatre actor. I want you to bring what you have and that is your Afro-Caribbean background. That to me is the richness of the piece and of the play.' So I explored and I revelled in that.

One pre-emptive conversation David Thacker had with his lead actor shortly before *Othello* opened may seem remarkable now. Walker says that the director told him: '"Look, I know exactly what the press is going to say about your performance. They are going to say either you're too western or you don't grasp the metre or whatever. They're not going to like you." And in fact he was absolutely right.' Problematic phrases pepper reviews of the production, reflecting negative stereotypes about African-Caribbeans' alleged lack of intelligence and propensity to anger, including 'this Othello appears more stupid than good' (*ES* 14 May 1984) and 'the Moor is seen to fall into a genuinely black rage' (*DT* 14 May 1984). The critics' reactions had as much to do with the perception of the production's politicization of Shakespeare as it did with the presence of a Black man playing a leading Shakespearean role.

For all the external pressures laid on him simply by being an African-Caribbean playing a leading Shakespearean role, Walker remains proud of the Young Vic *Othello*, not least because of the reaction of the audience. He fondly remembers a theatre 'packed with students' for whom 'a Black actor doing Othello appeared to them the norm, they responded to it normally'. The emotional toll on the pioneering generation that made the initial breakthroughs was high, even as they blazed a trail into classical theatre. After the Young Vic production, Walker vowed that he 'wouldn't touch Othello again in this country. I became very critical personally of the way critics viewed the likes of me going in to do Shakespeare. It has changed, thank God, over the years, but how many years has it taken for that?'

3

From 'suitable roles' to leads, 1980–1987

The integration of British Shakespeare is inseparable from the industry-wide practice of segregation of performers of colour into 'suitable roles', or 'Black parts': characters for which the ethnicity is specified, e.g. the Boy in *A Taste of Honey* or Tituba in *The Crucible*. The idea of 'Black parts' was so ingrained that, when Rudolph Walker was offered a part in John Arden's *Sergeant Musgrave's Dance* in 1966, he did not understand what part he would be playing. As he explains, 'Automatically you look at the play and you think, *But there aren't any Black parts in it*, because everything is specifically written'.

To make progress within the Shakespearean microcosm of a wider industry, Norman Beaton adopted language that delineated parts into either 'Black' or, the default, white. In his counterargument to the BBC at the height of its dispute with Equity over casting James Earl Jones as Othello, Beaton wrote what amounts to a manifesto for 'Black parts' in Shakespeare:

> Shakespeare actually wrote two major parts for black men, Othello and Aaron. He specifically underlined and italicised the characters' nationality. What is more Shakespeare's plays are littered with references to blacks (blackamoors). Apart from *Othello* and *Titus Andronicus*, there is a certain reference to Young Gobbo in the *Merchant* going out with the blackamoor wench, and a reference to Hermia in the *Dream* being called an Ethiop by Helena. The list, as any academician would corroborate, is considerable.
>
> (*Guardian* 9 February 1979)

The sudden proliferation of African-Caribbean and south Asian Princes of Morocco in productions of *The Merchant of Venice*, three in 1980 alone, was an early indication that the 'Black parts' of the Shakespearean canon were beginning to expand.

A Midsummer Night's Dream also joined this embryo 'Black canon' in the early 1980s, initially through Ron Daniels' casting of Joseph Marcell as Puck at the RSC in 1981. Marcell had been with the RSC during Trevor Nunn's 1972 *The Romans* season, along with six other actors of African-Caribbean or south Asian heritage. At the time, owing to the RSC's narrow view of what roles constituted 'Black parts' in Shakespeare, Black and brown bodies were most often coded as servants, primitives or cannon fodder.

Joseph Marcell went from playing small parts in the 1972 season to the fourth-largest parts in two comedies in 1981: Speed in *Two Gentlemen of Verona* and Puck in *A Midsummer Night's Dream*. 'It's really difficult', Marcell observes, for performers of colour to carve a classical career in Britain, so his route back to the RSC is worth detailing. He stayed at the RSC from 1972 to 1974, doing *The Romans* in Stratford and London, followed by a season of new work that included an adaptation of *Sherlock Holmes*. As Marcell tells it:

> My luck was this: in 1974 we took *Sherlock Holmes* to Broadway – the Royal Shakespeare Company did – and so I went to Broadway where we did six weeks at the Kennedy Center in Washington, D.C. and just over five months on Broadway. I played a character called Lightfoot MacTague, which was not a Black role. And I discovered that I think *King Lear* was, *Lear* was on at the Public [Theater] at that time – I can't remember whether it was *Lear* or, anyway... James Earl Jones was playing some huge Shakespearean role at the Public, which I saw and there was some stuff happening in D.C. as well. So I realized that perhaps there is more of an opening in the USA than there is in Britain, so I pursued that.

Marcell stayed in America, developing a transatlantic career, including appearances at Shakespeare and Company in Lenox, Massachusetts. What he calls his 'luck' also meant that he 'didn't need the RSC' and he returned because 'I just hadn't played Puck before'.

A Midsummer Night's Dream would prove fertile ground for directors looking to cast inclusively. John Harrison also hired an African-Caribbean, Leo Wringer, to play Puck at the Leeds Playhouse in 1982. Harrison went much further than Ron Daniels had at the RSC: in his version, Shakespeare's fairy kingdom was entirely comprised of African-Caribbeans. The Leeds cast included Ewart James Walters ('a dignified but rather subdued Oberon'), Cassie McFarlane ('a dynamic and almost menacing Titania') and Jenni George ('a charming First Fairy') (*TSTT* 17 June 1982), as well as thirteen amateurs, children from a local school. Counting the children, the Leeds Playhouse *Dream* had a majority minority cast.

A Midsummer Night's Dream emerged as an important breakthrough in integrated casting in the early 1980s because it enabled the expansion of what were considered to be the Shakespearean 'Black parts'. Shakespeare constructed *Dream* using three interlocking subplots involving a quartet of lovers, a group of theatre-loving mechanicals and a tempestuous fairy kingdom, giving equal weight to each. That the breakthrough for performers of colour came within the framework of the fairy kingdom was not accidental. The plots involving the lovers and mechanicals are more rooted in a material reality, while Oberon, Titania and Puck are firmly in the realm of fantasy. Ripe for 'other-ing', *Dream*'s fairies are ephemeral characters, easily placed outside white normative society's understanding of the world.

Another landmark in the history of integrated casting was Michael Rudman's production of *Measure for Measure* at the National Theatre in 1981. Rudman set the play in the Caribbean largely because, as he wrote in the programme, 'there [were] a lot of very good West Indian actors' not getting the opportunities they deserved. Rudman's setting also allowed him to circumvent the dominant 'suitable roles' culture, using a locale in which the audience could plausibly expect to see African-Caribbeans. With 'Black parts' created, Rudman hired eighteen performers of colour out of a cast of twenty-two. Perhaps most importantly, African-Caribbeans played all three of the play's largest parts, its leads: the Duke (Stefan Kalipha), Isabella (Yvette Harris) and Lucio (Peter Straker). Rudman's *Measure* also included Norman Beaton as Angelo, who had last been in a Shakespeare play a decade earlier, when he played Ariel in Jonathan Miller's production of *The Tempest*.

With its appropriation of Caribbean accents and society, in a building still partly controlled by a largely hostile dominant white culture, the limitations of Rudman's production were not lost on Norman Beaton. He told the *Guardian* at the time:

> The fact that the play is set in some mythical Caribbean island means that the audience are being pandered to. I don't think that blacks in the National Theatre is some kind of trigger or artistic liberation. The entire relationship remains paternalistic. If we had a theatre to which we could invite Rudman to direct that would be different, but we don't.
> (14 April 1981)

Rudolph Walker had turned down Rudman's offer of a lead role in the production for similar reasons. He explains:

> I got home [from his meeting with Rudman] and I thought: *This is ridiculous*. It was a period when no Black actor was 'good enough' to play Othello, but yet I am 'good enough' to play the leading role in an all-Black cast of *Measure for Measure*? Regardless of how fantastic the production [of *Othello* with Paul Scofield] was, it's insulting. To me it was insulting. I'm not saying Paul Scofield wouldn't have been fantastic, but someone had to do something. I wasn't prepared to walk on stage in an all-Black cast of *Measure for Measure*. The time was

wrong. It didn't push us any further. That comes with Black actors just doing whatever they want.

Walker's reflection helps to illustrate a second, perhaps more elusive level of segregation within British Shakespeare. Performers of colour faced not only a glass ceiling for individual parts viewed as 'suitable' but also a genre bias. The major breakthroughs in the early 1980s came primarily through comedies, such as *Dream* or *Measure*, but actors of colour continued to be excluded from the great tragic roles and the histories, with one notable exception.

The RSC made tentative steps towards discarding its decade-long 'suitable roles' model of casting in 1982. Hugh Quarshie, the Ghanian-born, Oxford-educated son of a diplomat, had played the RSC's version of 'Black parts' – Aaron in *Titus Andronicus*, the servant Cleomenes in *The Winter's Tale* and an outlaw in *Two Gentlemen of Verona* – in the 1981 season. When the RSC opened the Barbican Centre with both parts of *Henry IV*, Trevor Nunn cast Hugh Quarshie to play two English noblemen: Sir Richard Vernon and Lord Hastings. Quarshie was the first African-Caribbean to play a named historical figure in one of Shakespeare's history plays. That alone was a seismic shift away from traditional methods of inclusion through 'Black parts', but Quarshie went on to play one of the most iconic of the history roles: Hotspur.

Alby James, the university-educated son of Jamaican immigrants, was assistant director on *Henry IV*. When the production's original Hotspur, Timothy Dalton, left halfway through the run, Trevor Nunn told Alby James that Dalton's understudy, Hugh Quarshie, should take over the role of Hotspur. With Nunn opening *Cats* on Broadway, James was responsible for overseeing the mechanics of replacing Dalton with Quarshie, including informing the company and re-directing the plays. 'The reality is that no Black actor played an historical role on a national stage', James told Tony Howard, and Nunn's elevation of Quarshie met resistance within the company. James recounts:

> I had to make the announcement [to the company]. They were shocked, to be honest. I would always have really the utmost respect and love for Patrick Stewart, because I think he saved the day. If it was ever going to break down, he stopped it happening. He declared that he was willing to change his schedule – he was instructing the BBC to create time in his schedule [Stewart was filming *Mayberry*, while appearing as Henry IV] for the re-rehearsal period to happen. He was determined to do this and the others, I think, fell in, but there was this feeling that we were going to fall on our faces.

Quarshie played Hotspur from October 1982 through the last performances of *Henry IV* in March 1983. 'It shouldn't be breaking ground, but it is', the actor reflected shortly after his debut in the part. 'I had thought it would be some time yet before the RSC broke out of the hidebound tradition of British theatre. Of course, this may still be the exception that proves the rule' (*Ms London* 25 October 1982). On one level Quarshie would prove prescient, as the histories remain the least diverse genre in performance and performers of colour were still playing parts in Shakespeare that conformed to stereotypes at the end of the decade. Nevertheless, progress would also be highly visible, and by the end of the 1980s performers of colour were also playing leads.

'Black roles' at the RSC

Cyril Nri won Best Actor at the prestigious National Student Drama Festival at the end of his first year at drama school. When he returned to the Bristol Old Vic Theatre School at the start of his second year, he recalls:

> Suddenly the same people who were a bit sniffy and had said, 'Oh well, you're not going to be cast like that, so just suck it up and see' were saying, 'You can play one of the knights in *Murder in the Cathedral* this term.' Oh how quickly it changes.

Nri learned a valuable lesson and he began thinking, 'Maybe I need to be a little more rebellious. Maybe I need to walk away more. Maybe I need to bunk off a bit and go "Fuck you, I'll do it over here."' Nri would put this sentiment to use a few years later at the RSC.

Cyril Nri's first job out of drama school in 1983 was with the RSC, beginning his career with 'two named parts. It was fabulous' and any young classical actor's dream. Given its propensity to cast performers of colour in roles that had evolved as 'Black parts', Nri inherited two parts from his predecessors: Lucius in *Julius Caesar* and Curio in *Twelfth Night*. By the time Nri arrived in 1983, both Curio and Lucius had become integral to the 'Black canon' the RSC had developed, but *Julius Caesar* better illuminates the RSC's casting practices at the time.

The RSC had staged *Julius Caesar* four times since 1968, when Alton Kumalo became the first actor of colour to play Brutus' servant, Lucius, in Britain. In each of its four subsequent productions, the RSC continued its pattern of hiring African-Caribbeans to play both Lucius and Pindarus (Table 1).

Although Cyril Nri followed in Alton Kumalo's footsteps by playing Lucius, unlike Kumalo he decided to leave the RSC. 'After Stratford and Newcastle, there was a feeling of "Oh I could get stuck playing these small roles"', he recalls. 'I could get stuck here [London, for the RSC's Barbican season] for nearly a year. So I auditioned for Manchester.' At the time, the Royal Exchange Theatre was forming a company of actors for four plays,

TABLE 1 *African-Caribbeans cast in* Julius Caesar *by the RSC, 1968–1983*

Year	Lucius	Pindarus
1968	Alton Kumalo	Oscar James
1972	Joseph Marcell	Jason Rose
1979	John Matshikiza	–
1983	Cyril Nri	Doyle Richmond

including Shakespeare's *Cymbeline*, J. M. Barrie's *The Admirable Crichton* and an adaptation of Charles Dickens' *Great Expectations*. Leaving the RSC for Manchester, Nri says:

> was a no brainer for me and it was also about moving on. You look at it and go, yeah OK. *Cymbeline* is really a small to middling role, but I'm getting the chance to do some Dickens. I'm also getting the chance to do *Class K*, which is a modern piece; it's a musical. Equally you've got Art Malik and Hugh Quarshie playing in *Cymbeline* so why wouldn't you? It's a great chance to learn from these people.

His decision to join the Royal Exchange was met with disbelief at the RSC. 'Nobody believed me when I said, "I'm leaving"', Nri remembers, but the decision was also calculated. 'You can stay in the RSC and do year after year after year and slowly build yourself up – hopefully – to greater parts. But at the time, for a young Black actor, it didn't seem like that was going to be the case.'

Macbeth, Young Vic, 1984

David Thacker followed his *Othello*, starring Rudolph Walker, with *Macbeth* five months later. One-third of Thacker's cast of twenty-one performers were from African-Caribbean backgrounds. 'That was a political decision on my part', Thacker recalls. 'We've got to give opportunities and so I cast Black actors.' With *Macbeth* Thacker was not just providing the chance to play Shakespeare but also discarding stereotypes many had embraced.

Instead of placing his *Macbeth* in Africa or the Caribbean, Thacker's production was unequivocally modern dress and, importantly, presented the characters as British. The Young Vic production also broke stereotypes in another important way. As Martin Hoyle begrudgingly noted, Thacker had cast the majority of the African-Caribbeans – the men – as 'the goodies' of *Macbeth* (*FT* 22 October 1984): Macduff, Banquo, Malcolm and Ross. In a country where the media has persistently portrayed African-Caribbean men as criminals, subservient or 'exotic', this broke new ground. Wyllie Longmore, who played Ross, recalls that Thacker's *Macbeth* 'was the first time I thought we were cast with no nonsense about whether we should be playing these roles or not – or whether we were Scottish or not'. It was also the first time that people of colour had played Macduff, Banquo and Malcolm on the British stage.

Jeffery Kissoon, T-Bone Wilson and Brian Bovell played Macduff, Banquo and Malcom, respectively. For Michael Billington, Kissoon gave 'the performance of the evening', as the 'cool, lethal and watchful' avenger and the actor 'establishe[d] Macduff as a palpable threat to the hero with his level-toned, "Wherefore did you so?" after the killing of the grooms' (*Guardian* 20 October 1984). Bovell's Malcolm was a good foil for Kissoon's character; Martin Hoyle found him 'spirited', observing that he 'makes much of his testing of Macduff's loyalty in that often interminable scene when the young prince depicts himself as guilty of every vice' (*FT* 22 October 1984).

David Thacker's *Macbeth* became a magnet for the burgeoning opposition to integrated casting. The presence of multiple African-Caribbeans in the cast attracted the attention of the far-right National Front, which protested outside the Young Vic. Thacker recalls the demonstrations lasted 'a couple of nights' during the run with 'people handing out leaflets because there were non-white actors in it. It didn't get violent or aggressive. It only meant us clearing them away, but it was horrible.' Some critics also vociferously registered disapproval in reviews. For example, J. C. Trewin voiced complaints ranging from 'we have to accept that Duncan [the white actor Clive Russell] had a West Indian son [Brian Bovell as Malcolm]' to stating that 'three of the Scottish thanes' – Macduff, Banquo and Ross – 'are coloured, sometimes difficult to fit into the Shakespearean scene' (*BP* 22 October 1984). In contrast to the complaints in print, Thacker remembers a more diverse audience than usual attended the production. In a comment that mirrors Rudolph Walker's experience playing Othello at the Young Vic, Thacker recalls, 'what was so thrilling about it was having Black children coming to see Shakespeare'. The Young Vic was one of the few places where they could see people who looked like them performing Shakespeare.

Leading roles, 1984

Role size, specifically the three largest roles of Shakespeare's plays, is a useful metric for gauging the progress of integrated casting in Britain and for the purposes of this volume, a play's three largest parts will be identified as leading roles. In 1984 nine performers of colour, appearing across seven productions, played one of these leading parts (Table 2): a major milestone. The presence of eight African-Caribbeans and one south Asian performer in roles of this calibre meant that almost all were also breaking stereotypes.

TABLE 2 *Performers of colour playing one of the three largest parts in Shakespeare plays, 1984*

Rank and role	Play	Actor	Venue
1. Prospero	*Tempest*	Ricco Ross	Liverpool Everyman
2. Posthumus	*Cymbeline*	Hugh Quarshie	Royal Exchange, Manchester
2. Theseus	*Dream*	Don Warrington	Haymarket, Leicester
2. Othello	*Othello*	Joseph Marcell	Lyric Hammersmith
2. Othello	*Othello*	Rudolph Walker	Young Vic
2. Paulina	*Winter's Tale*	Anni Domingo	Yorick Theatre Company
3. Iachimo	*Cymbeline*	Art Malik	Royal Exchange, Manchester
3. Helena	*Dream*	Angela Bruce	Haymarket, Leicester
3. Malcolm	*Macbeth*	Brian Bovell	Young Vic

Hugh Quarshie played a romantic hero (Posthumus), Angela Bruce appeared as one of the four young lovers in *Dream* (Helena) and Don Warrington was Duke Theseus, with absolute power over Athens. These productions were also the first times that actors of colour played the roles of Prospero, Posthumus, Paulina, Iachimo and Helena.

By 1984 only two African-Caribbean men had played the largest part in a Shakespeare play: Stefan Kalipha (Duke) and Roy Alexander (Romeo). The African-American Ricco Ross became the third when he played Prospero at the Liverpool Everyman. The contrast between productions is important because both Kalipha and Alexander appeared in productions that had manufactured both as 'Black parts'. The Caribbean setting of Michael Rudman's *Measure* enabled Kalipha to play the Duke, and Andrew Visnevski's *Romeo and Juliet* at the Young Vic (1982) was designed as a parable about race relations, with African-Caribbean Montagues and white Capulets. Set in a circus, Glen Walford's *Tempest* was less reliant on stereotypes. Glen Walford was also clearly aware of her radical choice for Prospero, telling the *Liverpool Daily Post*:

> No-one really knows what type of actor Shakespeare had in mind when he sat down to create the role of the old magician Prospero in *The Tempest*. But it is safe to assume that he didn't consider it for a 6ft 2in black American with a name like Ricco Ross.
>
> (16 January 1984)

Productions of *The Tempest* since Jonathan Miller's in 1970 had settled easily into the cliché that reinforced stereotypes of subservience. Out of the seven productions since 1970 that had been inclusive, six, like Miller's, hired an actor of colour to play either Ariel or Caliban. In hiring Ross to play Prospero, Walford was the first director to break with Jonathan Miller's postcolonial reading of *The Tempest*. In doing so, she also created an onstage power structure that placed a Black man at the centre of his drama. In Walford's *Tempest*, Prospero's island was a circus tent populated by clowns and acrobats, with Ricco Ross' Prospero a magus wielding power as the ringmaster.

Walford's second decision, which pushed the boundaries of integrated casting, was to give Prospero an African-Caribbean family: his daughter Miranda (Cathy Tyson) and his brother Antonio (Burt Caesar). Miranda was Cathy Tyson's professional Shakespeare debut, after having worked with Walford on the Everyman's *The Liverpool Blitz Show*. 'I was a trapeze artist and so was Ferdinand', Tyson recalls. 'That's why we were held in this moon, this trapeze. We sat in a moon above the stage.' Tyson remembers being placed on Ricco Ross' shoulders at the end of every show, a father–daughter balancing act. 'He'd walk on with me and I'd be on his shoulders and it was like, "Am I going to fall off?"'

Cathy Tyson was eighteen when she played Miranda, with a passion for Shakespeare that was encouraged by her mother. Tyson recalls how pivotal *The Tempest* was for her:

> When I first got into the Everyman, in 1984, I thought: *I want to go to the RSC*. And I think under a year later, I was there and it was unbelievable, although I wasn't doing major roles. I was play as cast, you know, so I was very happy about that.

Tyson played one of Ophelia's ladies in waiting in Ron Daniels' production of *Hamlet* at the RSC 1984:

> The gown was absolutely amazing. I didn't have anything to say, so I had to learn, which is good for filming, I think, to act without words. I remember being praised by the director, Ron Daniels, coming up and saying to Sarah Woodward and I, 'Well done' because we were Ophelia's handmaidens. 'Well done for your performance. That was really nice'. Even though, because when you don't have any words in Shakespeare, it's all about the words isn't it? We had to listen, so I just enjoyed listening to the language, you know, the way other people spoke it. Roger Rees. I remember Brian Blessed turning upstage and doing a vocal exercise with his mouth and then turning back towards the audience and being able to speak. I remember Frances Barber's performance as well.

Tyson was the third woman of colour to appear in a Shakespeare play at the RSC, following Josette Simon and Alphonsia Emmanuel.

Rosaline, RSC, 1984

Josette Simon recalls a conversation during her final year of training at the Central School of Speech and Drama:

> I was taken into the Principal's office and told that I should be aware that I probably would never do Shakespeare because of my colour. And I remember thinking, 'Well that's a really stupid thing to say' – not because it wasn't true, but because why would you put an obstacle in your head? Why would you just dismiss it like that and say, 'Right, I'm never going to do that'. I knew there would be challenges and obstacles – which there were – but I thought it best to address those as and when they came up. Try to overcome them rather than putting it in your head at the beginning that I'm never going to do this, so I might as well not bother.

Josette Simon became the first woman of colour to appear in a Shakespeare play at the RSC in 1982, fifteen years after that first male cohort of Alton Kumalo, Oscar James, Louis Mahoney and Ben Kingsley. Undeterred by her Principal's warning, Simon had been determined to get into the RSC, but, as she recounts, 'My agent and I had been trying every which way to get an audition for the RSC with absolutely no response whatsoever. No interest, no sniff, nothing. I could not get an audition for love nor money.' Her break came through a rehearsed reading of a new play by Snoo Wilson, which she had agreed to do 'as a favour for the director, Dusty Hughes'. In the audience was the white director Howard Davies and, as Simon recollects, 'The next day my agent got a phone call saying, "Could she come in and audition for the RSC?"'

Josette Simon joined the company in 1982 and stayed for four years, playing in back-to-back two-year season cycles. She was cast in four Shakespeares her first season and, as with her male predecessors, her early roles fell into the RSC's stereotypical casting patterns. She played two servants, a witch and a spirit in her initial season: Iras in *Antony and Cleopatra*, Margaret in *Much Ado About Nothing*, a Witch in *Macbeth* and a Spirit in *The Tempest*. Simon recalls it fondly as 'a wonderful, wonderful, wonderful season' with 'an incredibly close company'. For a young actor, the RSC was also an opportunity to learn from 'seasoned veterans. I was a real sponge and I used to just watch and soak it up'. The ethos was one in which an actor could theoretically climb the classical casting ladder, as Simon explains:

> Us youngsters would get a smallish part and if you did well, you'd get another bigger part and if you did well at that, you'd get a bigger part. Until you may or may not get to where the next step up would be, a leading role.

FIGURE 5 *Josette Simon as Rosaline.* Love's Labour's Lost, *Royal Shakespeare Company, Stratford-upon-Avon, 1984. Photo by Donald Cooper/Photostage.*

Josette Simon returned to the RSC for a second season cycle in 1984. 'At that time', she recalls, 'it was a year in Stratford and a year in London. I did a year in London and came straight back.' At that point, there was no indication that she would end the season with a central role in a main house Shakespeare. She was initially cast as Portia's maid Nerissa in *The Merchant of Venice* and starred in Louise Page's *Golden Girls* as Dorcas Ableman. Playing a maid and a role described in the script as a 'Black athlete', Simon's parts were a promotion but also within RSC's pattern of casting performers of colour in 'Black parts'. By the end of the season Josette Simon would gain another promotion, playing Rosaline, the play's romantic heroine, in *Love's Labour's Lost*.

The RSC staged five productions of Shakespeare for its 1984 season in the Royal Shakespeare Theatre, the company's main stage: *Henry V*, *The Merchant of Venice*, *Richard III*, *Hamlet*, with Barry Kyle's production of *Love's Labour's Lost* the last to open. Principal players for the latter were announced in January, including the white actors Roger Rees (Berowne) and Kenneth Branagh (King of Navarre), but Rosaline was yet to be cast. Josette Simon recalls that Barry Kyle's casting of her as Rosaline 'caused major controversy' within the RSC: 'There was a lot of chat before they made that decision'. As she recalls, the arguments against Simon playing Rosaline were similar to those levelled at Alton Kumalo when he objected to continually being cast as a servant during his tenure with the RSC, 'Could they? Should they? Would the audience riot? Would they say "What's that Black face doing in Elizabethan England?"'

Without being privy to the internal disputes, it is impossible to know how Barry Kyle swayed those who were opposed to Josette Simon playing Rosaline. Clearly, however, the RSC's internal casting processes likely worked in the director's favour. 'Casting was obviously quite complicated' at the RSC, the white director Bill Alexander told Tony Howard. With multiple directors assembling a company that would be cross-cast across the season, 'that was a kind of natural limitation on each director being able to cast in exactly the way he wanted'. Alexander quickly realized 'that the more plays you were directing in a season, the easier it became to get exactly who you wanted. Because you could simply do your own through casting.' With two plays in the RSC repertoire, *Love's Labour's Lost* and *Golden Girls*, Barry Kyle was able to form his own mini repertory company: nine of the thirteen actors in *Golden Girls* also appeared in Kyle's *Love's Labour's Lost*.

In *Love's Labour's Lost*, Shakespeare 'plunges [his audience] into a world populated by a king and a princess, by lords and ladies' (Woudhuysen 2014: 1). Barry Kyle's production made class explicit by using a setting that hinted at the Belle Époque, with the women resplendently adorned in long, silk dresses with matching hats and parasols. Rosaline's attire immediately marked her as a woman of high status, as far from the maid stereotype as possible. The importance of Rosaline as the female centre of *Love's Labour's Lost*'s romantic entanglements also helped to refute stereotypes on the Shakespearean stage. Rosaline and her suitor, Berowne, are prototypes for Benedick and Beatrice in *Much Ado About Nothing*. Maria DiBattista describes these women as Shakespeare's 'peerless comic heroines', the originators of a tradition running from Shakespeare to Millament in Congreve's *The Way of the World* to the 'fast-talking dames' of 1930s American screwball comedy (DiBattista 2001: 31). Josette Simon uses similar language to describe Rosaline:

> A magnificent woman: so bright, so sparky, so accomplished, so witty, so self-possessed. I loved the fact of Rosaline that she gives as good as she gets. Rosaline and Beatrice are not dismissive, retiring types who are cowed by their male counterparts. They give as good as they get and they have the same amount of wit, if not more, and guile and intelligence [than Berowne and Benedick]. So that was, for me, was what Rosaline was about. It's a battle of equals.

For the first time on a major British stage, an African-Caribbean woman portrayed an intelligent, witty and strong leading Shakespearean character. Josette Simon was the first woman of colour to play Rosaline in Britain *and* the first person of colour to portray one of Shakespeare's lovers on the RSC stage. Like those who had come before her, she was a pioneer, the silent toll of which cannot be underestimated. 'Every part is hard', Simon observes, but Rosaline:

> was my biggest Shakespeare and I had this enormous light shining on me the whole time. It was really stressful. It's hard enough trying to make something as good as you could possibly make it. That job is hard without having a whacking great spotlight on you. You are the first and if you fail, people will say, 'Actors who are Black can't do Shakespeare. See, [casting this actor] didn't work, did it?' There was a lot of commentary about it and I remember thinking, 'I'm just going to go under if I let any of that in, because it's hard enough trying to do something well, so I've got to try and somehow tune this out and just focus on trying to do this thing well.'

Despite the glowing reviews for the production, some critics treated Josette Simon's casting as Rosaline as a novelty. John Barber ascribed Simon's casting to a 'witty director' who had taken Navarre's line 'By heaven, thy love is black as ebony' (4.3.243) as a description of skin colour. '[Shakespeare] only means she is a brunette', Barber opined (*DT* 5 November 1984). As late as 1990, even academics wrote of Josette Simon's Rosaline in terms of transience and novelty. In his Oxford Shakespeare edition of the play, George Hibbard refers to her casting as one of 'many experiments in staging that this highly experimental comedy has given rise to' (1990: 10). Speaking of integrated casting in terms of an 'experiment' is deeply problematic as it infers the practice is an aberration, rather than what it was by then: a common occurrence. Hostility to people of colour playing Shakespeare only grew more vociferous as the decade progressed.

'Othello was an Arab', RSC, 1985

In 1985 the RSC staged *Othello* for the first time since the BBC–Equity dispute had highlighted systemic inequality for African-Caribbeans in the industry. Terry Hands' choice for the title role was not one of the African-Caribbean men who had worked for the RSC since 1967, but a mixed-race actor of Gujarati and Russian descent. Ben Kingsley had first joined the RSC in 1967, one of four actors of colour who were the first to play Shakespeare on the RSC stage. His African-Caribbean contemporaries – Alton Kumalo, Oscar James and Louis Mahoney – struggled to play parts outside those deemed 'suitable'. Before arriving at the RSC, Ben Kingsley had changed his name from Krishna Bhanji out of what he described as 'a positive necessity' because 'every casting director in the land would expect me to speak fluent Hindi' (*Times* 21 September 1985). By changing his name, Kingsley largely avoided the overt racism heaped upon other performers of colour, although he sometimes straddled both halves of his mixed-race identity in the parts he played, as his 1974 appearances in the title role in *Hamlet* and the 'Coloured

Man' in Athol Fugard's *Statements After An Arrest* attest. His career path was equal to that of his white counterparts, however, and he was able to work his way up from supernumerary to leading actor. Kingsley had been playing the Yorkshire schoolmaster Wackford Squeers in the RSC's legendary production of Dickens' *The Life and Adventures of Nicholas Nickleby* when Richard Attenborough tapped him to play the lead in the Oscar-winning film, *Gandhi*.

Gandhi gave Ben Kingsley the kind of success that eluded his African-Caribbean peers. As an Academy Award winner, Kingsley was now an internationally acclaimed performer, highly sought and with impressive classical theatre credits to his name. Kingsley was filming in Marrakesh when the white director Terry Hands, joint artistic director of the RSC, reached him by phone to offer him the part of Othello; Kingsley accepted immediately. In his *Players of Shakespeare* essay Kingsley recounts that, as he continued filming in Morocco, a picture of his Othello began to emerge that was inextricably enmeshed with the North African landscape that surrounded him: 'Moor or Blackamoor?', the white actress Fabia Drake asked Kingsley, 'If the former you might find his physical counterpart here [in Marrakesh]' (Kingsley 1988: 169–70). Kingsley and Hands were united in this decision, opting to portray Othello not as an African-Caribbean but as a light-skinned North African Moor, a decision that also tapped into two centuries of prejudice, rooted in modern constructions of race.

By the early 1800s poets, philosophers and historians – including Samuel Taylor Coleridge, Charles Lamb, Immanuel Kant and the slave-holding third President of the United States, Thomas Jefferson – began writing treatises dehumanizing men and women of African descent. As Atesede Makonnen observes, 'The literary minds of the nineteenth century were thinking about race in changing ways, constructing paradigms that made blackness scientifically subordinate to whiteness, physically and morally' (2018: 348). These treatises intersect with Shakespearean theatre through Coleridge, whose writings were particularly influential in 'question[ing] the validity of portraying Othello as a black man' (Thompson 2016: 29). Coleridge projected his racist beliefs onto Shakespeare, claiming the playwright could not have been 'so utterly ignorant as to make a barbarous negro plead royal birth'. He was, in effect, positing the notion 'that Othello is not black but light-skinned' (Thompson 2016: 31). Coleridge's work influenced the actor Edmund Kean, who began playing Othello with lighter make-up, ushering in 'what has come to be called the great '"Bronze Age of *Othello*", the period in which Othello was portrayed as tanned, tawny, and off-white (i.e., definitively non-black)' (Thompson 2016: 31).

Coleridge's argument for, and Kean's physical embodiment of, a non-Black Othello had long-term consequences. A 'tawny Moor' morphed into an understanding of Othello as a light-skinned North African, enabling white actors and audiences to distance themselves from the African-Caribbean bodies they had begun to view as subhuman. As Kim F. Hall observes, in the age of slavery 'a bronze Othello [was] the best vehicle for engaging the audience's sympathy' (2003: 363). The portrait of Othello as, to use Ayanna's Thompson phrase, 'definitively non-black' still rears its head periodically. Four days after the announcement that Rudolph Walker would play Othello at the Young Vic, an upset reader wrote to the editor of the *Sunday Telegraph*: 'As Shakespeare's Othello was an Arab I am at a loss to understand why the Moor of Venice is so often portrayed as an African negro' (29 April 1984). At its root this argument aims to deny the legitimacy of portrayals of Othello by African-Caribbean men.

Twenty-three male performers of colour appeared in the RSC's Shakespeares between 1967 and 1985. Seventeen were of African-Caribbean decent and six from south Asian backgrounds (the first east Asian, Daniel York Loh, would not be cast in an RSC Shakespeare until 1993). Only three African-Caribbean men had played one of the three largest roles in any Shakespeare play at the RSC by 1985: Calvin Lockhart (Aaron), Jeffery Kissoon (Caliban) and Hugh Quarshie (Aaron, Hotspur). Not even Hugh Quarshie – the only African-Caribbean man to have been cast in a prominent role, Hotspur, that was not stereotypical or written as Black – seems not to have been considered as a potential Othello at the RSC in 1985.[1]

Even as the RSC cast Ben Kingsley, other productions of *Othello* continued to feature African-Caribbeans in the title role. Jeffery Kissoon appeared in a streamlined version of *Othello* at the Mercury Theatre, Colchester in March 1985 and Colin McFarlane played the part at the Chester Gateway in November. Of all the productions of *Othello* staged after the 1979 dispute between Equity and the BBC, the National Youth Theatre's 1985 production cemented the shift that Rudolph Walker and Joseph Marcell had begun. Even before the National Youth Theatre's *Othello* had opened, the Nigerian-born, Bristol Old Vic Theatre School student Hakeem Kae-Kazim was being lauded as an emerging talent: 'He speaks Shakespeare better than most white actors. He has a feeling for it', the NYT's founder, Michael Croft told the *Sunday Times* (15 September 1985). Martin Hoyle concurred, saying Kae-Kazim 'speaks the verse as well as many professionals' (*FT* 18 September 1985). While the RSC continued to deny African-Caribbean men the opportunity to play Othello, Kae-Kazim proved more than equal to the task at the end of his summer holiday.

Emergence of a new 'Black canon'

As regional and fringe theatres began to include performers of colour in Shakespeare productions, a new 'Black canon' began to emerge. Old patterns remained, as African-Caribbeans continued to be cast as Shakespearean servants or slaves, including Nerissa and Pindarus. At the same time,

---

[1] Quarshie suggested in a 2015 interview in the *Sunday Times* that it was not until 1995 the idea was broached (*STimes* 24 May 2015).

productions of *A Midsummer Night's Dream*, *Macbeth* and *Othello* were used to create a new stratum of 'Black parts'.

Between 1980 and 1987, actors from African-Caribbean or south Asian heritage were cast three or more times in a number of roles (Table 3).

These fresh entrants into the 'Black canon' continued to reflect dominant stereotypes, particularly parts that could be exoticized as 'other': the witches in *Macbeth*, and Puck, Hippolyta, Oberon and Titania in *Dream*. As blacking up became unacceptable, both Othello and the Prince of Morocco also entered as a more traditional type of 'Black part', the casting of which was determined by the ethnicity identified in the script. Only Banquo, Theseus and Hermia defy stereotyping, although a closer look at Hermia underlines why she emerged as a part in which directors were willing to cast a woman of colour.

The two female *ingénue* roles in *A Midsummer Night's Dream* are Hermia and Helena, both in love with their male counterparts. In 1984 women of colour played both parts for the first time in Britain at the Haymarket Theatre, Leicester: Angela Bruce (Helena) and Vicky Lickorish (Hermia). African-Caribbean women played Hermia four times between 1980 and 1987, but Helena only once. Two lines in the text stand out, both descriptions of Hermia given by her lover Lysander while under a spell: the seemingly innocuous 'Who will not change a raven [Hermia] for a dove [Helena]?' (2.2.118) and the more direct 'Away, you Ethiope!' (3.2.257). Eric Shorter's comment, that 'Angela Bruce's opening line "Call you me fair?" sets the ironical tone' (*DT* 30 October 1984), illustrates how casting was policed in the mid-1980s. Guided by the language of implied skin tone, directors either self-consciously or unconsciously allowed the textual epithet 'Ethiope' to be ascribed to a Black woman as Hermia, instead of casting a woman who was the opposite of 'fair' as Helena.

TABLE 3 *Parts in which actors of African-Caribbean or south Asian heritage were cast three or more times, 1980–1987*

Play	Role (number of times)
Dream	Hermia (4)
	Puck (4)
	Hippolyta (3)
	Oberon (3)
	Theseus (3)
	Titania (3)
Othello	Othello (10)
Merchant	Prince of Morocco (7)
	Nerissa (3)
Macbeth	Witch (4)
	Banquo (3)
Julius Caesar	Pindarus (3)

While the new 'Black canon' was forming, one director provided a rare glimpse of an alternate reality that had potential to move away from casting people in 'suitable roles'. The Yorick Theatre Company's production of *The Winter's Tale* in 1985 was one that broke stereotypes. Leo Wringer, who had played Puck for John Harrison at the Leeds Playhouse three years earlier, was cast as Autolycus. 'Mr. Wringer has the buoyant irreverence [*sic*] of the natural comic', wrote Rosalind Carne, 'and thanks to his wickedly endearing West Indian Autolycus, Act 4 is the most interesting part of the show' (*Guardian* 16 April 1985). Michael Batz's production also cast Shope Shodeinde as the first woman of colour to play Hermione. Despite these two examples, a subsequent lack of imagination continued to blight the careers of people of colour. The south Asian actress Priyanga Burford became the second Hermione of colour (Shakespeare's Globe, 2018), thirty-three years after Shope Shodeinde; Felix Dexter followed Leo Wringer as Autolycus sixteen years later (RSC 2002). Erica Whyman cast two African-Caribbean women in her 2020 RSC production as Hermione (Kemi-Bo Jacobs) and Autolycus (Anne Odeke). The coronavirus pandemic shut the theatres and it was never staged for a live audience, but filmed and broadcast on BBC Four in 2021.

One reason for the undercasting of these two roles is that they fall largely outside pervasive stereotypes. Although Autolycus does not appear until Act 4, he is a pivotal protagonist in *Winter's Tale* and the play's fourth largest role. On the surface the part conforms to stereotype, as Autolycus shares with Lucius in *Julius Caesar* the status of servant; as he puts it, he has 'served Prince Florizel' (4.3.13). The audience, however, sees Autolycus in a different guise: as a 'pedlar' (4.4.183) of ballads and trinkets, an entrepreneur earning a living.

Hermione is also outside the parts most often played by women of colour: maids, prostitutes or the exotic others of the canon. Hermione is a queen, the consort of Leontes, king of Bohemia. By casting Shodeinde, Batz broke a major taboo in placing a woman of colour at the heart of a royal court. Seeing a woman of colour making Hermione's journey through the play as a multifaceted character was also a major advance. Hermione is a strong woman who experiences a multitude of emotions: happiness, grief, anger, forgiveness. She is also highly intelligent and her spirited defence against a false accusation of adultery concludes with a rhetorical flourish: her husband's accusations are against the rule of law ("Tis rigour and not law' [3.2.116]). Instead of being on the periphery of the action, a woman of colour as Hermione was a fully formed, complex human being, who by her very presence broke all the stereotypes.

RSC 1986

Patrick Robinson was in his final year at LAMDA in January 1986, newly signed with an agent, when he got an audition with the RSC. The job was 'for the lowest form of contract', Robinson recalls, what the RSC calls play as cast, but taking it was 'a no-brainer'. That initial contract was for twelve months and, as he explains, 'in those days, you had to do your forty weeks to get your Equity card. For me, that was brilliant because I was at the Royal Shakespeare Company at twenty-two and I'm from Deptford, southeast London'. Robinson left LAMDA early for the RSC's Stratford base that spring, where he appeared in Aphra Behn's *The Rover* and three Shakespeares: *Romeo and Juliet*, *Macbeth* and *The Winter's Tale*.

Robinson joined the RSC at a time of significant change: 'When I'd first joined the RSC in '86, it was the biggest influx of non-white actors that they'd had. There was eight of us, out of ninety-odd actors.' The eight included five African-Caribbean men (Hugh Quarshie, Patrick Robinson, Tony Armatrading, Trevor Gordon and Joseph Mydell), two African-Caribbean women (Caroline Johnson and Jenni George) and one east Asian (Togo Igawa). This record influx coincided with the opening of the 450-seat Swan Theatre, a space loosely replicating Jacobean theatres and intended for the RSC's exploration of Shakespeare's contemporaries.

Five of the eight performers of colour in the 1986 Stratford season appeared on the RSC's main stage (Table 4), in three out of five productions, and two productions had all-white casts: *Dream* and *Richard II*. The lack of any actors of south Asian heritage and the omission of Togo Igawa from the company's Shakespeare repertoire highlights the groups' continuing exclusion from classical theatre. Equally important is the lack of a substantial role in the RSC's main house for the majority of African-Caribbeans. Returning to the RSC for his second season, Hugh Quarshie was the notable exception. Although both Quarshie's castings were important – as the first performer of colour to play Tybalt in Britain and the first to play Banquo at the RSC – they also speak to a level above which no person of colour could yet reach.

The opening of the Swan had long-term effects on the RSC's integrated casting practices, a trend that began in its first season in 1986. The RSC used its smaller stages to showcase ethnic-minority talent, while continuing to

TABLE 4 *Performers of colour in the Royal Shakespeare Theatre, 1986*

Actor	Role		
	Romeo and Juliet	*Winter's Tale*	*Macbeth*
Jenni George	Lady	–	–
Trevor Gordon	–	Pastoral Servant	–
Caroline Johnson	Lady	Dorcas, Lady	–
Joseph Mydell	–	–	Bloody Sergeant, Scottish Doctor
Hugh Quarshie	Tybalt	–	Banquo
Patrick Robinson	Policeman	Pastoral Servant	Seyton

marginalize performers of colour on the main stage. While Hugh Quarshie had prominent roles in productions at the Royal Shakespeare Theatre, they were relatively low in the pecking order. Quarshie played the sixth-largest part (Banquo) in *Macbeth* and a small though flashy role who speaks only seventeen times in two scenes: Tybalt in *Romeo and Juliet*. In contrast, Quarshie played second leads in the Swan. He was cast in the second-largest part in Shakespeare and Fletcher's *The Two Noble Kinsmen* (Arcite) and as the second male lead (Belville) in Aphra Behn's *The Rover*. The white actors Gerard Murphy and Jeremy Irons, respectively, played the largest parts in these plays. Together, Table 4 and Table 5 illustrate the distribution of the RSC's performers of colour throughout its repertoire: virtually every person of colour in the RSC in 1986 appeared in *The Rover*. No performers of colour were cast in Ben Jonson's *Every Man in His Humour*, and Joseph Mydell appeared in no Swan productions.

John Barton's production of *The Rover* was the most visible manifestation of an RSC response to growing pressure to be more inclusive. Barton shifted the action from Behn's setting of Carnival time in Naples to what Patrick Robinson describes as 'a generic Caribbean island'. Like Michael Rudman's Caribbean-set *Measure for Measure* five years earlier at the National Theatre, Barton's *Rover* created 'Black parts' by relocating the action. Unlike Rudman's production, *The Rover* was neither Shakespeare nor staged in the main house. While the RSC gave opportunities to people of colour, most worked at the company's margins, away from the works of its house playwright.

Opposition met the visibility of the cohort of eight performers of colour on the Stratford stage, despite their muted presence in Shakespeare. Local residents wrote to the *Stratford-upon-Avon Herald* to voice their outrage. One complained about Hugh Quarshie's appearances as Banquo, a Scottish thane, and Arcite, a Theban prince. These objections were rooted in ideas of

TABLE 5 *Performers of colour in the Swan Theatre (X), 1986*

Actor	Two Noble Kinsmen	The Rover	The Fair Maid of the West
Tony Armatrading	–	✓	✓
Jenni George	✓	✓	–
Trevor Gordon	–	✓	✓
Togo Igawa	–	✓	✓
Caroline Johnson	–	✓	–
Hugh Quarshie	✓	✓	–
Patrick Robinson	–	✓	–

historical ownership of Scotland, Thebes and Shakespeare. 'What [*Macbeth*] is really about', Quarshie responded:

> is a man confronting his own conscience of going too far and having to live with the effects on his psyche of a bad conscience. I don't think it makes any less sense for me to play Banquo than it makes for Vanessa Redgrave to play Cleopatra or for Antony Sher to play Richard III.
> (*Newcastle Journal* 2 February 1987)

The reaction to Hugh Quarshie's prominent place within the RSC's 1986 season was a symptom of wider societal attitudes, which were also apparent inside the company. The white director Graham Watts, who was then deputy stage manager at the RSC, recalls that the 'only incident of direct racism I witnessed' was an older member of the acting company saying, 'If the Black actors want to get on, then they should be prepared to white up'. At the time, Watts says, the attitude that performers of colour should white up to play Shakespeare 'was pretty prevalent. I don't think she was unusual in that respect.'

Patrick Robinson also remembers an occasion when the South African ambassador had been invited to a performance and Robinson had been asked if he was going to be whiting up:

> I said, 'Well, if he's coming, why should I do something just for one person? I'm a professional. And as far as I'm concerned, it's irrespective of what colour I am. I'm playing a character, so I'm going to do the show as I would do the show. Let him see my Black face. Up there on the stage.' I wanted him to see this [*gestures to his face*] doing it.

While no one whited up during the performance, Watts recalls, 'when the company came on for their curtain call, all the Black actors had whited up' in protest.

'They're nurturing you'

For Patrick Robinson the RSC was an important part of his development as an actor: 'You're doing understudies. You're working with Cis Berry. You'd done [Berry's] *The Voice and the Actor* book in drama school and there she is, talking to you. So I was like, "Wow!"' Fresh out of LAMDA, Patrick Robinson had been astonished to learn he would be understudying the white actor Sean Bean as Romeo: 'It was a bit of a shock because I thought, *I'm definitely understudying Hugh Quarshie because he's playing Tybalt and he's Black*. I'm the only other Black man [in the *Romeo* cast].' Sean Bean never missed a performance while he was in the RSC, but, when he was preparing to leave the company early, Robinson recalls Bean took him aside to give him the news:

> Sean Bean came up to me, because we got on great. He's a genuine guy. He said, 'Pat, I'm leaving. I'm leaving, so get your agent on to it.' I went, 'Oh. Really?' 'Yeah', he said. And I thought, *They won't use me.* Anyway, I do ring my agent and she said, 'Okay, Pat, I'll get onto it.' She came back with a thing, 'Oh no. They're nurturing you, Patrick. They're looking for someone with a bit more experience.' 'Oh. Right. Okay.' That was that.

The acting company received a memo on 22 June 1987, informing them that the white actor Greg Hicks would replace Sean Bean as Romeo. Graham Watts recalls the company being 'shocked' when the news came through.

Although Patrick Robinson was never *cast* as Romeo, he was the first performer of colour to *play* the role at the RSC. As Robinson recalls, the company was rehearsing fight sequences in preparation for Hicks' debut when the incoming Hicks was injured and one performance was cancelled. Robinson picks up the story:

> Then we all come back next day and I'm pulled aside and told, 'Oh could you go through Romeo for the other principals and everyone else for the show this afternoon?' Right. Okay. Come to five, six o'clock, we're waiting and another knock on the door, 'Right, you'll be on tonight.' And that was it. That was it.

Patrick Robinson played Romeo at the Barbican Theatre for eight performances between 22 and 28 July 1987. He became the first African-Caribbean to play a named Shakespearean tragic lead at the RSC, and the first actor of colour to play Romeo there.

Graham Watts was never privy to the decision to recruit an outside actor to play Romeo, but he feels it was a mistake, as Patrick Robinson 'was the best man for the role. Beyond a shadow of a doubt.' Paterson Joseph, who had started at LAMDA when Robinson was in his third year, recalls going to the production to see Robinson:

> He was beautiful. He was physically very capable and able. He was on the text. I remember watching him and not feeling any sense of a man being out of his depth. We all went to see him because we were all still at LAMDA.

Robinson also recalls Dilys Laye, who played the Nurse, telling him 'You were the best [Romeo of the three]' and that Jonathan Pryce, who was also appearing in the RSC that season, had come to see his Romeo: 'I was chuffed and he said, "Good job." So that was the biggest endorsement that I needed for confidence to believe that I can do Shakespeare wherever it is, not just at the RSC.' It would take the RSC another decade finally to *cast* an African-Caribbean actor, Ray Fearon, to play Romeo in his own right.

Antony, Contact Theatre, 1987

Although African-Caribbeans were regularly playing Othello by the mid-1980s, performers of colour remained excluded from what most consider the male pinnacles of classical acting: Hamlet, Macbeth, King Lear and Antony. Wyllie Longmore became the first performer of colour to play the male lead in *Antony and Cleopatra* in 1987. Staged at the Contact Theatre in Manchester by Brigid Larmour, the production's simple set had a classical plinth representing Rome and a honey-coloured cloth to suggest the Egyptian desert. Longmore felt that he was 'miscast. I think I didn't have the authority to play him, I thought I was too young':

> Because I am so slender, to me he was more mercurial and as temperamental as she was. He would sound off, the scene in which he chastises the servant, the messenger, for example, was a link to me about his energy. It felt to me as if he had got caught in this relationship with this woman – to whom he had almost given over his entire being – and then every day was regretting this. He was missing his authority in Rome and all of that. But because I was light – physically lighter than Antony usually is – I thought he was more a diplomat. So I was dressed in Italian-like garments, very loose trousers and very loose jacket and sort of pale cream. It looked wonderful, actually. But I thought he was more diplomat than soldier, so I found the soldier bits hard and the scenes in which he runs, when he loses the battle, and the scene with servants I found the hardest, because I couldn't quite reconcile [them] with who I was, really.

Despite his reservations, *Plays and Players* found Longmore a 'subtle, commanding and intelligent Antony', partly because:

> the shift from overconfident, charismatic hero to dazed and frustrated loser is made believable and moving, and Longmore lets us see the elements of wisdom emerging from defeat. He delivers his lines with a fluency that allows them to yield all their poetic rhythm without once breaking the illusion of natural speech.
>
> (August 1987: 31)

Although Longmore's Antony was a breakthrough for integrated casting, it forms the exception that proves the continuing lack of access to Shakespeare's highest levels for people of colour. Only three African-Caribbean men have followed in his footsteps since 1987: Jeffery Kissoon (1991, 2010), Paul Barber (1995) and David Harewood (1996).

Isabella, RSC, 1987

Josette Simon returned to the RSC for Nicholas Hytner's production of *Measure for Measure* in 1987. 'The first thing I remember about playing Isabella', Josette Simon recalls:

> was, it was again a very good lesson in learning how to tune out other people and their opinions. It's stood me in good stead. Once you start playing these classical leading roles – and of course you've got a whole plethora of actresses who've played these parts – they'll tell you, 'I saw Vanessa Redgrave. Marvellous, she was' and all those 'I saw the production where...'. So this was the first time that I learned to tune out other people and their opinions. Because everybody who found I was playing Isabella, everybody did the same thing: they all said to me, 'How are you going to say that line? "More than our brother is our chastity"'. Everybody said this to me. 'What are you going to do about that line? How are you going to play that line?' I don't know! You don't take a line out of context and just say, 'Oh, I'm going to do...' It's all part of the whole. People were obsessed with it. So many people asked me about that.

As the play begins, Isabella is a novice in the Order of Saint Clare in Shakespeare's Vienna. Her opening line, spoken within the walls of the nunnery, is a question: 'And have you nuns no further privileges?' (1.4.1). In introducing Isabella within the convent, Shakespeare establishes her faith and sets up the conflict that leads to that famous line.

Measure for Measure examines the moral and philosophical tension between law and mercy. As Abigail Rokison-Woodall observes, Hytner's production exposed the 'moral and sexual corruption' of Vienna by showing 'that while the ruling classes were legislating on the lives of the common man, they were themselves indulging in seedy sexual behaviour and drug taking' (2017: 40). Angelo, the bureaucrat left in charge of Vienna while the Duke has purportedly absented himself, reveals his corruption in his encounters with Isabella over the fate of her brother, Claudio. 'More than our brother is our chastity' (2.4.185) comes at the culmination of two bruising encounters between Isabella and Angelo.

Claudio has been sentenced to death for fornication, having impregnated his fiancée. When Isabella comes to Angelo to plead for her brother's life, he posits a bargain:

> Which had you rather, that the most just law
> Now took your brother's life, or, to redeem him,

> Give you your body to such sweet uncleanness
> As she that he hath stained?
>
> (2.4.51–4)

In Hytner's staging, this encounter escalated as Angelo blindsided Isabella, his sly suggestion becoming a blunt demand:

> You must lay down the treasures of your body
> To this supposed, or else to let him suffer
>
> (2.4.95–6)

The scene became physically dangerous for Isabella; in arguing with Angelo, she reached a point at which she threatened:

> I'll tell the world aloud
> What man thou art
>
> (2.4.153–4)

On those words Angelo, played by the white actor Sean Baker, grabbed Simon's Isabella, covered her mouth and shoved her down on his desk: 'Who will believe you, Isabel?' (2.4.154). Continuing the speech that illuminates her powerlessness, Angelo threw her on the ground and was on the verge of raping her. This was, as Rokison-Woodall notes, 'an extremely violent depiction' (2017: 45) of the scene and arguably went further than most productions. 'I do remember thinking that it was valid', Simon recalls. 'It was not just that he lost sexual control, he had stepped over a mark that he himself couldn't even believe. It's like he cut a rope, a literal tightrope that he operated.' With the stakes so high, in performance the impetus for Isabella's 'To whom should I complain?' was gut wrenching, the agony of her untenable position made clear.

Isabella is one of the few Shakespearean heroines whose story does not revolve around a current or potential marriage, but whose concerns 'are much bigger. Life, death, the soul and redemption' (Karmarelli 2005: 48). Isabella is the moral centre of the play and her faith, its guiding beacon. Josette Simon realized that many people assume Isabella makes the decision to enter the convent 'out of some negative reason, whereas I felt at the time she was making it out of a real, positive, joyous standpoint'. The course of Isbella's journey to the play's resolution tests her faith and the tenets she practises.

Near the end of the play, Angelo's corruption has been exposed and he is condemned to death, both for his assault on Isabella's honour and her brother's supposed death: 'measure still for measure' (5.1.410). Although Isabella believes her brother to be dead, she chooses to kneel and plead for Angelo's life:

> Look, if it please you, on this man condemned.
> As if my brother lived. I partly think

A due sincerity governed his deeds,
Till he did look on me: since it is so,
Let him not die. My brother had but justice.

(5.1.443–7)

'I think that just shows what an extraordinary person she is', Josette Simon observes:

> You start off this play where you've got this young woman who wants to be a nun, totally committed to that life and is tested beyond belief in terms of her resolve. And the person who put her through such horror is the person whose life she pleads to be saved. That tells you everything you need to know about this person. She shows an extraordinary level of compassion. I mean, it's a surprise to everybody except her because she can find it in herself to plead for his life. Amazing.

After this moment Isabella does not speak another line in the play, although she is reunited with her brother, whom the Duke has saved. Simon's Isabella stood motionless, clutching Claudio as the Duke proposed marriage:

Give me your hand and say you will be mine.
He is my brother too. But fitter time for that.

(5.1.493–4)

The Duke's (the white actor Roger Allam) proposal was tender and shy. He kept looking at Isabella, whose back was to him for the rest of the scene, wanting to speak but being unable to do so. 'Isabella says nothing to the Duke's proposals', Allam writes:

> I stammered hesitantly on the first one, and Josette used to look at me in disbelief at the Duke's crass timing. It got a wonderful laugh on 'but fitter time for that', but I was trying to show the Duke's realization of the anguish and pain he has put Isabella through.

(1993: 39)

For Josette Simon, Isabella's silence was key to unlocking the ending of the play:

> I can't remember how many pages it is. Eleven pages or something at the end where she stops speaking. She doesn't speak again. Now, Shakespeare doesn't write anything without a good reason for writing it, or not writing it. She doesn't speak for all those pages. Why? I decided – and so did Nick [Hytner] – that the reason she doesn't say anything is because she doesn't know. So rather than wrap everything up in a nice bow, the Duke asks her to marry him and it's all marvellous and they leave at the end and they're going to get married and so forth, we don't know. We don't know. So the

truest decision was to leave it as a don't know. She hasn't said anything, so that she walks away upstage on her own and then she turns round and looks at him and blackout. And you and your imagination as the audience has to think about what may or may not happen. Well we don't know. Neither does she. She doesn't say yes. This is the point. How can you wrap it up that they end up together when she doesn't say yes? She doesn't say anything. There's a reason for that.

After the final lines, Isabella and the Duke were left alone on stage. Isabella moved upstage, as if to leave, the Duke watching her retreat. At the last moment, she turned to look at him and the lights faded.

Josette Simon's Isabella, like her Rosaline in 1984, was another milestone of integrated casting, a beacon of what was possible. Like Hugh Quarshie in 1986, her presence stood out on the main stage. The RSC had continued the showcasing of performers of colour on its smaller stages, rather than in main house Shakespeares. In 1987 it did so largely through Heidi Thomas' *Indigo*, which told the story of the Liverpool slave trade. The RSC's segregation of talent was duly – if inadvertently – noted by Jeremy Kingston:

> Unequal though [*Indigo*'s] two acts are, both in interest and in achievement, I salute the young author's endeavour to create substantial black roles for the talented black actors of the RSC. For too long they have had to fall back on being the unexplained West Indian members of Henry V's court or Macbeth's clan.
>
> (*Times* 9 July 1987)

The inference that African-Caribbeans did not belong in Shakespeare illustrates the mindset that reinforced their exclusion. Hakeem Kae-Kazim, who had been praised as one of the best verse speakers when performing with the National Youth Theatre, was largely kept to the margins in the RSC's Shakespeares that season, playing supernumeraries in *Julius Caesar* and the Prince of Morocco in *The Merchant of Venice*. Nicholas Hytner had also cast him as Isabella's brother, eliciting praise from John Peter as a 'robust, tortured Claudio' (*STimes* 15 November 1987).

As more performers of colour took on Shakespeare's leads, resistance mounted in the press. Some critics refused to review Hynter's *Measure* because he had cast Josette Simon as Isabella; one reviewer claimed the casting was racist. As Simon noted at the time, she hadn't been on stage for two years, having concentrated on film and television, and had returned to find seventeen performers of colour in the company in both Stratford and London:

> ... and it seemed to me progress had been made. So this sort of reaction astounds me and disillusions me and made me very angry at the time –

the fact that some of the critics couldn't get past the Beecher's Brook of me being black, the fact that they couldn't see any further than that.
(*Newcastle Journal* 8 February 1988)

There had been a similar reaction to Wyllie Longmore playing Antony that same year. Robin Thornber wrote that Brigid Larmour's production of *Antony and Cleopatra* was 'of the well-meaning, worthy, earnest sort that casts a black Roman against a white Egyptian and expects you not to notice, for fear of censure by the Manchester City Council's race-relations unit' (*Guardian* 22 May 1987). Wyllie Longmore recalls that he:

resented the guy telling me that I shouldn't be playing [Antony], but I have every right to play the Roman nation. After all, that was made up of people from all over the world, so what difference if Antony had a streak of blackness in him?

Larmour herself responded with a letter to the editor, challenging Thornber's views:

He cannot let the casting of a black Antony pass without comment. Why? Is some sense of authenticity being infringed? How is authenticity to be defined? Would it be authentic to have an Italian, toga'd Antony, and a Greek Cleopatra? Or a beruffed Jacobean Antony and a boy Cleopatra.
(*Guardian* 30 May 1987)

When Nicholas Hytner was challenged about his casting choice for Isabella in a pre-production feature on *Measure* he responded: 'One knows a big fuss is going to be made about that, but you go on doing it so that in the end no fuss is made' (*Observer* 8 November 1987).

Julius Caesar, Bristol Old Vic, 1987

For all the progress made since the beginning of the decade, one production stands out as the theatrical equivalent of Robert Frost's the road not taken: Roger Rees' 1987 *Julius Caesar* for the Bristol Old Vic. Leon Rubin had inherited a financial crisis and falling audiences when he arrived at the Bristol Old Vic in 1986 to take up the post of artistic director. Where other regional theatres – such as Leeds Playhouse, Manchester's Royal Exchange and Leicester's Haymarket – and the RSC diversified their casting practices, the Bristol Old Vic had lagged behind, hiring only one actor of colour for a Shakespeare play between 1980 and 1986: Rudolph Walker as Caliban in *The Tempest* in 1980. It was Walker's first Shakespeare since playing Caliban in Miller's groundbreaking production a decade before. In an example of the 'distinctive and subordinated position' that 'black labour' occupied in Bristol (Joshua and Wallace 1983: 2), the production's programme omitted Walker's biography while including those of white actors playing minor roles. As part of the legacy of Bristol's involvement in the slave trade, the erasure of Walker's work cohered with a heavily segregated city whose theatre was not actively serving its full community.

When Leon Rubin arrived at the Bristol Old Vic, he wanted to change this. He found 'the audience was almost entirely white, the company was entirely white, the employees, everybody. It just seemed to me that the theatre needed to serve more of its community.' Using an Arts Council grant, Rubin set up a multiracial company at the Bristol Old Vic, called Company 3, which, he notes, would 'focus on the issue of trying to get integrated casting for classics'. This important initiative was meant to address the long-term consequences of exclusion from classical theatre for actors of colour. 'Some of the actors', as Rubin recalls:

> hadn't had the opportunity to hone some of their skills with Shakespeare. They just hadn't been given that chance. So I thought [Company 3] would be a kind of springboard. The idea was we would run a season or two and then gradually those actors would then integrate into the other companies.

The remit of Company 3 was thus not solely to deliver opportunities for actors of colour in the classics but to provide a training ground, intended to lead to promotion to main house productions. The first show by the fledgling Company 3 was *Julius Caesar*, directed by RSC associate artist Roger Rees.

By 1987 David Yip – the first east Asian to play a named part in Shakespeare in 1976 at the Young Vic – had developed a profile through his television work. Yip had starred as Detective Sergeant John Ho in the BBC series *The Chinese Detective*, which was the first, and to date the only, television drama series with a British east Asian lead (see Knox 2019). Yip recalls that, when Rees explained to him what he and Rubin were trying to achieve with Company 3, 'that it was an ensemble piece, basically a multicultural production', he had thought: '*How exciting. This is great.* I said to him, "Look, it sounds fantastic. What else isn't cast?"' Yip joined Rees' production as Mark Antony.

In a first for British Shakespeare, Rees assembled a cast and production team for *Julius Caesar* that was truly multicultural in the ethnicities and countries represented: Guyana, China, Nigeria, Ethiopia, Greece, Jamaica, Wales, Tanzania, Scotland, Zanzibar, Japan, Zaire, England and India. The casting was also a clarion call for more opportunities for people of all backgrounds, which Roger Rees stressed at the press launch for *Caesar*: 'There is not enough commitment to casting people from multi cultural background[s]. This play is a step towards expressing how we would like to be' (*Bristol Journal* 8 January 1987).

The Jamaican-born actor Leo Wringer, who played Brutus, was the most experienced classical actor in the company, having begun his Shakespeare career with a production of *Troilus and Cressida* at the Bristol Old Vic in 1979. By 1987, Wringer had amassed credits that included Puck in *A Midsummer Night's Dream* and Banquo in *Macbeth*, as well as being the first actor of colour to play Launcelot Gobbo in *The Merchant of Venice* in Britain, all in the early to mid-1980s. David Yip's experience at the Young Vic in the 1970s made him the second most experienced classical actor to join Rees' *Caesar*. Rees' Calphurnia, Shope Shodeinde, had only one Shakespeare credit to her name, as the first performer of colour to play Hermione, in the same production of *Winter's Tale* as Wringer. Peter Straker, better known as a musician, also had one Shakespearean credit, in Michael Rudman's Caribbean *Measure for Measure*, before playing Cassius for Company 3. For Ram John Holder (Caesar), Lucy Sheen (Portia) and Dhiendra (Octavius Caesar), Rees' *Julius Caesar* was their first professional Shakespeare.

Lucy Sheen reflected on playing Brutus' wife Portia, crediting Rees' experience with Shakespeare and his 'understanding of that character' as being 'much stronger than Brutus' as pivotal in helping her develop the character. As Sheen recounts:

> When we [Roger Rees and Sheen] came to discuss the speech she has when she indicates she's wounded herself [2.1.290–301], [he thought] it should be a wound much closer to her private place because that is indicative of the respect, but also the strength that she has. That gives Portia a very different quality. It's not just the wife that's saying, 'What's happening? I'm fearful for you'; it's a person, a woman who has an acumen or understanding and who also has a proud heritage of coming from political links and an understanding of how things work and how they don't work and what happens when they go wrong. And also the courage to stand with your convictions, to be better than the others that are going along.

The detail with which this scene was worked illustrates the quality of a production that the *Bristol Evening Post* called 'a very promising start' (20 February 1987).

Rees' production of *Julius Caesar* was a success on multiple fronts, achieving several of the aims set by Leon Rubin for Company 3, recognized as one of the most popular shows of Rubin's tenure (*BEP* 25 June 1987). For Lucy Sheen the success was measured by 'the amount of people who were not only seeing it when we were touring it, but coming back to the Old Vic, was amazing'. For Daniel York Loh, who had seen it at his college in Weston-super-Mare, the production had a profound effect: 'It tipped me over the edge to being an actor.' A roster of well-known people came to see the show, including theatrical stalwarts like the white actor Timothy West, as well as the rock star Freddie Mercury and his band Queen. Yet, despite its success, the climate within the establishment could also be hostile. Lucy Sheen recalls being called 'uppity wogs' when the company lobbied to have the run of *Caesar* extended because of difficulties with Company 3's second show, *Woyzek*.

Growing dissent in pockets of the media indicated the amount of progress that had been made in integrating Shakespeare in the 1980s. The further the casting of actors of colour moved from 'suitable roles' or 'Black parts', the greater the outcry. The *Daily Telegraph*'s sub-editor created an eye-catching headline: in a play on Caesar's uncomplimentary line about Cassius (1.2.192), it reads 'Let me have men about me that are black'. The lede, beginning with 'The introduction of black players in roles written for whites is increasing', makes the author's stance abundantly clear. With claims such as 'the colour of an actor's skin is crucial to the impact on the spectator', Eric Shorter's review brims with the same arguments articulated many times before in an attempt to exclude people of colour from productions of Shakespeare's plays. Instead of simply reiterating the cliché 'they can't speak the verse', Shorter elaborates on the theme: 'The black, brown or yellow-skinned player may speak English supremely, as to the manor born, but it may not sound as we are used to hearing it from the mouths of the leading Shakespeareans' (*DT* 27 February 1987).

Company 3 failed to achieve its ultimate aim of integrating its multicultural casts of *Julius Caesar* and *Woyzek* into the Bristol Old Vic's main house productions. Leon Rubin's experiment was cut short when he left in June 1987, after eighteen months as artistic director. The much-needed classical training ground of Company 3 was disbanded and a more traditional and English-centric repertoire was reinstated in the autumn 1987 season. Although *Julius Caesar* received a significant amount of press attention, both locally and nationally, it did not translate into a universal breakthrough for actors of colour playing major parts elsewhere. While a handful of performers of colour have played Brutus in subsequent productions, only one other African-Caribbean has played Julius Caesar since Ram John Holder: Jeffery Kissoon in the RSC's 2012 production.

The subsequent lack of progress since Roger Rees' multicultural *Caesar* also highlights the continuing exclusion of east Asian actors in Shakespeare. Lucy Sheen was the first actress of east Asian heritage to play Portia and few have followed her, male or female. Portia has also been her only Shakespeare role:

> It's just a shame that thirty years on, there have been very few actors – east Asians, let alone females – that have done major Shakespearean roles and that is a real sadness, that I'll still be able to say I was the first; I want to be able to say, it's been followed by so and so and so and so, they've gone on to do Juliet, they've gone on to do Cleopatra, they've gone on to do Beatrice, Miranda, whatever, they've been at the RSC, they've been at the National, they've been at the Globe.

4

Owning Shakespeare – Temba, Talawa and Tara Arts, 1988–1994

At age eleven Kulvinder Ghir began building his Shakespearean résumé at a performing arts school in Leeds with a small passage from *King Lear*, graduating to Seyton in *Macbeth* and finally moving on to Don Pedro in *Much Ado*:

> The school was really, really great at putting these productions on. It really built a great reputation for doing Shakespeare in a very professional manner. And you had these kids from the ages of eleven to seventeen doing these plays. And they came from very deprived areas to do this course on the other side of Leeds, in Bradford.

Ghir began his professional acting career in television, but in 1988 he was offered the chance to play Paris in *Romeo and Juliet* at the Albany Empire in Deptford, London: 'Anytime Shakespeare pops up, yes please. Because you want to take that man on, and his words and his rhythms and his humour and his tragedy and his pathos.'

Few traces remain of Teddy Kiendl's production, but the advertising material has an evocative description of its concept:

> Trinidad in the 1930s. In the heat and the dust young men play with a fire they cannot control. Conflict flares up between two great Black and Asian families. And the passion of lovers threatens to ignite a racial tinderbox.

Kulvinder Ghir recalls the Capulets were portrayed by actors of south Asian heritage and the Montagues were African-Caribbeans. Carlton Chance was Romeo and Janet Steele – who went on to run Kali Theatre Company for thirteen years – played Juliet. Sharon D. Clarke and Madhav Sharma were also in the cast, Sharma as Friar Laurence and Clarke, according to one of the few extant reviews, as a singer. Kiendl's production was also the first since Peter Coe's *The Black Macbeth* to have a cast comprising solely performers from minority heritages.

The Albany Empire *Romeo* was staged to serve its community, and Ghir recalls specific reasons for putting on that play with a mixed cast of African-Caribbeans and south Asians:

> At that time, it was a lot of gangs and a lot of fighting going on and it was right for Deptford to go and put *Romeo and Juliet* on. And because it's about cultures, it's about differences, and at the end of the day, you know, it's their love and hope.

Ghir also remembers the young audiences' engaged reaction to the play:

> It was a very, very Afro-Caribbean, Black audience who came. And you could hear them sucking their teeth, vexing, 'Why!' You could hear the comments. We need that raucousness sometimes, we need that energy from the audience to actually make those comments. And Deptford, it was very much like that. Especially the way the set was designed because he had two voms [entrances through the audience] that came into a playing area and the audience completely surrounded it. And what I remember of Albany was young people. They stayed there in the theatre afterwards, because the theatre would change into a club and they put the big screens up. So the kids and the young people that were there, they not only came and watched a bit of Shakespeare, they stayed for the night and listened to music. It was a great place at that time, the Albany, because it was quite vibrant.

The Albany Empire *Romeo and Juliet* was one of several productions in the late 1980s and early 1990s – including Roger Rees' *Julius Caesar* – whose diverse casts and audiences collectively put pressure on the industry to integrate British Shakespeare.

Three minority-led theatre companies – Temba, Talawa and Tara Arts – provided a major platform for performers of colour by expanding their repertoire into classical theatre, giving opportunities to African-Caribbeans and south Asians to produce work they were denied elsewhere. Oscar James and his fellow RSC alumnus, Alton Kumalo, set up their theatre company, Temba, in 1972, partly because of Kumalo's growing frustration at the RSC. Tara Arts was established in 1977 in the aftermath of the murder of Gurdip Singh Ghaggar, who had been killed in a racist attack the previous year. Jatinder Verma, who was finishing university at the time, recalled it had been the 'sense of anger and of trying to understand what's happened and of trying to say something, [which] led us to make our theatre' (qtd in Hingorani 2006: 175). A quartet of women of colour – Mona Hammond, Carmen Monroe, Inigo Espejel and Yvonne Brewster – formed Talawa Theatre Company nearly a decade later.

Although none were envisioned as a classical theatre company, each has an important place in the history of Shakespearean integrated casting. As Brewster noted in 2016, 'At Talawa theatre company, our policy was to give black actors work they weren't being offered – and nobody was offering them the chance to do Shakespeare' (*Guardian* 1 February 2016). Between them, Temba, Talawa and Tara Arts produced four important productions of Shakespeare between 1988 and 1994 that helped to reclaim parts of the canon that were largely still out of reach. The three companies also put down a marker, demonstrating that they had as much right to Shakespeare as their white counterparts.

Romeo and Juliet, Temba, 1988

Alby James' experience as an assistant director at the RSC proved formative for Temba. As a university-educated director, James recognized his privilege. He recalls:

> Hugh [Quarshie] and I had been to university. I realized that without such a background it would have been difficult for us as blacks to get into the RSC. I decided that black actors needed experience in textual investigation. I wanted to run a company with similar values to the RSC and the Royal Court.
>
> (*Times* 13 January 1990)

While at the RSC James had advocated greater representation within the company in terms of Shakespeare's leading roles. James recounted to Tony Howard that Terry Hands, then joint artistic director of the RSC with Trevor Nunn, had told him:

> The ideal thing to do was for me to go and form my own company where I could then train the actors from Black and Asian backgrounds in the ways that the RSC work. If I were able also to enable them to have high profiles through being very good at what they do then they, in a sense, are becoming sufficiently high profile enough for the RSC to then bring them in to play the lead roles I'm talking about. That was his plan.

With this advice in mind, Alby James left the RSC and sought experience elsewhere, landing the job as artistic director of Temba in 1984.

Temba's first and, it proved, only Shakespeare was Alby James' 1988 production of *Romeo and Juliet*. Staging Shakespeare was the logical conclusion to the director's conversations at the RSC, but the choice of play also filled a major gap in representation. Audiences never saw, James observed, realistic portrayals of people of colour in contemporary drama. James described how, in television and theatre 'blacks and whites are antagonistic to one another. The black people are mad, hysterical, aggressive. In those dramas, no black person can love any white person… it reinforces the fear the white person has of black people' (Carpenter and James 1990: 33). With a love story at its centre, *Romeo and Juliet* was chosen partly to assuage those fears, but also because 'We can't be so easily stereotyped if we have dimensions and humanity' (Carpenter and James 1990: 34). The production featured a young David Harewood in his first professional job out of RADA as Romeo, opposite Georgia Slowe's Juliet. Although Romeo would quickly become a staple of integrated casting in the 1990s, Harewood was only the second performer of colour to play the part, after Roy Alexander at the Young Vic in 1982.

In his documentary *David Harewood: Psychosis and Me*, the actor recalls that, when he won the role after leaving drama school, he thought 'Great. Nice job, lead role', but then the reviews came out:

> I suddenly started realizing that they were all prefaced by 'Black actor David Harewood', 'Black theatre company, Temba Theatre Company', the 'Black production of Romeo and Juliet'. I thought I was just doing *Romeo and Juliet*. No, no, no. You're doing the 'Black' production of *Romeo and Juliet*. And you're a 'Black' actor. Although I was conscious of myself as a Black person, it wasn't until I got out of drama school that the world said to me: 'You are Black'. Your aspirations, dreams, your hopes are now restricted. I'm starting to wonder how much my psychosis was connected to the racism I was dealing with.

What should have been an achievement, as it would have been for any white actor, became one of the catalysts for Harewood's breakdown. As Temba broke down barriers by being the first minority-led theatre company to stage a Shakespeare play, the response from critics had unleashed the worst aspects of an industry refusing to see performers of colour as equals.

Antony and Cleopatra, Talawa, 1991

Doña Croll was born in Jamaica, arriving in Britain at the age of four. She began her career in 1976 and was finally cast in a Shakespeare play in 1987: something she says she had always wanted to do (Croll 2020). She played Nerissa, Portia's maid, in a production of *Merchant of Venice* at the Royal Exchange, Manchester. By then, she had worked professionally for ten years outside classical theatre, while her white colleagues had gained, or were gaining, the work in Shakespeare she had been denied:

> I realized I was working with people who'd just left drama school and they were doing Shakespeare. Why haven't I been allowed to do it? Things were very different in the eighties. In the seventies and eighties. I'm working with all these, what I thought were very posh actors, and I thought they were all much better than me. And then I realized, working with them, that they weren't, they were just whiter than me. And that production changed my life. When I finished it, I said to my agent, "I'm not doing any more repertory theatre," which is what I'd been doing.
> (Croll 2020)

That her first Shakespeare role was a maid speaks volumes about the location of the glass ceiling then and, to some extent, now for women of colour in classical theatre: they are more likely to play servants than tragic leads. By 1991, when Talawa staged *Antony and Cleopatra*, only one woman of colour had played any of Shakespeare's female title roles: Julie Spencer[1] as Juliet at the Latchmere Theatre (now Theatre 503), a pub theatre in the London district of Battersea.

Doña Croll became the first woman of colour to play Cleopatra in Britain, for Talawa Theatre Company in 1991, in an *Antony and Cleopatra* directed by artistic director Yvonne Brewster. Croll recalls that the scrutiny was intense:

> I didn't understand what all the fuss was about. I realized later it was because Cleopatra is seen as a symbol of great beauty and Black women in this society are not regarded as beautiful. I mean, things have changed a little now, where you have Lupita Nyong'o on the front of magazines. That wasn't happening in 1991 and it didn't occur to me because I've always thought I was beautiful. My parents told me I was. And so I assumed I was. And that I realized, I didn't realize it at the time, but that was what that argument was about. "How dare this Black woman take on the part in Shakespeare, which is the most revered and beautiful part." That's what that was about. But I didn't notice it.
> (Croll 2020)

Cyril Nri, who played Eros in the production, reflects, 'It was great to be doing a version of the play which had a Cleopatra who was of colour. This is 1991 and we haven't gone that far and that's fantastic to have that.'

The production design incorporated elements that hinted at Egypt: a 'sandy type floorcloth with half a pyramid' and a large square quilt the 'colour

---

[1] Julie Spencer was then working professionally as Julie Saunders.

of the sea on one side – and on the other side there was the most enormous appliqué, in raw silk, of Isis' (Schafer 1998: 181). Yvonne Brewster also hired an Egyptian movement consultant to work with the cast and Ben Thomas, who played Octavius Caesar, recalls the director 'encouraged the cast to create shapes, patterns and physicality within that'. Brewster's *Antony and Cleopatra* also had what was billed in the programme an all-Black cast. The cast and crew came from a combination of African-Caribbean, south Asian and east Asian heritages. Cyril Nri observes, 'It was important to have an all-Black cast. It was important, too, for all of us that were in it. It again was another first.'

Set in Egypt with a multi-ethnic cast, Brewster's production raised important questions about identity and the ownership of Shakespeare's works. When Michael Rudman transported *Measure for Measure* to the Caribbean and had his actors use Caribbean speech rhythms, he positioned his performers as foreign. By contrast, Brewster's cast used English dialects in *Antony and Cleopatra*, positioning themselves as British. Cyril Nri says:

> We were all just with our own English accents, so it wasn't a matter of putting on anything. We didn't go, 'Well we're setting it in Egypt, we need to have Egyptian accents.' That just came as read. We are Black and therefore we are dealing with this Nubian place.

What this describes is equivalent to British actors playing Henrik Ibsen's *A Doll's House* in Received Pronunciation (RP), rather than Norwegian accents. For Michael Billington, Talawa's *Antony* also showed 'that we have a sizeable corps of black actors who speak verse with ringing authority' (*Guardian* 20 May 1991).

Talawa's ambition was to 'occupy the mainstream', as Brewster's successor as artistic director, Patricia Cumper, observes (Igweonu 2015: 244). The genesis of the production of *Antony and Cleopatra* has an important sidebar that illustrates that desire. The African-American actress–singer Eartha Kitt was performing in London in the summer of 1990. In a radio interview, she mentioned that she had never been asked to play Cleopatra. Then planning Talawa's production of *Antony and Cleoptara*, Yvonne Brewster and Talawa's administrator, David Hoare, approached Kitt and offered to remedy that situation; negotiations between the parties ensued.

Talawa's archive clearly shows that at least one West End theatre was interested in welcoming a Talawa production of *Antony and Cleopatra* starring Eartha Kitt: the Old Vic. Given that British actors of African-Caribbean heritage were traditionally passed over for jobs in favour of imported African-American actors, there is a certain amount of unintended irony in a Black British theatre company looking to an American star to headline its show. It also reveals the relationship of the upper tier of British theatre to celebrity and its exclusion of British performers of colour, who are frequently sidelined for famous white performers. Had the casting of Earth Kitt come off, it would have been a major publicity coup and provided

Talawa with its commercial West End debut, raising the company's profile and perhaps its status. Kitt's casting, however, would also have deprived Doña Croll her place in history as the first woman of colour to play Cleopatra in Britain.

Troilus and Cressida, Tara Arts, 1993

In the mid-to-late 1980s Tara Arts' artistic director Jatinder Verma began what Dominic Hingorani has described as a second theatrical movement (2006: 175). The company's previous work had produced theatre that either interrogated colonialism from a south Asian perspective or chronicled the community's experience in contemporary Britain. 'I didn't feel capable enough before the nineties [to produce Shakespeare]', Verma says: 'Part of not feeling capable was a) technically not capable, but b) not having figured out: how does this fit into our project?' Work on classic texts of the western canon such as *The Government Inspector* and *Tartuffe* made 'thinking about Shakespeare much more possible' because 'it's another form of dialogue. You're now having a dialogue, if you like, with the traditions of the country that you're in, represented in.'

Jatinder Verma's production of *Troilus and Cressida* was as much a dialogue between Britain and its colonial past as it was about contemporary events. 'The choice of *Troilus*', Verma explains, 'was really to do with what was going on in the world, the breakup of Yugoslavia.' The conflict gained the attention of the western world in 1991 when Bosnia and Herzegovina declared independence from Yugoslavia. It triggered a war that lasted four years and brought genocide back to Europe, as nationalist Croat and Serb forces carried out 'ethnic cleansing' against Bosnian Muslims, most notoriously with the slaughter of eight thousand Muslim men and boys in the town of Srebrenica in 1995.

Before the war, Bosnia's population had been 'a multi-ethnic mix of Muslim Bosniaks (44%), Orthodox Serbs (31%) and Catholic Croats (17%)' (*Atlantic* 13 April 2012). The destruction of the country's multiculturalism resonated with Verma, helping to shape his production of *Troilus and Cressida*:

> In a way it became, I suppose for me, this sense of a kind of eulogy on the death of Troy, or civilizations like Sarajevo. What had struck me about the cosmopolitanism of Sarajevo before the war was what we could identify with it: there was a very evident multiculturalism there. And that was what was absolutely at threat and simply got demolished during the war.

For Verma, Shakespeare's warring factions – the Trojans and the Greeks – had their parallels in Yugoslavia, as cosmopolitan Troy was besieged by the 'very rigid' Greeks.

Verma's *Troilus and Cressida* incorporated 'classical Indian dance, with accompanying rhythms provided by bamboo sticks striking the wooden stage floor' (*Guardian* 21 March 2016). There was also delineation between the Trojans and the Greeks through language. For the multicultural Trojans, Verma recalls that he:

> made a deliberate choice for the Trojans to use whatever ways in which people spoke in my cast for the Trojans. And I'd gone even further: I knew there was a bilingual French actor, there was a Bengali actor, Hindi actor, bringing those languages in. And didn't do that with the Greeks.

Provocatively, Verma had the actors playing the Greeks 'white up', to make the inference clear.

Perhaps the most direct form of Verma's dialogue with Britain was replacing Shakespeare's Prologue with a cardboard cut-out of Queen Elizabeth I issuing her 1601 proclamation that Africans should be 'discharged out of this, Her Majesty's dominions' (*Guardian* 2 October 1993).[2] This image emerged, Verma explains, because of the:

> connection with the expulsion of the Moors from Elizabeth's time. It came about because of the era I was working in, the Yugoslav war, and this whole notion of ethnic cleansing had reared its head yet again. What was interesting about that is that, as a way of bringing it home to us that it's not just over there, is that we had an equivalent kind of ethnic cleansing with the expulsion of the Jews [in 1290]. And indeed later on in the Reformation, which I didn't allude to that much other than the figure of Elizabeth, is a kind of physical ethnic cleansing with the defacing of all the statues of saints outside cathedrals.

Verma also experimented with gender roles: a man (Yogesh Bhatt) played Cressida and Helen, while a woman (Shelley King) portrayed Thersites and Diomed. Feminist performance readings of the play since the mid-1980s had been more sympathetic to Cressida's actions once she reaches the Greek camp, portraying her as a victim (see Rogers 2014). Verma's choice to cast a man as Cressida reflected these new performance sensitivities, but for a more visceral reason. With Bosnian Serbs then enslaving Muslim women at rape camps, the director 'felt uncomfortable, given what was going on in the news at the time in Yugoslavia and all that, for it to be a woman actress in that role'.

Troilus and Cressida was Verma's and Tara's Shakespearean apprentice work, the first time a south Asian company had staged a production of a

---

[2] See Emily Weissbourd's article, '"Those in Their Possession": Race, Slavery and Queen Elizabeth's 'Edicts of Explusion' in *Huntington Library Quarterly* 78, no. 1 (Spring 2015) for an alternative interpretation.

Shakespeare play. The director readily admits, 'the one thing the production did not lack was a surfeit of ideas'. He feels that 'with hindsight' a woman playing Cressida 'may have been better. Equally if I had gone this way with crossing of gender, then it would have been really interesting to have got Odysseus [Ulysses] and Achilles and Hector played by women'. Verma also believes he did not execute the Elizabethan parallels, introduced by the image of Queen Elizabeth, as well as he could have:

> I think that that, on reflection, may have been too crude a device. I don't disagree with having used it, but I didn't bring it into the rest of the text. So it was a little bit of a kind of frame and then you got on with the play. And that I think was a pity. It could have been much more pulled out from that. If I would do it again, then one very simple thing would be that I would do it in Elizabethan costume.

Though flawed, *Troilus and Cressida* began a decades-long, if intermittent, conversation between Tara Arts and the Shakespearean canon.

King Lear, Talawa, 1994

Yvonne Brewster's second Shakespeare production was Talawa's 1994 *King Lear*, chosen, as she recalls, 'because Norman Beaton wanted to play King Lear' (qtd in Schafer 1998: 133). Talawa's archive provides a glimpse of how Beaton would have interpreted Shakespeare's tragic hero: 'Norman Beaton sees Lear not as a benevolent, misled, ill-treated old man but as a spiteful, vain, divisive man who deliberately sets his daughters at each others' throats.' King Lear would have been Beaton's third major Shakespearean role, after Ariel in Jonathan Miller's 1970 *Tempest* and Angelo in Michael Rudman's 1981 *Measure for Measure* at the National Theatre, and his first tragic lead. Beaton would also have been the first man of African-Caribbean heritage to play King Lear since Ira Aldridge, 135 years previously.[3]

Ben Thomas was already cast as Edmund when Beaton fell ill. He recalls, 'I got a phone call from Yvonne one night, saying "Are you a big man?"' She asked him to replace Norman Beaton as Lear. As Thomas recalls:

> I was aware that this was a step up to the biggest challenge I could possibly have. One, for myself, but also, two, for her to take that risk because it meant changing the whole ball game really. Norman would have played the old man. How do you deal with a thirty-nine-year old strapping fella playing him?

---

[3] The Burmese-Jewish actor Abraham Sofaer was the second performer of colour to play Lear, in a production at the Shakespeare Memorial Theatre in 1943.

Thomas and his director approached the age differential partly by incorporating a heart ailment into Lear's narrative. Brewster gave Lear an attendant physician (Evroy Deer) who doled out medication to his patient at moments of high stress. They also dug into theatrical history and discovered that the white actor Donald Wolfit had also played King Lear at thirty-nine, a fact they drove home in the publicity.

Ben Thomas' replacing a man nearly twenty years his senior also led to a different focus for his interpretation of Lear. The actor recalls that he and Yvonne Brewster:

> both decided that the best way was to have a look at the emotional arc of this character, rather than depend on the decrepit-ness that his age brings. It's a play that rips you to pieces, if you're going for it in an honest way. You start as God of the Kingdom to dying of a broken heart. That arc, and playing it twice in a day [on matinee days], is extraordinary.

Much of Lear's emotional arc takes place within the context of the king's familial relationships. The father of three daughters, Lear famously gives up his kingdom in the first scene of the play. Lear insists each daughter catalogue her love for him to gain her rightful third of his kingdom. In Brewster's production, the youngest daughter Cordelia (Diane Parish) calmly asked, 'Why have my sisters husbands, if they say / They love you all?' (1.1.99–100), goading her father into an apoplectic rage. Lear's propensity to fury provided Lolita Chakrabarti's Goneril with motivation for her character's rupture with the king. As she recalls, 'I thought that her father looked like he was raging and was not of sound mind at all'.

Having given his kingdom away and banished his youngest daughter, Lear and his retinue must live on the charity of his elder daughters. When Chakrabarti's Goneril entered to find the chaos Lear caused in her household, the tension was immediately palpable. Goneril did not return Lear's affectionate hug and quietly seethed when he pinched her cheek as though she was still a child. Receiving no response, Lear's intemperate chiding of her silence reduced him to yelling at Goneril 'Methinks you are too much of late i'the frown' (1.4.182) in exasperation. Her reply, when it came, was withering: Chakrabarti's Goneril reminded him, 'As you are old and reverend, should be wise' (1.4.232), emphasizing the last three words. This sent him into an uncontrollable rage and, eventually, reaching for his heart medication. Chakrabarti observes, 'I think Goneril is absolutely right, her father is losing his mind, needs to be contained. It makes total sense. You don't need all these people around you, draining money off you, just so you can be a drunken old sot.'

The original concept for the production, laid out in Talawa's archive, was to set *Lear* in a 'pre-historic Africa' that depicted 'three tribes, Black, white and brown', which was to be explored by using a multiracial company. The director eventually decided to set the play in a futuristic Britain, but Brewster kept the skeleton of the original concept. She assembled a cast that included performers from south Asian, east Asian and African-Caribbean heritages, as well as two white actors playing Gloucester and Albany. The design reflected the heritages of *Lear*'s multiracial cast, crafting an aesthetic by appropriating clothing in the way that British culture has absorbed immigrant culinary traditions until curry became the nation's favourite dish: 'traditional African hats, Arab head scarves and Indian frock coats' (*Times* 22 March 1994).

FIGURE 6 *Ben Thomas (Lear) and Mona Hammond (Fool).* King Lear, *Talawa Theatre Company, 1994. Photo by Donald Cooper/Alamy Stock Photo.*

Hints of non-Anglophone cultures were also injected into the production in other ways, with the most striking example the transformation of David Webber's Duke of Kent through disguise into the servant Caius. Kent's alter ego wore dreadlocks and shifted vocally to West Indian cadences as Caius, transforming both visually and aurally from gentleman to servant. David Webber's transition also stood out because the rest of the cast spoke in RP. Webber was the lone performer who used an accent other than a British dialect.

The importance of actors using RP in the two Talawa Shakespeare productions from the early 1990s cannot be underestimated. It was first and foremost a departure from productions helmed by white directors such as Peter Coe and Michael Rudman, who exploited diasporic cultures for *The Black Macbeth* and the National Theatre's *Measure for Measure*, and emphasized their actors' difference from white, English Shakespeareans. Particularly with *King Lear*, Brewster presented an unequivocally British production of one of Shakespeare's greatest tragedies. It positioned the company 'as black-British rather than West Indian or African... in order to proclaim its Britishness and that of those it represents' (Igweonu 2015: 249). Talawa's use of standard English is an important shift in the integration of Shakespeare in Britain as British-born and British-raised children of immigrants, including Ben Thomas, entered the profession. The Leeds-born actor says: 'I was born in England and half of my family is white and the other half were colonials. So I'm an Englishman.'

One of the more eyebrow-raising assumptions critics brought to Talawa's *Lear* was that because the company is Black-led, its Shakespeares would, or should, depict African or Caribbean customs. For example, Gerald Berkowitz noted in *Shakespeare Bulletin*:

> rather than Afro-Caribbean style, the strongest influence on this *King Lear* seemed to be orthodox British: the quiet and intimate playing continually produced striking and no doubt unconscious echoes of the Laurence Olivier television version of a decade ago.
>
> (1994: 32)

Writing in *Shakespeare Survey*, Peter Holland claimed the publicity heralding Talawa as a multicultural company was false advertising, saying the leaflets amounted to 'a suggestion of something more substantially different from what the company actually offered'. Holland also noted:

> But precisely in the measure that the company achieved that aim they obscured any reason to foreground the ethnic identity of the leading actor or the multi-racial company. The company's own publicity emphasis was effectively denied by the conventional classicism of the physical movement of the cast and the Received Pronunciation of most of the voices.
>
> (1996: 196)

With their observations, Holland and Berkowitz were denying the British identities of Talawa's performers of colour. The majority had trained at the country's élite drama schools, including RADA (Lolita Chakrabarti, Mona Hammond, David Harewood, Diane Parish), Central (Jeff Diamond) and Rose Bruford (Yvonne Brewster, Ben Thomas, David Webber), where the use of RP in classical work was standard. Critics would have made no comment about the use of RP had the actors been white.

This reaction encapsulates the exclusion of African-Caribbeans, south Asian and east Asian performers from the dominant white culture. Instead of accepting that a production by British artists of colour could be set in Britain, critics were baffled. They found fault because the production did not transport them – white, male Shakespeare scholars – to where the performers were, to co-opt a loaded phrase, 'actually from'. By contrast, Tara Arts had, with *Troilus and Cressida*, staged a production that was more overtly 'foreign', using Indian classical theatre, foreign languages and Indian attire, which fulfilled an image of what critics expected a minority-led theatre company should be producing: a production that was 'other', not British. Critics thus used a different form of exclusion for *Troilus*, insisting the approach had promise but was not up to the standards expected of Shakespeare in performance. Irving Wardle wrote, 'I feel an attack of blimpish nationalism coming on: damned outsider gate-crashing the club, doesn't know the rules... '. After a catalogue of what he felt to be both good and bad practice in *Troilus*, he concluded, 'Eventually, if not quite yet, the [English] club will have to find room for [multicultural Shakespeare]' (*Independent* 3 October 1993).

To varying degrees, the four productions chronicled in this chapter all broke boundaries and interrogated British identity and ownership of the national playwright. The resistance that actors, such as David Harewood and Doña Croll, and the productions as a whole encountered show the continuing exclusion of artists of colour from Shakespeare. As Alby James observed in 1988, 'as far as some whites are concerned, Temba ought to be doing its own thing – always separate. Another thing is they don't wish to see us integrated into the *mainstream* of English theatre' (Carpenter and James 1990: 32). As we will see, these four productions also ran parallel to an era of much greater change as performers of colour made further inroads into that mainstream.

5

Cracking the glass ceiling, 1988–1996

In 1988, five years after his first professional job at the RSC, Cyril Nri was on the verge of abandoning his career. He explains:

> I never felt like I was being included in the intellectual kernel of the play. I was always what I call the bra salesman as opposed to within the inner family. I was the guy who knocked on the door: the postman, the whatever. And I'd had enough of that.

Nri was in Nigeria contemplating his future when his agent lured him back to Britain to finish a BBC radio series: 'Otherwise they will sue you', she warned. With the actor back in England, his agent phoned with news of two auditions: for David Hare's film *Strapless* and with Jonathan Miller, then running London's Old Vic Theatre.

Miller's revival of *The Tempest* in 1988 was simultaneously progressive and symbolic of the glass ceiling, the 'Black canon', which had evolved since his 1970 production. Miller felt that the 'thinking in these fields has matured and expanded in those two decades, and I need to amplify and improve on the ideas I had then' (*STimes* 9 October 1988). The director's casting pattern had remained static and, in the 1988 revival, performers of colour once again played Ariel (Cyril Nri), Caliban (Rudolph Walker, reprising his 1970 role) and the female spirits: Iris, Ceres and Juno.

By the early 1990s the white theatre critic Michael Billington was finding productions like Miller's *Tempest* 'problematic' because he felt the 'conceptual casting' reinforced stereotypes, rather than broke them. Using the casting of Walker and Nri as his example, Billington observed:

> Both actors were very good. But the unspoken implication was that black actors had access to a world of colonial oppression and non-human

spirituality denied to whites. The truth is, of course, that black actors living in Britain today inhabit the same god-awful, materialist mess as everyone else.

(*Guardian* 1 November 1990)

Reflecting on the production two decades later, Nri observes, 'You've got the three women of colour, you've got Ariel and Caliban. That was interesting' and yet 'the central family of the piece is still white'.

Playing concurrently with Miller's production, Peter Hall also staged *The Tempest* in 1988, along with *Winter's Tale* and *Cymbeline* at the National Theatre under the banner *The Late Shakespeares*; the three NT productions had all-white casts. The juxtaposition of one director (Miller), whose production utilized stereotypes to cast performers of colour, with another (Hall), who totally excluded them, provides a snapshot of the state of integrated casting at the end of the 1980s. Compared to Hall's, Miller's 1988 production of *The Tempest* was progressive. The issue was that while Miller's production had been revolutionary in 1970, in 1988 it symbolized stunted progress.

Despite gains chronicled in previous chapters, actors from Britain's minority communities were still regularly denied access to classical theatre. By 1988 Cyril Nri's professional Shakespeares had amounted to a line of servants for the RSC in 1983, inherited from the performers of colour preceding him, and minor roles in the Royal Exchange's 1984 production of *Cymbeline* (chapter 3). While a young actor recently graduated from drama school could reasonably expect to play such parts, for performers of colour they rarely led to larger roles by which young white actors climbed the classical casting ladder, e.g. Laertes or Claudio. In addition, Nri inherited the role of Ariel from Norman Beaton when he joined the cast of Miller's *Tempest*. Nevertheless, the production was a considerable promotion for Nri because, as he puts it: 'Even though Ariel is outside of the central family, he's definitely within the central, intellectual kernel of the piece.' That chance to work within the central story, as Ariel, convinced Cyril Nri to continue his acting career in Britain.

Like the two *Tempest*s, productions of Shakespeare's history cycles in 1988 also provide a sense of a split screen of contrasting images, in terms of casting practice. The English Shakespeare Company continued to tour its cycle of eight history plays; like Hall's *Tempest*, they all had all-white casts. By contrast, in 1988 both Adrian Noble and Deborah Warner cast Patrick Robinson for their productions of history plays at the RSC. When finishing his first two-year season cycle at the RSC in 1987, Robinson was advised by fellow actors: '"Tell your agent you want to go back to the RSC." – So I did.' He was offered 'slightly more featured parts' than the previous season and was no longer on a play-as-cast contract. As well as Conrade in *Much Ado About Nothing* in the 1988 Stratford season, Robinson appeared in Adrian Noble's truncated history cycle of *Henry VI* and *Richard III*, staged collectively as *The Plantagenets*, and Deborah Warner's production of *King John*. Robinson's inclusion in Shakespeare's history plays is an underappreciated milestone in the RSC's history of integrated casting. Robinson's line of parts – including noblemen such as Catesby in *Richard III* and Melun in *King John* – was less stereotypical and far more diverse than Cyril Nri's had been just five years before.

'You can't have a West Indian actor playing a Welsh poet... '

Joseph Marcell was among very few actors of colour – along with Wyllie Longmore as Antony and Leo Wringer as Brutus – who had played a Shakespearean tragic lead (other than Othello) by 1988. Joseph Marcell's path to Brutus began in the early 1970s when he auditioned for John Dexter at the National Theatre. As Marcell recalls, Dexter 'said to me: "Look, I'm sorry we can't use you. You'd be wasted here." And that was the end of that.' A decade later, Marcell remembers Dexter:

> came backstage after *Othello* and said, 'I'm going to do something for you' and I think it was three years later, he called up my agent and said, 'I'm getting my company together and these are the plays I'm doing and I'd like Joseph to play Brutus and I'm getting Stephen Spender to write him the part of Creon [the title role in Spender's amalgamation of Sophocles' Oedipus trilogy].' And my agent said, 'Are you serious?' and he said, 'Yes. He's the one I want to do these.'

John Dexter casting Marcell as the lead in a double bill of two classical plays illustrates the power directors can wield.

Although Marcell's experience with Dexter appears straightforward, resistance to people of colour performing Shakespeare remained high. The difficulty David Thacker encountered in bringing Rudolph Walker with him to the RSC in 1989 provides one example. Casting at the RSC is an onerous process, as multiple directors negotiate over actors to fulfil their individual requirements. Thacker's 1989 *Pericles* was part of a half-season comprising three Shakespeares in the main house, alongside three shows in the Swan Theatre: Thacker's *Pericles*, *The Duchess of Malfi* and Peter Flannery's epic about postwar Britain, *Singer*. Even with a truncated season, Thacker still had to agree with five other directors in order to cast *Pericles*.

The RSC expects actors to work across multiple productions and, because of budgetary restraints, discourages hiring an actor for a single show. Thacker wanted to cast Rudolph Walker as Gower in *Pericles*, the second-largest part, but, as he explains, other directors 'kept saying in relation to Rudolph, "I don't think he's right for this" or "I don't think there's a part for him [in their productions]."' These attitudes recall the 'suitable roles' culture that had inhibited the integration of performers of colour into the classical repertory for decades. What Thacker found most shocking, however, was:

> the reasons cited for why Rudolph shouldn't play Gower: 'West Indian actors can't do the verse' as a statement of fact and also 'You can't have a Black actor playing – (I doubt whether the word "Black" was even used, probably West Indian) – playing a Welsh poet.' Absurd reasons.

Stratford's history made these arguments more absurd: another actor from the Caribbean, Edric Connor, had graced the Stratford stage as Gower in 1958.

One way to solve casting disputes at the RSC, as Thacker learned, was 'to form alliances with other directors. If you could find a line of three parts for an actor, then they'd get into the company.' When that avenue failed with Walker, Thacker became creative. The RSC's artistic director, Terry Hands, was directing two plays that season, including *Coriolanus* with Charles Dance. When Thacker could not get another director to cast Walker, he approached Hands with a new gambit:

> 'Look, Terry, you've got Charles Dance playing Coriolanus and he's only in *Coriolanus*. He's not doing anything else. So I can have Rudolph Walker just doing Gower in *Pericles*? He doesn't have to be in anything else. That's right, isn't it? Because what's right for you is right for me?' To give him credit, he said, 'Well, yes, if he wants to, but he probably won't want to just do that, will he? Just come and do Gower?' And I said, 'I think you'll find he will because he'd love the opportunity of working at the Royal Shakespeare Company and he likes working with me and I think he'd think it was a great honour to be able to do that.'

Thacker's persistence paid off and Hands relented, which allowed Rudolph Walker to make his RSC debut. Walker recalls:

> Doing that one-off with David suited me fine because it was in rep and I had a certain amount of freedom. I could concentrate on playing Gower, not be pulled left, right and centre by other directors. Once again it's something that I feel grateful and thankful to David, for doing that.

Gower would be Rudolph Walker's only Shakespeare role at the RSC although he returned twice in the 1990s, appearing in Derek Walcott's version of *The Odyssey* (1992) and Naomi Wallace's *Slaughter City* (1996). In both, Walker played parts where the ethnicity of the character was specified.

... But West Indian opera singers can speak the verse?

The first African-Caribbean man to play Othello for the Royal Shakespeare Company was not a classically trained actor, but an opera singer with no classical theatre experience. This distinction between *actor* and *opera singer* is critical. While David Thacker ran into difficulty casting Rudolph Walker, Trevor Nunn hired the Jamaican-born bass baritone Willard White as Othello for his celebrated 1989 production. On an institutional level this was indicative of the continued exclusion of actors from African-Caribbean backgrounds from the Shakespearean role most associated with them.

A decade had passed since Equity's dispute with the BBC over the latter's attempt to cast James Earl Jones as Othello for the *BBC Television Shakespeares*. The BBC's argument that there were no home-grown performers of African-Caribbean heritage capable of playing Othello had been disproved by performers doing just that for nearly a decade, including RSC veteran Joseph Marcell and Rudolph Walker (chapter 2). By the time Nunn staged *Othello*, an ample talent pool was available, but he did not audition Marcell, Walker or presumably other actors of their stature, including Norman Beaton.

Trevor Nunn's casting of an opera singer over an actor as Othello was symptomatic of institutional issues that had dogged the RSC since the hiring of its first cohort of performers of colour in 1967. By 1989 the RSC's layers of exclusion had been in place for two decades, from Alton Kumalo pushing back against continually being cast in servant roles to Cyril Nri stepping into Kumalo's shoes to play those same servants. Change was incremental; for example, when the RSC had the opportunity to promote Patrick Robinson into the role of Romeo permanently, it brought in an external white actor instead (chapter 3). Returning to the RSC for a second season in 1988, Patrick Robinson saw the glass ceiling, as his white contemporaries entered the RSC several levels above him:

> I was like, *He's a similar age, but he's playing a lead. Okay.* And that's how it was. There was no one that I could see apart from Hugh [Quarshie] and Hugh wasn't there [in 1988] playing leads. And you're thinking, *Okay, [I] still can't get a decent gig at the RSC, even though I played Romeo.*

The narrative, Robinson felt, was one in which his experience of understudying Romeo was, as he puts it, redolent of 'Yeah, you got us out of a bit of a tight spot. Thanks for that, but you know, we're not really considering you for any leading roles at the RSC.' Two decades after the RSC first began employing performers of colour, it was still preventing many from rising through the ranks to fulfill their potential and become leading classical actors. It would take twenty years from the BBC–Equity dispute, with one south Asian (Ben Kingsley) and one Black opera singer (White) playing Othello in the interim, before the RSC hired its first African-Caribbean *actor* to play Othello: Ray Fearon in 1999.

Troilus

Three of the shows in the RSC's 1990 Stratford season stand out, showing the evolution of the RSC's casting practice: Nicholas Hytner's production of *King Lear*, Sam Mendes' *Troilus and Cressida* and Nick Dear's adaptation of Tirso de Molina's *The Last Days of Don Juan*, directed by Danny Boyle. Paterson Joseph recalls that season: 'There was a kind of wonderful sense that something was happening at the RSC. Or it was the end of something and the beginning of something new, with the youth of the directors.' Joseph was one of the RSC's intake of four performers of colour for the season, along with Julie Spencer, who agrees: 'I think it was a time when Terry Hands was leaving, a new artistic director [was] coming in and there were these new directors. Look at them now! Danny Boyle, Sam Mendes. And they just wanted new people.' Both Joseph and Spencer made their RSC Shakespeare debuts in Sam Mendes' production of *Troilus and Cressida* as Patroclus and Andromache, respectively. Clarence Smith and Rowena King completed the quartet of actors of African-Caribbean heritage in the RSC's 1990 season.

Nicholas Hytner was the only director at the RSC in 1990 to cast more than one person of colour in the five Shakespeare productions staged in the main house (Table 6); none were cast in *Much Ado about Nothing* and *The Comedy of Errors*. All four of that season's cohort had roles in Hytner's production of *King Lear*, although the women were supernumeraries.

TABLE 6 *Performers of colour in the Royal Shakespeare Theatre, 1990*

Actor	Role				
	King Lear	*Love's Labour's Lost*	*Richard II*	*Much Ado About Nothing*	*Comedy of Errors*
Rowena King	Lady	–	Lady	–	–
Paterson Joseph	Oswald	Dumaine	–	–	–
Clarence Smith	King of France	–	–	–	–
Julie Spencer	Lady	–	–	–	–

Paterson Joseph played Oswald, the servant of Lear's daughter Goneril, and Clarence Smith was the King of France, who appears in the first scene as one of two suitors to Lear's youngest daughter Cordelia. Concentrated in one show, the sight of the four Black bodies on the Royal Shakespeare Theatre stage provoked the ire of some in the press, including the *Mail on Sunday*'s Kenneth Hurran. He aggrievedly listed multiple objections to Hytner's modern-dress staging, including his observation that 'a few black characters fashionably intrude' (15 July 1990).

Objections to high-status characters – such as Hotspur, Banquo, Antony, Isabella – being played by people of colour had become increasingly vocal as the 1980s waned, so it is perhaps unsurprising that critics aimed their loudest objections at Clarence Smith's King of France, rather than the servants played by Joseph, King and Spencer. Charles Osborne was also unable to overlook Clarence Smith as a monarch:

> As too often with the Royal Shakespeare Company, there are several elements in this staging to make the willing suspension of disbelief as difficult to achieve as possible. Among others, there is a black King of France (yes, I know the audience isn't supposed to notice).
>
> (*DT* 13 July 1990)

Critics usually express displeasure at the appearance of an African-Caribbean actor on stage in a Shakespeare play through their individual media platforms, while white audience members write irate letters. As the white director John Caird observed, 'However colour blind directors and actors are, audiences are not colour blind. When Hugh Quarshie played Hotspur the RSC got dozens of letters protesting that it was ridiculous that a Black Hotspur should have white parents' (*Independent* 30 July 1990). Perhaps uniquely in contemporary British Shakespeare, hecklers in the theatre greeted Hytner's choice for the King of France. Clarence Smith had just uttered his first few lines, 'This is most strange' (1.1.214) when, in his recounting:

> Somebody in the audience says, "Well, yes, it most bloody certainly is [strange]!" and shouted. And every time I spoke, I was being heckled. And you can imagine, you look out into the auditorium, and it's just a sea of white faces, and I'm like, "This isn't happening. Something else is happening, Clarence. You [just] think that every time you speak somebody is saying you should not be speaking." And basically, there was someone in the audience who was French who said it was a disgrace that a black man was playing the King of France.
>
> (qtd in Thompson 2008: 6)

Julie Spencer remembers that performance vividly and her account of the reaction of her white colleagues provides a window into the experience of African-Caribbeans in the RSC and in Stratford during the era:

Clarence Smith played the King of France and on one of the first shows there was a protest in the audience, someone standing up and saying, 'The King of France would never have been black!' It was interesting how the white actors went [*intake of breath*]. I remember the reactions were really interesting and that they couldn't understand how we were not fazed by it. Someone [a white actor] was hyperventilating and I'm like, 'Yeah, it didn't happen to you.' Even walking in Stratford, even walking in Stratford, we had experienced that.

Paterson Joseph recalls in his memoir, *Julius Caesar and Me*, that 'Stratford was shockingly mono-cultural' to a young man who had grown up in multicultural London. 'I was stared at constantly on the street. I ignored it after a while but was always painfully aware that I was a curiosity' (Joseph 2018: 22). That performers of colour stood out in predominantly white Warwickshire and its predominantly white theatre spaces may be the subliminal reason for their continued segregation into the RSC's smaller spaces.

Paterson Joseph, Julie Spencer and Clarence Smith each played their most prominent parts in the Swan for the white directors Danny Boyle and Sam Mendes, both making their RSC debuts. Boyle directed Nick Dear's feminist adaptation of Tirso de Molina's *c*. 1620 comedy-parable *The Last Days of Don Juan*, while Mendes took the helm of the only Shakespeare play staged in the Swan that season, *Troilus and Cressida*. Away from the main house Shakespeare productions, there was no stereotypical casting, which seemed something of a breakthrough to Joseph:

> Julie and I in *The Last Days of Don Juan*: she's playing a Duchess; I'm playing a Marquis. These were big deals, comedy though it might have been. It was still an elevation for Black actors to play characters who had, in their own lives, some sort of authority, position of authority and they were being pulled down from there. A lady having her virtue threatened or a Marquis having his livelihood taken away by his own foolishness and foppery. These were really good characters. These weren't just working-class characters who were ciphers for some plot point; these were actually rounded-out people who could not be ignored or dismissed, as was often the case with the less prominent roles Black actors were getting in classical theatre at the time.

Sam Mendes also cast Paterson Joseph and Julie Spencer in *Troilus and Cressida* in ways that broke stereotypes. Joseph played Patroclus, Achilles' companion, while Spencer was Andromache, Hector's wife. They both understudied the eponymous couple and Spencer better recalls her work on Cressida:

> With *Troilus and Cressida*, you have the political and then you have the romance and you have the double entendre and you have the naughtiness.

So to be able to go through a play and experience all those things, even though Cressida's a minor role in the scheme of things, to play with the dynamics of it, it was just amazing. Fabulous.

Late into its London run in 1991 the original Troilus, the white actor Ralph Fiennes, left the RSC, and Paterson Joseph took over the role. With that cast change, Sam Mendes' *Troilus and Cressida* became an important and largely overlooked step forward for the RSC. While Patrick Robinson had played Romeo for eight performances as understudy, Paterson Joseph became the first African-Caribbean understudy to step into a title role permanently at the RSC. This was not, however, necessarily the panacea for equality that it may appear. The RSC would take another six years to cast an African-Caribbean man, Ray Fearon, to play a title role, Romeo, in his own right.

Young lovers

Adrian Lester joined the National Theatre fresh out of RADA in 1989, playing Puck and Lysander in an NT Education touring production of *A Midsummer Night's Dream*. As a Shakespearean subset, the play's young male lovers, Lysander and Demetrius, had remained almost exclusively white. In the 1980s and 1990s, as now, the media negatively stereotyped African-Caribbean men. The words most frequently used in the headlines of news stories between 1981 and 1986 were 'police', 'riot' and 'black' (van Dijk 1991: 54). These stereotypes seeped into dramatic form in appearances on television where 'the blacks are always about to mug people', as Peter Ansorge, then Channel 4's Commissioning Editor for Drama, observed in 1989 (qtd in Ross 1996: 109). As perceptions slowly changed, a few depictions of African-Caribbeans began to break these stereotypes, notably the popular television series *Desmond's*. Norman Beaton's eponymous barber was the head of a family unit that included two sons, one a banker and the second on track for a career as a university lecturer. As Beaton put it, those characters showed 'how we (that is, black people) have moved on from being just passive, to being socially mobile people' (qtd in Pines 1992: 118).

As perceptions changed on television, classical theatre slowly shifted so that, when young actors of colour began to graduate from Britain's elite drama schools in the late 1980s and early 1990s, they gained roles from which their predecessors had been barred. As we saw in chapter 3, when Cyril Nri left drama school in 1983 the roles he was offered were limited to stereotypes. By contrast, the young men of colour who followed him into the profession as little as four years later were cast, not as servants, but as young male lovers in Shakespeare's comedies (Table 7).

That Adrian Lester's first three Shakespearean roles were lovers in the comedies – Lysander, Florizel and an acclaimed Rosalind in *As You Like It* – testify to the tectonic shift taking place in the early 1990s.

TABLE 7 *First casting of actors of colour as young male lovers*

Year	Company	Play	Role	Actor
1987	Nottingham Playhouse	*Dream*	Lysander	Winston Crooke
1988	Theatre Royal, Stratford East	*Twelfth Night*	Orsino	Winston Crooke
1990	Royal Exchange, Manchester	*Winter's Tale*	Florizel	Adrian Lester
1991	Oxford Stage Company	*Tempest*	Ferdinand	Ray Fearon
1992	RSC	*Merry Wives*	Fenton	Peter de Jersey

Rosalind

Cheek By Jowl's all-male *As You Like It* emerged in 1991, the year after Prime Minister Margaret Thatcher lost power. Some critics read Declan Donnellan's production – along with his 1992 production of Tony Kushner's *Angels in America* at the National Theatre – as a canonical protest of Thatcher's notorious 1988 anti-homosexual legislation, Section 28 (Kirwan 2019: 87). Donnellan says *As You* had no 'direct agenda' (*Guardian* 12 November 2014), although a small programme note informed the reader that 'Ganymede', Rosalind's alias in the Forest of Arden, 'was shorthand for homosexual' in Elizabethan slang. Placing a Black man, Adrian Lester, at the play's centre was more clearly an act of radical protest, intentional or otherwise, against another form of discrimination in British society.

An Anglo-Irish Roman Catholic, Declan Donnellan once described his bond with England as one of 'You're in it, but not quite *of* it' (*Guardian* 15 June 1994). This status as both insider and outsider may be key to Donnellan's championship of actors of colour as early as 1982, long before he cast Adrian Lester as Rosalind. For example, four years after the BBC asserted that no British African-Caribbean men were capable of playing Othello, Donnellan cast Doyle Richmond as Othello, the ultimate outsider, for Cheek By Jowl's second production.[1]

---

[1] Between *Othello* and *As You Like It*, Declan Donnellan cast five other performers of colour: Anthony Dixon (Lennox, *Macbeth*, 1987), Cecilia Noble (Miranda, *Tempest*, 1988), Paterson Joseph (Adrian, *Tempest*, 1988), Peter de Jersey (Laertes, *Hamlet*, 1990), Patrick Miller (Rosencrantz, Marcellus, *Hamlet*, 1990).

Adrian Lester recalls that, early in his career, he 'became aware of how different things were' for him, treated as a perpetual outsider in the industry:

> I began to realize that people perceived my skin colour to have a character all of its own. When I walked into a room, before I opened my mouth, judgements had been made on the kind of character that I was, based on the colour of my skin. This 'character' exists purely in the eye of the beholder and for them creates a huge contrast with any Shakespeare character I choose to play.

Donnellan's and Lester's unique, but parallel, experiences of being in the society, but not of it was the perfect crucible for Lester's Rosalind.

Lester was initially frustrated with Rosalind: 'I started rehearsals trying to play a kind of "Everywoman". Thank God nobody saw the funny, sexist diatribe of nonsense that I first brought into the room.' This soon yielded to an interpretation anchored in the experiences of a person perpetually excluded from society. He explains:

> I realized that me becoming Rosalind wasn't some huge idea of female appearance that I needed to put on. It's rules that shape Rosalind. I realized she's not my male idea of 'Everywoman', she's me, without artifice, obeying the rules that society has laid down for women and their behaviour.

Assisted by Lester's six-foot frame, Rosalind's physical awkwardness became one manifestation of society's rules, as Donnellan recounted at the time:

> Adrian Lester (Rosalind) is a strapping lad. I said to him: "You're a woman. Now look in the mirror and tell me what you feel about it." He said: "Oh God, I'm much too tall." "I know," I said, "there are 6 ft strapping women; what do you do about it?" So the shoulder slips and the knees dunk".
>
> (*Independent* 24 November 1991)

Lester's description of this revelation is an eloquent expression of empathy for the often-overlooked ways in which society disadvantages the under-represented:

> I started thinking of the women I know who are statuesque, tall and beautiful. Women that nature has decided most men would have to look up to. Because they occupy a space that society says is too tall, they start to collapse themselves slightly. Rosalind is too big, she takes up too much space, so therefore she's trying to make herself smaller because the physicality of every woman in this society is one that says, "I will shrink my physicality in order to take up less space." Every woman does it.

There's no space. It's always instinctive, it's always smaller. It becomes a form of natural female body language. So, in rehearsals I thought: *Right. I must adopt that thought that I'm too big.* Then I thought: *My voice is too low.* And so on… Imagine this poor nineteen-year-old girl: too quick witted, too tall, too big, completely flat chested. She's nineteen, she's thinking, *Shit.* There's all that stuff going on with how she feels about herself and then Bang! She falls in love. Absolutely has her stomach ripped open with passionate love for this man, this boy who appears to be completely lost and have no one, which is exactly how she feels.

The physicality Lester created vividly displayed Rosalind's insecurity at Court. Rosalind begins the play existing on the charity of her uncle, who has usurped the crown and banished her father, the legitimate Duke. She remains at Court as companion to her cousin, Celia, and Lester's bookish and bespectacled Rosalind crouched on the side of the stage when her uncle appeared with his retinue (1.2). In the archive video,[2] Celia (Simon Coates) held out her hand and Rosalind grabbed it for protection. Rosalind walked with her head down, shoulders bent, looking at the ground; she simultaneously exhibited the female propensity for not taking up space, combined with the terror Rosalind feels.

In that same scene, she also fell awkwardly in love with the second son of Sir Rowland de Boys, Orlando, whom Rosalind and Celia first saw taking part in a wrestling match with the Duke's wrestler, Charles. Collaborating with his colleagues and Donnellan, Lester gave a complex and nuanced portrayal of a relationship that was far from straightforward. Lester explains:

> We discovered in the middle of the play that it's not the meeting of powerful, beautiful mind meeting powerful, hunky, beautiful, powerful mind because that's f-ing boring. It's actually what Declan called the meeting of the underdogs, the meeting of the uglies. It's the meeting of the two people who thought they would never find anybody.

In winning the match, Orlando the underdog also won Rosalind's heart. 'Wear this for me' (1.2.235), said Lester's Rosalind, holding out a gold chain she had taken from around her neck, hesitating, unsure. She ran off quickly, abandoning him there, skittish. That moment was another key one for Lester:

> Suddenly, for me, the play started to take off in that moment. He's about to leave the stage, I stop him with 'Sir!' He stops and turns. Rosalind is thinking: *Fuck he's looking at me. Oh, shit. All I've got is this. I'll give*

---

[2] The archive video was filmed during the 1994 revival of Donnellan's production. In the original 1991 production, Tom Hollander played Celia and Patrick Toomey was Orlando.

him this. Maybe he can sell it and get something. Here. Have this. All without looking at him – I remove the chain from my neck and hold it out at arm's length. Orlando came forward thinking, *She's a princess. What the fuck should I do?* So Orlando knelt down and put his head forward for Rosalind, for me, to put the chain over his head. After a beat Rosalind realizes the chain hasn't been taken, she looks up to see Orlando kneeling and patiently waiting. Her blood runs cold when she realizes... *fuck, I've got to go **close** to him now*! We raised the stakes, took our time and made sure that nothing took place between them without a sense of risk. For that to work, nothing about their vulnerability could be flippant. When we found that truth behind every physical, painful, loving moment – the laughter that I heard in the audience was young and it was female. I was really excited. I came off stage thinking – *Got it! I've got it right. I'm actually giving voice to something rather than commenting on it.* I felt that was the correct way.

When Rosalind and Celia, disguised, met Orlando again in the Forest of Arden, he took them at face value as Ganymede and Aliena, respectively. Upon seeing Orlando, Lester's Rosalind approached him to touch the necklace, still around his neck. She was trying to tell him who she was, but Orlando batted her away and, feeling spurned, Rosalind's anger rose, a choice which both showed what Lester describes as Rosalind's 'pure, unadulterated love' along with her 'anger and bitterness':

> I said to Declan, 'She is angry. She's angry. I don't know why she's angry, but she's angry.' He asked, 'What do you mean?' I said, 'If she's doing it all for a joke, fine, but the joke's over half way through the first meeting. Why does she carry on and on? What is she doing? It's like she's saying, you don't love me enough.' Three days later, Declan came in to rehearsal and said, 'I know why she's angry.' And I went, 'Yeah, why? Why is she angry?' And he said, 'Because when she first meets him and presents herself to him, he doesn't recognize her.' I just looked at him and nodded, smiling. Sometimes a director gives you a perfect note. This was a perfect note. In that moment he didn't trap my instinct for her anger, he released it by giving it absolute and complete logic.

Rosalind's anger was so potent that she screamed 'I am your Rosalind' (4.1.62) at Orlando in complete frustration, when he arrived late for their appointed meeting. For all her anger, Rosalind never lost her love for Orlando, which perhaps manifested itself in no better place than a pause taken by Lester when Rosalind tells Orlando that he will marry his Rosalind when his brother marries Celia. 'Believe me if you will, I', Rosalind says and into the vast emptiness of silence, her confession of 'I love you' seemed on the tip of her tongue. Time stretched out and Rosalind, having nearly made her feelings known to Orlando, continues, 'can do strange things' (5.2.57–8).

FIGURE 7 *Adrian Lester (Rosalind) and Patrick Toomey (Orlando). As You Like It, Cheek By Jowl, 1994. Photo by John Haynes.*

Adrian Lester's performance fully displayed the 'complexity of human love', as Donnellan called it (*Guardian* 12 November 2014).

For all the plaudits Lester received as Rosalind, including an Ian Charleson Award commendation, and the forensic detail and originality he brought to her, some audiences and critics showed an element of Orlando's obliviousness. 'Wasn't Josette Simon good?' he heard one audience member say when leaving the theatre (*STimes* 1 November 1998). 'Lester's as black and as tall as Josette Simon, whom he uncannily resembles', wrote Michael Coveney (*Observer* 1 December 1991). These comments rendered Lester, the Black man, unthreatening, but also denied his presence, as though the British stage had room for only one African-Caribbean performer of Shakespeare.

Portia

Three years after graduating from the Welsh College of Music and Drama, Rakie Ayola became the first woman of colour to play Portia in *The Merchant of Venice*, for Jamie Garven at the Sherman Theatre in Cardiff in 1992. Although the cast was majority white, Garven also gave prominent roles to two African-Caribbean men, Kenneth Gardnier (Shylock) and Marcus Heath (Duke/Solanio), as well as Ayola. Garven also went against stereotype and cast an east Asian man, Paul Courtenay Hyu, to double the Prince of Morocco with the young lover, Lorenzo. This last was arguably the most radical piece of casting, in part because few east Asians had yet spoken a line of Shakespeare in professional British theatre by 1992.[3]

Ayola never discussed the casting with her director, but she reflects that Garven's reasons for his multicultural *Merchant* were intentional:

> It absolutely wasn't colourblind casting. He really wanted you to think about it all. He found actors that he wanted to work with, but then he knew that he could manipulate his audience with those two people. So Black Portia, Black Shylock. There's an awful lot you might be forced to think about as a regular theatregoer in Wales, in Bangor, in Gwynedd. You might have found yourself instinctively rooting for – or absolutely not rooting for – either of them, based on what you were seeing. You might have found yourself listening more keenly to their argument as a result.

Jamie Garven's casting evolved during the audition process, although he had Rakie Ayola in mind for Portia from the beginning. He recalls:

> I'd worked with her just previously and I'd known her in the [Welsh College of Music and Drama]. And at that time she was a very radiant young actress. She really had a kind of star quality about her. A warmth that was good for Portia. I really rated her. Shylock probably became a Black actor during the casting process and perhaps the same with Lorenzo actually, who was the Asian actor, Paul.

Although the multiracial casting had evolved, it had breadth across the production including in an authority figure (the Duke) played by an African-Caribbean. Garven also had performers of colour playing the friends of the male romantic lead, Bassanio, as well as Portia and Shylock. The choice was linked with the complexity of audiences' ingrained perceptions of race and, as Garven puts it:

> It was to do with colourblindness, so you don't have a Black family and a white family. That just took a bit of balancing really. You had to have a sufficient number of Black actors. You couldn't just have one. You couldn't just have two, it becomes too much of a statement. So you have to make sure it spreads across [the cast]. So it all seemed quite logical following on from the first idea [of Ayola as Portia].

---

[3] They were: Denise Wong as Juliet in *Measure for Measure* (Young Vic, 1985) and as Hippolyta/Titania in *Dream* (Derby Playhouse, 1987); David Yip as Mark Antony and Lucy Sheen as Portia in *Julius Caesar* (Bristol Old Vic, 1987); Julian Lyon as Ariel and Toshie Ogura as Miranda in *Tempest* (Phoebus Cart, 1991); Daniel York Loh as Fortinbras and Lucianus in *Hamlet* (Riverside Studios, 1992).

Navigating the racism embedded in *Merchant* can be difficult for a contemporary performer. For the actress playing Portia, one major difficulty is her line about Morocco, 'Let all of his complexion choose me so' (2.7.79). Directors sometimes deal with this by cutting it. With an African-Caribbean Portia and an east Asian Morocco, it brought an inversion of the racist behaviour audiences expect. Ayola recalls she took the line at 'face value and it meant "I don't mind someone that looks like me or looks like you [white Nerissa], I just don't want someone who looks like him [east Asian Morocco]."'

Portia's encounter with the Prince of Morocco is the result of her status as an heiress, trapped by the provisions of her father's will which stipulates the only method by which she may gain a husband. As in medieval romances, her suitors must negotiate a trial: three caskets of gold, silver and lead, one of which holds Portia's portrait, signifying the winner. Portia's only companions at her mansion in Belmont are her servants and, in Ayola's interpretation, a doll. Ayola found in Portia's secluded existence 'an overgrown child-woman'. She describes Portia as:

> very well educated, very well read but she hadn't quite grown out of things because she hadn't needed to. I don't know why, but I decided I liked the idea that no one had told her to stop playing with things.

Garven supported Ayola's instinct, providing a straw doll for Portia to play with and incorporated a hammock into the set design for Belmont. Ayola remembers lying with one leg hanging out of the hammock, waving her doll around as she dismissed each unwanted suitor.

The fairy-tale nature of the audience's initial contact with Portia gives way in Act 4 to her appearance in a courtroom, disguised as a male legal scholar. Aiming to save Antonio, the friend of her fiancé Bassanio, Portia travels from Belmont to Venice's law courts in an adventure that ends in the condemnation of Shylock and the forfeiture of his bond, half his wealth and his Jewish religion. Ayola built on the image of the overgrown child for her motivation, asking the underlying question, 'What if nobody told her not to [go to Venice]? Why shouldn't she do it?' Primed for impulsive action, Ayola's Portia thought to herself: '*I have the knowledge to sort that out [Antonio's legal defence]. I'll dress up and I'll go and sort it out. That's what I'll do. And it'll be fine.* She was going to get this wrapped up by tea.' For Ayola, the scene held another layer of complexity, stemming from Portia's sheltered existence while waiting for a successful suitor. She recalls:

> I liked that idea of someone who was not prepared for the world **not** to go the way she wanted it to go. She became really confused and really hurt and then almost out of petulance going, 'Well, I can trump that, actually. You're forcing me to do this.'

After the bruising encounter with Shylock, Ayola's Portia longed to return to a place of innocence in which 'everything else will be as I expect it to be'.

With Ayola, a Black woman, cast as Portia, the courtroom scene became another way in which Garven subverted expectations. With few exceptions, in Shakespeare women of colour in the early 1990s were playing roles such as Nerissa (a servant) or Bianca (a prostitute) in *Othello*. Women are rare in Shakespeare and Rakie Ayola was one of that even rarer breed: a woman of colour who had, by 1992, played a fully developed, multifaceted female Shakespearean lead. One other woman of colour would play Portia in the 1990s, Cathy Tyson at the Birmingham Rep in 1997, and, as of going to press, only five productions have had a performer of colour as Portia. That two of these five were men illustrates the continuing lack of opportunity afforded to women of colour in Shakespeare's major female canon.

The Shakespearean glass ceiling, 1988–1996

Between 1988 and 1996, just under half the total number of parts cast using performers of colour occurred in only six of the thirty-seven plays in Shakespeare's main canon, including the three that began this history: *Macbeth*, *The Tempest* and *Othello* (Table 8). Those early productions set a template that continued into the mid-1990s. Two out of the other three, *Dream* and *Romeo*, had also been early additions to the 'Black canon', another indication of how opportunities continued to be narrow for performers of colour in Shakespeare. Looking at the most recent addition to these 'Black canon' plays, *Twelfth Night*, helps to illuminate both the progress classical theatre had made and the location of the glass ceiling by the mid-1990s.

Out of the plays with the most number of roles played by performers of colour, *Twelfth Night* makes an interesting case study because, unlike the two other comedies in Table 8, it has a social structure that revolves around two households: those of Orsino, Duke of Illyria and the Countess Olivia. Both have a number of characters in service as steward, a waiting-gentlewoman, a jester and attendants: Malvolio, Maria, Feste and Fabian serving Olivia, and Curio and Valentine in Orsino's household. Viola and her twin brother Sebastian are both from the upper class, despite their low fortunes during much of the play. Countess Olivia has a kinsman, Sir Toby

TABLE 8 *Total roles played by people of colour by play, 1988–1996*

Play	Roles cast
Macbeth	76
Romeo	74
Dream	54
Twelfth Night	51
Tempest	39
Othello	36

Belch, who resides in her household and has a companion, Sir Andrew Aguecheek. Class politics drive much of the comedy, particularly the subplot of Olivia's steward, Malvolio, who is gulled into believing his mistress is in love with him.

Fifteen productions of *Twelfth Night* staged between 1988 and 1996 had some form of inclusive casting.[4] Table 9 shows the breadth of change in casting practices from the 1980s to the 1990s. In the 1980s, people of colour almost exclusively played servants, except for Suzette Llewellyn and Anthony Phillips as Viola and Sebastian in a production that set Illyria on a generic tropical island.[5] As Table 9 also shows, the following decade

TABLE 9 Twelfth Night *characters by number of times cast*

Roles	Actors of colour cast	
	1980–1987	1988–1996
Maria	2	7
Antonio	2	6
Orsino	0	5
Olivia	0	4
Feste	1	4
Curio	2	4
Viola	1	3
Sebastian	1	3
Valentine	0	3
Sir Toby Belch	0	2
Fabian	0	2
Sir Andrew Aguecheek	0	1
Malvolio	0	1

[4] There were at least seven other productions in that time frame that had all-white casts, including Ian Judge's 1991 production at the Royal Shakespeare Company.

[5] The Northumberland Theatre Company's 1983 production also had Kenneth Gardnier as Feste. The production was well received and Richard Kelly in the *Guardian* provides a flavour of the reception:

> *Twelfth Night*'s latest transplant is to a tropical island in the twilight of empire and it works a treat. The shipwrecked twins are played by coloured actors (Suzette Llewellyn and Anthony Phillips) and this enables the Northumberland Theatre Company's director Martin Troughton to add a dimension of racial harmony to the play without detriment to the text. Even more successful is the casting of the West Indian actor Kenneth Gardnier as the clown Feste. Never have I heard Shakespeare's language, even the nonsense, sound so melodious.
>
> (7 September 1983)

found performers of colour playing a wider variety of characters across the play's social strata, although the bias for casting people of colour as servants remained. For example, between 1988 and 1996, directors of almost 50 per cent of productions staged cast a woman of colour as Maria, Olivia's waiting-gentlewoman.

Table 10 reveals remaining inequalities in the discrepancy between the parts most and least frequently played by performers of colour within this chapter's time frame. Two parts in the 'Black canon', Othello and the Prince of Morocco, were also two of the most frequently cast roles between 1988 and 1996. In contrast, performers of colour played Portia and Shylock in *The Merchant of Venice* only once during this time period: Rakie Ayola and Kenneth Gardnier, respectively, in Jamie Garven's production.

This table also makes explicit other lines of exclusion, as many of the apparent breakthroughs chronicled in this and previous chapters happened only once between 1988 and 1996. Adrian Lester, Rakie Ayola, Kenneth Gardnier, Ben Thomas and David Webber were the only people of colour to play Rosalind, Portia, Shylock, King Lear and Kent, respectively, throughout the nine-year span. Casting practices still, subliminally or otherwise, often defaulted to casting people of colour in subservient positions (Ariel, Caliban) or as those outside a family unit (Edmund, King of France). Without Talawa's production of *King Lear* (chapter 4), no actors from African-Caribbean backgrounds would have played either King Lear or Kent. The lack of a single Hamlet of colour between 1988 and 1996 also illustrates the complex levels of inequality that had begun to emerge. That twenty African-Caribbeans played Othello during this period, including both experienced actors (Jeffery Kissoon, Leo Wringer) and those just starting out (Ray Fearon, David Harewood, Danny Sapani), while not a single performer of

TABLE 10 *Roles most and least frequently played by performers of colour, 1988–1996*

Play	Role (number)
Merchant of Venice	Prince of Morocco (12)
	Portia (1)
	Shylock (1)
Tempest	Ariel (7)
	Caliban (4)
	Prospero (1)
King Lear	Edmund (4)
	King of France (4)
	Lear (1)
	Kent (1)
Hamlet	Laertes (4)
	Hamlet (0)

colour was cast as Hamlet, shows both the persistence of the glass ceiling as well as greater access to Shakespeare since the 1970s.

'Are we saying we're white people?'

The only representations of south Asians that Paul Bazely saw on television as a child were in stories that revolved around corner shops or arranged marriages. Bazely trained at the Manchester Polytechnic School of Theatre and recalls that, when he left drama school in 1989, he 'was desperately trying to break away from those tired Asian storylines'. In 1992 Bazely found himself working for the National Theatre in Richard Eyre's 1990 production of *Richard III*, which had been re-cast for an American tour:

> I'd just played Macbeth for a small theatre company in Manchester, so I was feeling quite confident with Shakespeare. I'd just moved to London, just got my London agent and they got me in [to audition]. When I turned up on the first day [of rehearsals], I was still so green, particularly about the politics of colour, but I looked round the room thinking there was a few of us there. There was myself and Dominic Hingorani.

When Bazely and Hingorani were cast in *Richard III* in 1992, the National Theatre was still at the beginning of its journey towards a more inclusive Shakespearean repertoire. Since the company's inception, the National Theatre had staged twenty-nine Shakespeare productions on its main stages: the Old Vic from 1963 to 1976 and then the three theatres in its purpose-built residence on the South Bank.[6] Only nine of those twenty-nine had any performers of colour in their casts (Table 11). For the first thirty years of the National's existence, 68 per cent of its Shakespeare output had been exclusively white. The National Theatre cast no actors of colour in its productions of: *Hamlet* (1963, 1975–1976), *Othello* (1964, 1980), *Love's Labour's* (1968), *Merchant* (1970), *Coriolanus* (1971, 1984), *Macbeth* (1972, 1978), *Richard II* (1972), *Tempest* (1974, 1988), *As You* (1979), *Richard III* (1979), *Much Ado* (1981), *Antony and Cleopatra* (1987), *Cymbeline* (1988) and *Winter's Tale* (1988).

The National Theatre began its journey towards greater inclusion after Richard Eyre succeeded Peter Hall as artistic director in 1988. One of Eyre's first major tasks had been to increase cultural diversity on its stages, as required by Arts Council initiatives (Rosenthal 2013: 497). Eyre's first foray into Shakespeare at the head of the National was marginally more diverse

---

[6] This excludes NT Learning productions and NT Studio production as they were designed for schools or experimental productions, rather than produced for the theatre's main stages.

TABLE 11 *Performers of colour in National Theatre Shakespeare productions, 1963–1992*

Year	Production	Performer(s)	Role(s)
1967	*Much Ado*	Sam Dastor[7]	An Inanimate
1967	*As You*	Sam Dastor	Lord, Page
1977	*Julius Caesar*	Olu Jacobs	Soothsayer
1981	*Measure*	Stefan Kalipha Yvette Harris Peter Straker Normal Beaton + 14 others	Duke Isabella Lucio Angelo Multiple roles
1982	*Dream*	Marsha Hunt Edward de Souza	Hippolyta Theseus
1986	*King Lear*	Roshan Seth	Fool
1990	*Richard III*	Hakeem Kae-Kazim	Tyrrell
1990	*King Lear*	Hakeem Kae-Kazim	Edmund
1992	*Dream*	Lolita Chakrabarti Indra Ové Jeffery Kissoon Trevor Thomas Abraham Osuagwu	Hippolyta Hermia Oberon Egeus Moth
1992	*Richard III* (re-cast)	Paul Bazely Dominic Hingorani	Marquess of Dorset First Murderer/Lord Lovel

than Hall's 1988 valedictory trio all-white Shakespeares: *Winter's Tale*, *Cymbeline* and *The Tempest*. In 1990 Ian McKellen and Brian Cox led a company at the National, the former playing Richard III for Eyre with the latter taking the lead in Deborah Warner's production of *King Lear*. That original company included one actor of colour, Hakeem Kae-Kazim, who had been praised in 1985 by the founder of the National Youth Theatre ('He speaks Shakespeare better than most white actors' [*STimes* 15 September 1985]). He had played two Shakespearean leads, Othello and Henry V, for the National Youth Theatre, joined the RSC in 1987 (chapter 3) and had recently reprised Othello at Theatr Clwyd in Mold, Wales. Kae-Kazim was the first African-Caribbean man to appear in a main-stage Shakespeare at the National since 1981, but his characters were the stereotypical murderous outsiders: Tyrell in *Richard III* and Edmund in *Lear*.

---

[7] Sam Dastor was part of the sixth and final cast of Zeffirelli's production of *Much Ado*, joining in 1967. He was credited as Saam Dastoor in the programme.

Richard Eyre's *Richard III* famously placed Shakespeare's play about dynastic political power in 1930s England, framing the eponymous character as a quintessentially English prototype of Hitler. Eyre was 'fascinated by the idea of portraying an English tyranny' (qtd in Rogers 2012: 102) and settled on the decade that had given rise to Oswald Mosley and his British Union of Fascists. Although Eyre was producing an alternate vision of English history, the production was designed in ways that evoked imagery of English national identity. As Eyre puts it, 'There *are* specific references, to our own country. The banner of Richard bears the cross of Saint George, which is the English flag, his uniform is a British uniform' (1990: 135). Eyre also incorporated arguably the most potent symbol of national identity into his production, the monarchy, through Shakespeare's Edward IV and the Duchess of York who bore more than a passing resemblance to their regal counterparts, King George V and Queen Mary.

The reconstruction of national identity was crucial to Eyre's production, but it also mimicked an exclusionary version of Britain then being constructed on film and television, particularly in period dramas such as Granada Television's *Brideshead Revisited* and ITV's *Jeeves and Wooster*. What these period dramas portrayed was a past that was exclusive, rich and white. As Lez Cooke notes, it was 'not the industrial heritage of coal mines, factories or shipyards... but the upper-class and aristocratic heritage of country houses and stately homes' that dominated popular consciousness of the past (2003: 167). These portrayals banished contemporary multicultural Britain from the country's screens and, consequently, the stage of Richard Eyre's *Richard III*.

Although Eyre's production of *Richard III* became more diverse in 1992 with the addition of Paul Bazely and Dominic Hingorani, it also became more 'white'. As Bazely notes, 'I remember it was still like we were pretending to be Europeans, most certainly. We were pretending to be white people of the thirties.' This became problematic for the two south Asians when they arrived in sunny America in the summer of 1992. As Bazely recalls, one senior member of the company:

> was worried that we were all getting too tanned and we weren't looking like people from the thirties anymore. And, for instance, me and Dominic said, 'Well we're Indian. I start brown and I go a bit browner.' But what are we saying? Are we saying we're white people? Because we're not.

Both Bazely and Hingorani played *Richard III*'s smaller roles, but were expected to subsume their ethnicity for whiteness; this illustrates one problem with the practice known as colourblind casting. As Hingorani notes, the principle:

> may appear laudable but it fails on two significant levels: it attempts to disavow the ethnicity of the performer and refuses to acknowledge the cultural difference between the performers; and it does not begin to

address the causes that lead to the discriminatory practices against actors from minority communities.

(2009: 165–6)

Eyre's colourblind casting for *Richard III* was meant to preserve the status quo of national identity and, while inclusive in terms of casting two south Asians, still painted a picture of an exclusively white Englishness.

'That wouldn't have happened here'

Julie Spencer became the first woman of colour to play Juliet in Britain since at least 1930, when she took the female lead in *Romeo and Juliet* for the London Actors Theatre Company in 1988. Spencer got a second chance to play Juliet in 1996 when the Haworth Shakespeare Company, an annual summer festival based in the United States at Haworth, New Jersey, staged the play. That production, directed by Simon Stokes, went on a tour of America, playing in locations as disparate as Kansas, Indiana, Louisiana, Ohio, Pennsylvania and New York City. Their appearance at Aaron Davis Hall, a performing arts centre in Harlem, the epicentre of African-American arts excellence, provides Spencer with her most enduring memory of the tour:

> You remember how it feels [playing Juliet] and being in New York, in the Aaron Davis Hall and just saying these words. I know it's not a sob story, but from where I come from and being on this stage and saying these words, the epitome of Britishness. And this girl – who came from a single parent, who worked as a cleaner at the age of eight before going to primary school – and saying these words on that stage. And that sense of achievement. I actually remember being on that stage in New York and actually saying 'No one will ever take this away from me.' I actually remember saying that before going on, thinking no matter what happens from here, no one's ever going to take this away from me.

By 1996 the Haworth Shakespeare Festival had staged three productions of Shakespeare with imported British actors, all with connections to the RSC and its performers of colour.

The white South African director, Stephen Rayne, initially staged a production of *Hamlet* for the Haworth Festival in 1990, headlined by the white actress Susannah York's Gertrude. Rayne had been an assistant director at the RSC, and in 1991 he directed his second production, a version of *Macbeth* set in Africa. Patrick Miller, who played Malcolm in the production's first incarnation, recalls:

> It was essentially a Black cast because it was meant to be Idi Amin's Africa. But you had a white actor there, who was playing this great white hunter character in Seyton [Desmond McNamara] and then Bhasker

Patel playing Ross. So you did get a sense that it was Africa but a real one, just status was in reverse. The audiences loved it. It worked really, really well. Caroline Lee Johnson was stunning as Lady M. She used to get a standing ovation after her first speech. I wish it had been seen here because I thought it was really, really good. Really, really good. That wouldn't have happened here.

Miller's 'here' refers to both the standing ovations and the RSC, where he had first worked with Stephen Rayne during the 1988 Stratford season. The director had become aware of racial disparities growing up in his native South Africa. In 1995, he recalled the genesis for the Haworth *Macbeth* had been his time at the RSC, where he had seen at first hand the discrimination actors of colour endured in regularly being overlooked for roles:

> Those people (producers/directors at the RSC) still think of Shakespeare as actors running around in woolly pants... I was amazed at how they showed such an inability to see the society we're living in today, a society that is first and foremost a multi-racial society.
> (*The Tennessean* 8 February 1995)

Rayne directed at least three incarnations of *Macbeth* – in 1991, 1993 and 1995 – and assembled an impressive cast for each, led by the Macbeths of John Matshikiza, Hakeem Kae-Kazim and Patrick Robinson, respectively. That each played the leading role in America and not Britain speaks volumes about what was possible for actors of colour, even as opportunities were expanding in 1990s Britain.

Birmingham Repertory Theatre, 1993–1996

The white director Bill Alexander left the RSC in 1993 to become artistic director of the Birmingham Repertory Theatre, forty miles north of Stratford-upon-Avon. The contrast between the two theatres – the Shakespearean behemoth and the regional theatre founded in 1923 by Barry Jackson – in their inclusion in Shakespeare productions between 1993 and 1996 could hardly be starker. Bill Alexander had built on the work of his immediate predecessor, the white director John Adams, who put in place 'a theatre policy which at long last was to address the multi-ethnic Birmingham community' (Cochrane 2003: 127). Adams staged a production of *The School for Scandal* in his first season with a cast that included two performers of African-Caribbean heritage: Michael Buffong and Ram John Holder. Its programme 'detailed the extent of the black population in eighteenth-century England thus justifying the more radical casting of black actors in an English classic play' (Cochrane 2003: 127). Joseph Marcell, who played Sir Toby Belch in a Caribbean-set *Twelfth*

Night at Birmingham in 1989, recalls of his frequent collaborator: 'When John Adams took over the Birmingham Rep, he decided that it's been a long time since there'd been non-white actors in that theatre.' For the first time since Zia Moyheddin played Shylock in 1968, the Rep under John Adams included performers of colour in its Shakespeares, twenty-one years later.

Bill Alexander built on Adams' legacy, creating an informal multi-ethnic company for the Rep's classical work that included Jeffery Kissoon, Rakie Ayola, Pal Aron and the white actor Richard McCabe.[8] The director opened his tenure with *Othello* in 1993, beginning a prolific working relationship with Jeffery Kissoon, who played the title role. Alexander told Tony Howard that he had asked Kissoon whether other performers of colour should be cast in it. 'I think part of the power of Othello is that he is the only Black character', was the actor's reply, according to Alexander. The director credits that conversation as the genesis of his multiracial productions of Shakespeare at the Birmingham Rep.

Bill Alexander's second Shakespeare at the Rep was a production of *The Tempest*, in which Jeffery Kissoon played the lead, Prospero:

> I thought, 'Right, Jeffery's playing Prospero and he's a Black actor. Therefore – because it is in one sense a family play – I want to cast Miranda, his daughter, as Black and I want to cast Antonio, his brother, as Black.' Which I did, because that had a logic to it. And because Ariel is the spirit of the man, I want that actor to be Black as well. So for reasons of… I suppose you'd call them 'internal realism' those actors were in those parts. The actor who played Caliban, [Richard] McCabe, we made very white – like he was someone who never ever saw the daylight, like the creature from H.G. Wells' novel *The Time Traveller*, the ones who live underground and never see daylight.

Along with Kissoon as Prospero, Alexander cast Ginny Holder, Tony Armatrading and Rakie Ayola as Miranda, Antonio and Ariel, respectively.

Alexander set his production in the Victorian era and, within this context, Michael Billington found in Kissoon's Prospero 'not just a wronged Duke but a mixture of Victorian magus and Darwinian explorer seeking to discover the roots of civilisation' (*Guardian* 15 September 1994). Alexander explains:

> There are echoes of the idea of the white man colonizing the lands of the Black man, which was just beginning to happen, so you have the seeds of racism there. And quite often, to make that point, productions of

---

[8] For a more detailed account of Alexander's multiracial productions at the Birmingham Rep, see Rogers (2016).

The Tempest had made everyone white except for Caliban, who was cast as Black. So, I suppose [his casting choices] almost became a conscious inversion and challenge to that way of seeing the play, as a sort of proto-colonialist piece.

Rakie Ayola makes the point that Alexander's *Tempest* was British, as were the island's inhabitants:

To be honest, I really, really loved the fact that we weren't trying to take people to some other [country]. I mean, it's on an island, but we weren't saying it's an island off the coast of Sierra Leone. I liked that. We were always people from here. We were always as we are. We were always using our own voices.

Although Alexander initially considered Ariel to be 'the spirit of' Prospero, in creating her character Ayola had one major question: why does she stay with Prospero? Embedded in the text are clues to the closeness of the relationship between Ariel and Prospero. As Katherine Brokaw observes, Prospero is the only character that '*sees* him as Ariel', rather than in one of the shape-shifting disguises Ariel adopts in the service of the island's magus: 'Ariel is described most frequently by Prospero' and the adjectives he uses 'merely signal that Ariel is a pleasing servant to his master' (Brokaw 2008: 28). The master–servant relationship remains in the text, regardless of a director's vision, and Ayola's crafting of her character led her to the question:

Who is this person who could just keep flying, but like a trained dog just keeps coming back? That was the essence of it for me. Who is this that has the ability to just keep walking but doesn't even realize? And that for me said damaged. Ariel can do all this stuff and could just go, so why not go? Because in that really damaged way, she was beaten down and was really obedient and didn't understand that she actually had the key the whole time. She didn't know she had it. So she's just waiting for someone to say, 'You can go.' It was as simple as that.

Rakie Ayola was the second woman of colour to play Ariel in Britain, after Diane Parish who played the character for the Oxford Stage Company in 1991. Alexander's *Tempest* was also the first time Ayola had been in a rehearsal room with another woman of colour:

I was always very excited to get these jobs, I didn't even ask when I met him. It didn't occur to me to ask. So it was only when I arrived on day one, I went, *Oh, we're all Black. Okay.* And I probably did just go, *Oh, we're all Black. Oh, there's another woman who's about the same age as me. That's never happened before. Okay.* So there's Jeff. There's

Ginny playing Miranda. That was definitely the first time, going all the way back through my career to that point, this is 1994. Going all the way back through drama school, I had never on day one sat there with another Black woman. Going back through National Youth Theatre of Wales, I'm struggling to find the time. In fact, maybe that was the very first time I had entered a rehearsal room with another Black woman. Yeah, it had never happened. In fact, I'm going right back to some point in high school, when a Black girl played Queen Elizabeth I and I played her page.

Ayola felt a sense of release that accompanied the inclusion of another woman of colour, a feeling that comes with not having to subsume part of your identity when you are 'other' and a minority:

So should it have mattered? No. Did it matter? Yes. It's a bit like when you get used to using force and then you don't have to. It's that kind of thing, you go, *Oh, I don't need to push that hard; oh, I don't know how hard to push now*. So it was a bit like going, *And now I can relax*. And of course Ginny and I met and had a chat, had a cuppa; we were very different. It makes me frown to think about how uncomfortable I was because I didn't know how to be. I would expect somebody to feel the same way if they spend their life as a green Mohican and then walk into a room and see another green Mohican.

The Birmingham Rep's achievement in integrated Shakespeare under John Adams and his successor Bill Alexander was immense. Few theatre companies could boast a similar ratio of productions to performers of colour in major roles, particularly at the two major national companies. Between 1993 and 1996, the Birmingham Rep staged four productions of Shakespeare: *Romeo and Juliet*, *Othello*, *The Tempest* and *Macbeth*, the latter three directed by Alexander. In each, performers from African-Caribbean backgrounds had played at least one of the play's two largest parts: Jeffery Kissoon (Othello, Prospero, Macbeth), Josette Bushell-Mingo (Juliet) and Rakie Ayola (Ariel).

During the same time frame, 1993–1996, the National Theatre staged five major productions of Shakespeare, and only one had a person of colour playing either of the two largest parts: Aaron in *Titus Andronicus*, one of Shakespeare's few explicitly 'Black parts'. The RSC's output of Shakespeare was far greater than either the National or the Birmingham Rep, but its record in the integration at these highest levels was poor. Out of twenty-six new productions of Shakespeare staged between 1993 and 1996, the RSC cast just two performers of colour in the first or second largest parts: Jeffery Kissoon as Brutus (1993) and Zubin Varla as Romeo (1995). In other words, 100 per cent of the Birmingham Rep's Shakespeare output in three years had a performer of colour playing the first or second lead (or both, as in the case of the 1994 *Tempest*), in contrast to the National Theatre's 20 per cent and the RSC's 8 per cent. The failure of both major national companies to regularly provide opportunities at the highest levels of classical theatre shows the placement of the glass ceiling at the major companies.

6

'Monarchs to Behold': 1997–2003

Louis Mahoney had been part of the RSC's first cohort of performers of colour, joining the company in 1967. It took thirty years for Mahoney to return to the company, playing Montague in Michael Attenborough's 1997 production of *Romeo and Juliet*. An avid cricketer, Mahoney had played for Gambia before emigrating to Britain to study medicine at the University of London. In England he continued to be active in the sport, joining the ground staff at Essex in 1960 and then Ilford as a fast bowler (*BP*, 27 March 1967). Mahoney gave up medicine to pursue an acting career, becoming increasingly involved with Equity for twenty-five years, including serving as the union's Vice-President. Mahoney was one of the leading advocates of integrated casting and in 1983 was one of the speakers at a conference on integrated casting. In a special issue reporting on that event, Mahoney eloquently refuted arguments opposed to integrated casting, reprinted in a special issue of Equity's in-house magazine:

> ... we know that television can determine what the relationship between a young Afro-Asian and a young English kid becomes. It is therefore the responsibility of people here today to determine what sort of society we are going to have in the future... I don't believe that racialism can be found within the viewer. I think that it comes from what the viewer sees and is fed.

Mahoney's work with Equity was crucial in forcing the door open for the generations of African-Caribbeans, south Asians and east Asians that followed him.

Michael Attenborough's 1997 production of *Romeo and Juliet* was a symbolic passing of the torch from one generation of performers of colour to the next. Mahoney's pioneering appearance at the RSC in the late 1960s, along with advocacy by him and his colleagues, had resulted in greater opportunities for those who followed. Joining Mahoney in Attenborough's cast were several performers of colour who had entered the profession in the early 1990s: Nigel Clauzel (Tybalt), Joplin Sibtain[1] (Mercutio) and Ray Fearon (Romeo). For Fearon, *Romeo and Juliet* was the culmination of his desire to become a leading classical actor, an ambition he had harboured since leaving Rose Bruford six years earlier.

At Rose Bruford Fearon played Berowne in *Love's Labour's Lost* and Othello with the head of acting, Vladimir Mirodan, encouraging Fearon in his classical work. While at drama school, Fearon won the Society for Theatre Research's prestigious William Poel competition for excellence in the performance of early modern drama. Around the time David Thacker sought to cast Rudolph Walker as Gower in *Pericles* at the RSC and was told 'West Indian actors can't do the verse' (chapter 5), Fearon was also learning that these attitudes remained common in the industry:

> I kept hearing, 'You've got a natural talent [with Shakespeare].' But what followed it was: 'But I don't think you'll get the parts.' I remember Vladimir saying, 'I want you to go out there and really do this.' But he said, 'Man, I tell you, the way those people are, they make out like Black people can't speak the verse.' I kept hearing this but he was like, 'You're going to go to the RSC and you're going to do all of this.' When I started to get into Shakespeare and I really started to love it, I thought: *Do you know what? I'm not going to let anybody deny me this. And this thing of Black people can't speak the verse is a load of rubbish. If you're telling me I can't do this, that's just racist. I've never heard anything so racist in my life.* But that's what was being said. There were good Black actors. But you had to prove you were good enough to go on that stage and trade with anyone up there. You had to.

Fearon's topic for his final-year thesis at Rose Bruford was the state of integrated casting in British theatre. His research looked at performers of colour working at the RSC, the National and the Royal Court between 1960 and 1991. Fearon's findings were stark:

> There was one person [across those three theatres] who played a title role: Josette Simon. She played Vittoria in *The White Devil* [in Philip Prowse's production at the National Theatre]. But Shakespeares? No one played a title role part. And I remember thinking, *This is a shambles. This is terrible.* And it was my main aim to come to the RSC. I thought: *I'm going to come and I'm going to stay in there and I'm going to change it. I'm going to stick around and learn this because I want to be doing what they're doing up there. I want to be a good actor. I want to be doing*

---

[1] Joplin Sibtain was credited as Chook Sibtain for much of his career, including *Romeo and Juliet*.

Shakespeare. I'm going to stick around and I'm going to become a lead actor in the RSC.

After leaving drama school in 1991 Fearon built an impressive set of classical credits in regional theatre. His first professional job was playing Ferdinand in *The Tempest* for the Oxford Stage Company, becoming the first performer of colour to play the part in Britain. He then spent 1992 at the Liverpool Everyman and Manchester's Royal Exchange playing Othello, Charles Surface in Sheridan's *The School for Scandal* and Longaville in *Love's Labour's Lost*.

At the Royal Exchange, Fearon was working with white performers who had recently played leading roles for the RSC, including Edgar in *King Lear* (Linus Roache) and Marina in *Pericles* (Suzan Sylvester). A formative moment occurred when Fearon's agent came to see *Love's Labour's Lost*. He recalls her conversation with the theatre's casting director:

> She went, 'You have to have a crack at lead parts and great parts to improve as an actor. Everybody else on that stage, they've had cracks at certain parts and they've improved. He [Fearon] has to get those parts. He has to play those kinds of parts to improve as an actor.' And I remember listening thinking, *She's right. For me to become a good actor, I have to play those bloody things*. Pippa [Markham] said that and it's stayed with me.

In 1992, the RSC continued its pattern of showcasing performers of colour outside its Shakespearean repertory, using a diverse cast for both Derek Walcott's *The Odyssey* and Terry Hands' production of Marlowe's *Tamburlaine*. Only four of the seven performers of colour cast in the RSC's 1992 season were also seen in its main house Shakespeares.

Fearon turned down offers for parts in *The Odyssey* and, a year later, the Barbican transfer of *Tamburlaine*. For the latter, Fearon remembers reading one part for his audition and then being told, 'Well, I can't really offer you this part [the larger one Fearon had read for], but I'll tell you what: I'll guarantee that it will be a great part.' Having been warned by his peers about the perils of play-as-cast contracts, Fearon was determined to enter the RSC at a level where he could, as his agent had observed, play the parts that would enable him to improve as an actor. Fearon bided his time.

Fearon's next contact with the RSC was an audition with David Thacker for his 1993 production of *The Merchant of Venice*. Fearon recalls:

> I got to the fifth line [of Morocco's speech] and [Thacker] stopped me. And he just went, 'Yep. Of course. I've had enough. I really like you. You're really, really good' and stuff. 'I'm sure some of the other directors will see you and we'll see how it goes.' Fine, fine, fantastic. He said, 'I definitely will see you again.' I looked at him and I thought, *Do I really want to go there and do the Prince of Morocco? What else have they*

got? Anyway, Steven Pimlott called me in for [T. S. Eliot's] *Murder in the Cathedral* and he had me read the fourth templar knight – I think he had Hugh Quarshie down to play Becket. So Becket's alter ego would have been me. So he [Pimlott] said, 'Depending on what [Quarshie] does, I'll give you this part. If not, I'm going to have to give you the other one.'

In the end the white actor Michael Feast played Becket with Fearon as the first templar knight, but Fearon had avoided the RSC's play-as-cast contract: 'I did take [the job]', he recounts, 'And I didn't understudy. And I played the third lead in *Moby Dick*. I knew I could do something with those parts to make them noticed.'

Ray Fearon had been with the RSC for two seasons, working his way up through the ranks, when he won the lead in Michael Attenborough's *Romeo and Juliet*. The director originally intended that two white performers, both promising young actors who had been with the RSC for one season in 1996, would alternate Romeo and Mercutio (as Laurence Olivier and John Gielgud had done in 1932 at the Old Vic). Both eventually bowed out, opting for film or television projects rather than another season at the RSC. After the first performer declined, Attenborough asked Fearon to join the production and alternate Romeo and Mercutio with the remaining actor. When the second actor left, Fearon recalls Attenborough came to him and said, 'You can have any part you want. You want to play Romeo, play Romeo. You want to play Mercutio, play Mercutio.' Fearon chose Romeo, the fulfilment of his ambition to be a leading actor at the RSC. He was also the first actor of African-Caribbean descent to be cast in a title role at the RSC, thirty years after the RSC's first performers of colour, including Louis Mahoney, had played servants in Shakespeare's plays.[2]

'I belong here'

Born in Birmingham to immigrant parents, Nicholas Bailey dates his interest in performing Shakespeare back to his school days. Frequently involved in school productions, he 'never really had anybody say to me, "Go to drama school. You should give it a go because I think you'd be good at it."' His epiphany came when he was eighteen. Intent on pursuing a career as a barrister, Bailey was interviewing for a place at an Oxford college to read law when:

> I realized that the things that appealed to me [about law] were things I already had in my life: being on stage, playing different characters,

---

[2] As discussed in chapters 3 and 6, Patrick Robinson and Paterson Joseph were both understudies who played Romeo and Troilus, respectively, but they were not originally cast in those roles.

entertaining people, expressing myself through other people's words. That was already there and was actually to do with legal dramas and things that I saw in the 1980s – and wanting to be Blair Underwood from *L.A. Law*.

Bailey began his acting career in the early 1990s, after training at LAMDA and the National Youth Theatre. He cut his professional teeth on Shakespeare in regional theatre with productions of *Julius Caesar*, *Winter's Tale* (Florizel) and *Hamlet* (Laertes) at the Royal Exchange and Library theatres in Manchester.

Like Ray Fearon, Nicholas Bailey had the ambition to perform Shakespeare at the highest levels: 'I used to beg my agent every day, "What's going on at the RSC? What's happening?" That's all I wanted to do: be in the RSC and make movies.' When Bailey got the opportunity to audition for Richard Eyre's 1997 production of *King Lear* at the National Theatre – with the white actor Ian Holm in the title role – he was ecstatic:

> I'd seen productions at the National over the years – brilliant productions – and Richard Eyre was almost this mythical creature to us as young actors. All of my heroes were Shakespearean actors at that time. And that's what I wanted to be. I wanted to do what they did. I wanted to be like them: McKellen, Olivier, all those guys. People like Hugh Quarshie. Who had [all] done incredible things in Shakespeare.

Eyre cast Bailey as the Duke of Burgundy with another young performer of colour, Adrian Irvine, playing the King of France:

> I didn't really think about it at the time too much. We were the only two Black actors in the cast. I went to the costume fitting and was eager to see what we were wearing. They showed us kaftans, the silk kind of kaftans, bright colours. So the idea was that [the kingdom of] France was this sophisticated and Moorish type of culture. They had the wealth and there was also an exotica to France, an otherness to France, which made that scene and what happens in the scene more uncomfortable, more polarising.

When France and Burgundy arrive in the middle of the first scene, they enter into the political chaos created by Lear. Having split his kingdom, banished his trusted courtier Kent and disowned his daughter Cordelia, whom both Bailey and Irvine's characters had come to woo, Lear addresses Burgundy first, a sign of the Duke's status. Bailey explains:

> The Duke of Burgundy was as powerful as the King of France. Burgundy was the big financial centre [of early modern Europe] and I thought: *The one thing I'm not going to do is pander to status in the scene.* I

wanted Burgundy to have presence and dignity. I didn't want him to get exasperated and start throwing toys out of the pram; it's not there. What is there is a negotiation and he's decided, *Look, you may think that you've got the upper hand in this negotiation, but you don't; I do.* And that was it.

For Bailey, being part of *King Lear* at the National Theatre was 'a fantastic experience' and the production 'like a masterclass':

I'm watching all these guys, masters at the work, doing their thing and then I'd pick their brains. And I just remember being hugely inspired. I mean, the people that came to see it! Whoopi Goldberg came; Delroy Lindo and people like Paul Newman and John Gielgud. I just thought: *I belong here. I belong here doing this, feeling like this.*

Richard Eyre's *King Lear* closed in October 1997, and would be Bailey's last professional Shakespeare for nearly twenty years. 'All I wanted to do when I left drama school was be in the RSC and play Macbeth, Othello, Coriolanus, you name it. The big ones', he says. 'I just always thought Shakespeare would be my life.'

Othello, National Theatre, 1997

David Harewood became the first African-Caribbean performer to play Othello at the National Theatre in 1997, nearly twenty years after the BBC's dispute with Equity over James Earl Jones (chapter 2). The production's director, Sam Mendes, originally asked Adrian Lester to play Othello, but brought Harewood in after Lester won a role in a major Hollywood film, *Primary Colors*. Mendes' casting was predicated on the age of the leading actor:

I wanted a believable sexual relationship between Othello and Desdemona,... which I'd somehow never seen before. Othello is always treated as a father figure, whereas I wanted electricity; I wanted to feel that embryonic relationship which is destroyed.

(*NYTimes* 1 February 1998)

The production drew plaudits from John Peter, who found Mendes' *Othello* to be 'one of the finest Shakespeare productions in the National's history'. Praising its leads, Peter found it 'one of the rare productions in which Othello and Iago are evenly matched. They clash like thunderbolts' (*STimes* 21 September1997). Harewood's status as the first African-Caribbean Othello at the National Theatre also provoked a not-so-subtle backlash against integrated casting.

Several critics made similar claims to those of Carole Woddis, who wrote:

> It's over a decade since the National Theatre last staged *Othello*, with Paul Scofield in the title role. Since then, new cultural sensitivities over 'blacking up' have almost driven one of Shakespeare's greatest tragedies off the British stage.
> (*Independent* 16 September 1997)

Although the National had last staged *Othello* in 1980 with the white actor Paul Scofield, the play had not, in fact, disappeared from the British stage. In the eight years preceding Mendes' production, theatres across the country had staged over twenty productions of *Othello*.

Like Woddis, Charles Spencer began his review of Mendes' production by claiming *Othello* was 'a rarity' on the stage, the result of 'political correctness', but a more troubling argument accompanied his selective amnesia:

> It is no longer considered acceptable for white actors to black up for the title role, yet there are relatively few black actors with the authority and technical accomplishment to play Othello successfully.
> (*DT* 18 September 1997)

Spencer's argument that few actors of African-Caribbean descent were capable of playing Othello echoes the false assumptions that sparked the dispute between Equity and the BBC over *Othello* in 1979. Replicating, without evidence, that decades-old charge illustrates that negative perceptions still infused the discourse around inclusive casting. Michael Billington provides the antidote to these reactionary views, writing that Mendes' 'brilliant' production 'boast[s] a first-rate Othello in David Harewood – thus nailing the racist lie that there are few good classical black actors' (*Guardian* 18 September 1997).

Women of colour: pushing against the glass ceiling, 1998–1999

When Canadian-born, RADA-trained Tanya Moodie played Rosalind in *As You Like It* at the Bristol Old Vic in 1997, she was one of twenty-three actors of African-Caribbean and south Asian heritage to play a leading role in Shakespeare that year, a high-water mark in the integration of Shakespeare. Women of colour comprised a third of those twenty-three performers and Moodie was one of several following in the footsteps of trailblazers like Josette Simon in the 1980s and Rakie Ayola and Doña

Croll in the 1990s: the first women of colour to play Isabella, Portia and Cleopatra, respectively.

Alphonsia Emmanuel became the second woman of colour to play Cleopatra in Britain, six years after Doña Croll, in a fringe production at London's Bridewell Theatre in 1997. Having immigrated to Britain with her parents at the age of two, the Dominican-born Emmanuel grew up in Kensal Rise, London. A pioneer in her own right, she was the second woman of colour playing Shakespeare at the RSC, first in *Measure for Measure* (1983) followed by *Love's Labour's Lost* (1984). In a 1997 interview promoting the Bridewell *Antony and Cleopatra*, Emmanuel referred to the lack of opportunities for women of colour at the highest level: 'Like Hamlet, Cleopatra is a wonderful part to get your teeth into and see how far you can go and nobody was offering me it at the RSC so I thought, yeah why not have a go' (*Lowdown* 11 April 1997).

Clare Bayley praised Emmanuel's performance as Cleopatra:

> [Emmanuel] seizes the opportunity afforded by Shakespeare's wonderfully rich characterisation and elegantly combines regality and playfulness, political wit and emotional vulnerability, eroticism and intellect. Even in jealous outbursts or moments of immoderate rage, she maintains a crucial edge of self-knowledge and carries it off without ever appearing petty, weak or mean-spirited
>
> (*Times* 15 April 1997)

Another critic wrote Emmanuel 'ought to be giving her Cleopatra on stage at the Barbican [the RSC's London base], accompanied by trumpets and profiles in the national press' (*Midweek* 16 April 1997). The hierarchies of British theatre, with fringe theatre at the bottom and organizations like the RSC at the top, and the concomitant levels of media coverage meant Emmanuel's performance never received the attention it deserved. Cleopatra was also her last known Shakespeare role in Britain.

The English Shakespeare Company took the unheard-of step of hiring two women of colour to play leading roles in *Antony and Cleopatra* and *As You Like It* in 1998: Cathy Tyson and Ivy Omere as Cleopatra and Rosalind, respectively. *Antony and Cleopatra* was Tyson's eighth Shakespeare since *Tempest* at the Liverpool Everyman in 1984, while *As You* was Omere's first professional work. Despite her previous experience, Tyson lacked confidence in playing Cleopatra:

> What I found difficult was this sensuality, getting that mix quite right. How much to push that. I was just too self-conscious, I think, in that. Ill-equipped, I think, as well, you know, looking back on it.

Both of Michael Bogdanov's productions came in for a fair amount of criticism, including repeated complaints about actors mumbling. Despite the lacklustre reception, the reviews convey the power both women brought to their roles:

> Cathy Tyson seizes the role of Cleopatra and plays it at full strength.... This is a woman who combines regality with playfulness: a practical-joking, hard-drinking success in her own right.... In Tyson's Cleopatra, one can clearly see the conflict between the head that wears the crown of Egypt and the heart that loves Mark Antony.
> (*Independent* 26 August 1998)

Robert Smallwood had high praise for recent Webber Douglas graduate Ivy Omere's Rosalind, calling it an 'immensely promising professional début' (1999: 233). Born in Britain to parents who had emigrated from Nigeria in the 1960s, Omere incorporated her heritage into her portrayal of Rosalind, adopting a Nigerian accent when disguised as 'Jove's own page' Ganymede:

> The accent came and went very tellingly in the main wooing scene with [the white actor] David Shelley's refreshingly straightforward, gracious, and intelligent Orlando – what a pleasant change not to feel that Rosalind is throwing herself away – its presence or absence a barometer of her level of personal commitment.
> (Smallwood 1999: 233)

While Smallwood was complimentary, Jeremy Kingston felt Omere was 'spoiling the verse' (*Times* 19 October 1998) by using the Nigerian accent. Kingston was essentially rejecting the validity of Omere's choice to use her background for her performance. Choosing 'spoiling' to describe her verse speaking was a more coded method of saying that she 'couldn't speak the verse'.

Although women of colour were playing leading roles such as Rosalind and Cleopatra in regional theatre, equivalent opportunities were almost non-existent at theatre's highest levels in the late 1990s. Rakie Ayola had played a succession of leading Shakespearean parts by 1998, including Portia in *Merchant of Venice* at the Sherman Theatre, Cardiff, and Ariel in *The Tempest* at the Birmingham Rep (chapter 5). At the same time, Noma Dumezweni took on her first professional Shakespeare: Helena in *A Midsummer Night's Dream* for London Bubble. The juxtaposition of the two actresses' successes in regional theatre with their respective encounters with the RSC helps to illustrate the Shakespearean glass ceiling for women of colour.

Rakie Ayola auditioned for the RSC's 1998 season, which included a production of *Measure for Measure* directed by Michael Boyd. As shown by the descriptions of the white directors David Thacker and Bill Alexander, the RSC's audition process can be complicated. As Thacker notes in chapter 5, getting the actor you want can depend on forming alliances with other directors. Michael Boyd seems to have been unable to strike such a bargain with his colleagues. Ayola remembers:

> I auditioned [for Isabella in *Measure for Measure*] and my agent at the time was told they were looking for another part for me. The way that was sold made us believe that Isabella was mine. I met two more directors for other parts, the whole time assuming it was simply a matter of 'Let's find her a second or even third part in the season.' There was no sense from them that might not happen. After several weeks the call came in that they hadn't been able to find that other part and therefore couldn't offer me Isabella. My agent was in tears when she told me. Neither of us had understood that to be a possible outcome. I've never cried about not getting a job like I cried over that one.

Ayola went on to play Ophelia in *Hamlet* for Bill Alexander at the Birmingham Rep in 1998 and the following year she once again auditioned for the RSC. The 1999 Stratford season included an adaptation by Biyi Bandele of Aphra Behn's anti-slavery novella *Oroonoko* and Steven Pimlott's production of *Antony and Cleopatra*. Ayola recalls:

> I was offered a lead part in *Oroonoko*. I was offered, alongside that, a small part in *Antony and Cleopatra* and the chance to understudy Frances de la Tour [as Cleopatra]. The reason I said, 'No, thank you' to that was because it didn't make sense to me that an actor would be trusted to carry a lead role in the 'Black play' [*Oroonoko*], but wouldn't be trusted to carry a lead or second lead in any of the other plays. So I was very grateful for the offer, but declined.

Noma Dumezweni's experience stands in contrast to Ayola's, in part because of the level at which she entered the RSC. While Ayola had reached a point in her career that the RSC was considering her for leading roles, Dumezweni was several rungs below her on the casting ladder. Her first audition for the RSC was with Gregory Doran for a small part in *Oroonoko*. She did not get that job, but:

> It must have been about three months later, I got a phone call from my agent saying, 'Greg Doran would like to speak to you.' And there was a conversation we had on the phone. He said, 'Look, I knew I was going to be doing a production of *Macbeth* later on. So after seeing you for *Oroonoko* – I didn't want you in for that because you wouldn't have been able to do it – but can I bring you in to audition for one of the witches in *Macbeth* I'm going to be doing with Antony Sher and Harriet Walter?' I was like, 'Yes!! Yes, yes, I would audition again!'

Noma Dumezweni joined the RSC for Doran's production of *Macbeth*, the centrepiece of the RSC's 1999 winter season in the Swan Theatre. She played one of the witches, parts that had by then been part of the 'Black canon' for performers of colour since 1966. While the RSC was willing to hire Dumezweni to play a part mired in stereotypes, the company remained reluctant to cast women of colour as leads. Its glass ceiling meant that by 1999 only two women of colour had played leading Shakespearean roles at the RSC: Josette Simon (Isabella) and Naomi Wirthner (Kate).

RSC, 1999

Ray Fearon was still on tour with *Romeo and Juliet* in 1998 when its director, Michael Attenborough, first broached the subject of Othello:

> Mike said to me, 'Would you come back to the RSC?' And I said, 'Yeah, but you have to make me an offer I can't refuse.' That's exactly what I said. Then he said, 'Would you play Othello?' And I went, 'I didn't know you were going that far.' I'd played the part twice [while training at Rose Bruford and at the Liverpool Everyman in 1992], but by now I'd learned a lot more. I said, 'Mike, if you want me to do Othello, yeah, I'll do it.' He said, 'Right. I'll tell you what: I'll have a word with Adrian [Noble, the RSC's artistic director].'

In 1999, Ray Fearon became the first African-Caribbean man to play Othello for the RSC on its main stage, the Royal Shakespeare Theatre (and the first Black *actor* to play the part for the RSC).[3] Having been the first performer of African-Caribbean descent to play a title role in his own right for the RSC as Romeo, he was also the first to play a title role in the RST as Othello. Despite having regularly cast performers of colour since 1967, the RSC had taken over thirty years to reach this milestone.

A Midsummer Night's Dream, *Antony and Cleopatra*, *Timon of Athens* and *Othello* made up the RSC's 1999 main-stage season. While the RSC was prepared to consider an African-Caribbean (Rakie Ayola) to understudy a white actress playing the Egyptian queen Cleopatra, the first woman of colour to play a leading role returned to play Titania in *A Midsummer Night's Dream*. Josette Simon relished returning to play the Fairy Queen, a character she describes as:

> So exciting, powerful, fearsome and intelligent and magical and complicated, delicious. That's what I think of her. Again, you know, she and Oberon, absolute equals, absolute equals. And she can't be controlled, the only way you can control her is to drug her.

---

[3] As described in chapter 6, the first African-Caribbean man to play Othello at the RSC was not a trained classical actor, but the opera singer Willard White. For the RSC is also a crucial distinction here, as both Paul Robeson (1959) and Ira Aldridge (1861) had played Othello in that theatre when it was the Shakespeare Memorial Theatre, but Fearon was the first to play the part on that stage after the RSC was incorporated in 1961.

Simon was also the first performer of colour to play Titania at the RSC, which was her only Shakespeare role that season. Another eighteen years would pass before she again returned to the RSC, finally given the opportunity to play Cleopatra.

The presence of fourteen performers of colour, the largest number the RSC had employed in any single season, was perhaps the most significant aspect of the RSC's 1999 Stratford season. There were twelve actors of African-Caribbean heritage, including Ray Fearon and Josette Simon, one actress from a Middle Eastern background (Sirine Saba) and one south Asian man (Sam Dastor). Ray Fearon recalls the importance of that season's cohort:

> [1999] was the first season that there was a big spread [of performers of colour]. But before that, there was one or two Black actors. I was the only Black guy here [Stratford-upon-Avon] playing speaking [roles in his first season] that wasn't play as cast. There wasn't one Black actress here in that season. Of one hundred actors and actresses. In 1999, that's when I saw more Black actors at the RSC more than any other season. *Oronooko* was going on and a lot of them were spread out around the company. It was great to see, do you know what I mean? To see David [Oyelowo] in *Volpone*. That was great, that those guys came and were seeing me play Othello out there.

What makes this 1999 RSC season significant is not just the number of performers of colour in the season, but their inclusion across it. We have seen in earlier chapters how they were largely excluded from the RSC's main-stage Shakespeare productions. In 1999, however, the fourteen performers of colour were cast across the repertory and thirteen of them were included in the RSC's main house Shakespeares. The company usually staged five Shakespeare productions in the RST every season, two of which had all-white casts throughout most of the 1990s. By contrast, out of ten productions – five of which were Shakespeares – staged across its three theatres in 1999, only one had an all-white cast, a revival of T. S. Eliot's *The Family Reunion*. The 1999 season was a remarkable shift in the RSC's casting practice.

Gregory Doran directed both Biyi Bandele's adaptation of Aphra Behn's *Oroonoko* in The Other Place and Shakespeare's *Timon of Athens* in the Royal Shakespeare Theatre. That *Oroonoko* was an anti-slave-trade story, partly set in Africa, also meant that this single production was the primary driver of the RSC's 1999 inclusivity, with ten of the season's twelve African-Caribbeans included in *Oroonoko*. It was therefore no accident that Doran's production of *Timon of Athens* was also the most diverse of the RSC's main-stage Shakespeare productions, as he was able to cross-cast the two productions to form a mini-company of his own. Seven of the eight performers of colour cast in *Timon* were African-Caribbean and appearing in *Oroonoko*. The eighth was Sam Dastor, the Mumbai-born performer who was making his RSC debut after over thirty years' experience as a professional actor.

Dastor's route into the RSC and its main-stage Shakespeares illustrates the difficulties performers of south Asian heritage continued to encounter in classical theatre. At the beginning of his career, Dastor's classical pedigree was equivalent to those of his white peers at Cambridge and RADA. He won the Forbes Robertson prize for Shakespeare at RADA in 1965, in an era of blatant discrimination against performers of colour (see Errol Hill's recollections of RADA in the Introduction). Shortly after leaving RADA he joined the National Theatre at the Old Vic and became the first actor of colour to appear in Shakespeare with the company, then run by Laurence Olivier. Dastor went on to play Ariel opposite Paul Scofield's Prospero in John Harrison's production of *The Tempest*, first in Leeds in 1974 and London's West End the following year. As Dastor says:

> My entire life was built around Shakespeare and I became an actor for Shakespeare. So it was a great disappointment to me, after I played Ariel and I got very good reviews as Ariel, I never got any offers from the RSC.

His route into the RSC came via working with the white director Tim Supple. Dastor recounts:

> I didn't do any Shakespeare for ages and ages and ages and then it happened by accident. I was in India doing *Such A Long Journey*, which was a film of the Rohinton Mistry novel, which we were filming in Bombay, Mumbai as it is now. Somebody told me, 'Did you know that they're doing [an adaptation of Salman Rushdie's] *Haroun and the Sea of Stories* at the National?' I wrote to Tim Supple and, to his credit, he said, 'Come along and see me.'

Dastor was cast in *Haroun and the Sea of Stories*, which played at the National Theatre at the end of 1998:

> I got on very well with Tim [Supple] and Tim said, 'Well I'm going to Stratford to do *Tales from Ovid*. Would you like to do that?' I said, 'Yes I'd love to do the season.' So I did that. I did Tireseus in *Tales from Ovid*.

Dastor's training and experience should have allowed for an easy transition between Ted Hughes' *Tales from Ovid* to the RSC's Shakespeare productions, but his journey from the Swan to the Royal Shakespeare Theatre was far from straightforward. Dastor explains:

> They had this ludicrous casting system at the RSC, which is you have to do at least two plays or three plays. And none of the other directors

wanted me, so Adrian Noble [RSC artistic director], I thought, read the riot act [to the directors] and said, 'Look, Tim Supple wants Sam Dastor and we can't afford to have him just do that. So what else is there?' So eventually Greg Doran said, 'I could fit him into *Timon of Athens* somewhere.' So I went and saw him and he said, 'What would you like to play?' And I said, 'I'd like to play Apemantus' and then he said, 'Well I'm afraid that's cast. [Richard] McCabe's playing that.' And I said, 'Well, yes, I thought he would be.' And so I said, 'Well I'm too old for Alcibiades.' And he said, 'Yes.' And he said, 'Well, anything else you can choose.' So I said, 'Well, I think the Poet is probably the best one.' So I played the Poet for him.

As the Poet, Sam Dastor had the largest role played by a performer of colour in *Timon*, but the initial difficulty in finding him another role is reminiscent of both David Thacker's experience in casting Rudolph Walker in 1989 and Rakie Ayola's encounter with the RSC a decade later when she was considered for Isabella in *Measure for Measure*. Sam Dastor was in the most diverse RSC company to date, but his experience highlights continuing structural inequalities for performers of south Asian descent in classical theatre.

Troilus and Cressida, National Theatre, 1999

Trevor Nunn's production of *Troilus and Cressida* signified the differences between the Trojans and Greeks along racial lines. In Shakespeare's bitter anti-war satire, Nunn cast white actors as the Greek invaders and had fourteen African-Caribbeans playing the Trojans under siege. *Troilus* was part of a six-play repertory and originally devised as a cross-cast companion to the final play of Nunn's ensemble season, a revival of Peter Shaffer's *The Royal Hunt of the Sun*. Subtitled 'a play concerning the conquest of Peru', Shaffer's 1964 work chronicles the Spanish conquistadors' destruction of the Incas. When Shaffer withdrew the rights, Nunn's motif of white Greeks versus Black Trojans remained intact (Rosenthal 2013: 614–5).

Trevor Nunn put the actors of colour playing Trojans in the traditional robes of north Africa, an unequivocal statement of difference. Shakespeare's parable became literally one of Black and white to Alistair Macaulay, who saw racial conflict in Nunn's motif, stating that the:

> … production makes *Troilus* a war of whites (Greeks) versus blacks (Trojans). The whites, dressed in a mixture of Oriental and modern attire, are ruthless schemers; the blacks, in traditional Arab/African dress, are honourable, open-hearted, noble.
>
> (*FT* 17 March 1999)

FIGURE 8 *Michael Wildman (Margarelon), Dhobi Oparei (Hector), Chu Omambala (Paris), Oscar James (Priam), Vernon Douglas (Helenus), Peter de Jersey (Troilus), Mark Springer (Deiphobus).* Troilus and Cressida, *National Theatre, 1999. Photo by Donald Cooper/Photostage.*

Buried in Macaulay's language was another stereotype, that of the noble savage, a point made by Paul Bazely, who was working at the National at the time:

> When they did *Troilus and Cressida*, they should've [cast] it the other way round. The wily, sophisticated Greeks should've been Black and the doomed heroics should've been white. And how would that have felt? I think that would have felt uncomfortable. For good reason, because of the assumptions we make about the noble savage. So that was why I felt they [the NT] thought they were being really amazing and I felt it was already old fashioned because it was a white sixty-five-year-old man who made that call. And you ask a young actor of colour [what to do] and he'd go, 'Switch it [Nunn's casting].'

By casting the Trojans as Black, Nunn also reinforced the primacy of whiteness, because the white Greeks would successfully conquer the African-Caribbean Trojans. Instead of breaking stereotypes, Nunn was replicating ingrained notions of white superiority over people of colour.

Nunn could have made another choice for the Trojans, which would also have been better aligned with the play's production history. In dressing his Trojans as Africans, Nunn subverted a long-standing tradition of equating Troy with England. Tyrone Guthrie's influential 1956 Old Vic production, for example, placed the Trojans in replica Horse Guards jackets and opted to paint the Greeks as Germans sporting spiked helmets and Kaiser Bill moustaches (Shirley 2005: 33). At the RSC in 1990, Sam Mendes' Trojans resembled English officers of the Empire, stiff-backed and immaculately dressed in khaki uniforms, while the Greeks were dishevelled and unkempt. Instead of othering his performers of colour as African, Nunn's *Troilus and Cressida* could have gone some way towards breaking the stereotypes he was replicating by depicting his Trojans as British officers in British uniforms rather than the African robes chosen for costumes. Nunn's production would then have made a statement both about belonging and being British, rather than reinforcing narratives of colonization. Instead, he chose to cast his fourteen African-Caribbean performers in ways that played into the worst instincts of a nation that continues to find its multiculturalism difficult to accept.

Identity and colourblind casting

Adrian Lester played Bobby in Sam Mendes' 1995 production of *Company* at the Donmar Warehouse: the first time a performer of colour had played a lead in a Stephen Sondheim musical, on either side of the Atlantic. The production's original advertising was a drawing of an everyman flicking a wedding ring into the air: by default an image of a white man. Audience members unused to African-Caribbeans playing leading roles were confused. The Donmar's front-of-house staff overheard comments such as 'He was marvellous; gosh, I mean he's brilliant, but you know, it's a shame we didn't catch the real person', and relayed them to Lester, who recalls:

> Because I am a Black actor playing that role the assumption for some audience members was that I was the understudy. I went to Sam and asked if we could have a Black man on the poster. Sam listened but was a little puzzled as to why I wanted to be so racially specific with the image. We don't see the guy's face as he is only viewed from above. I completely understand his point of view, he just wanted the image to be an everyman, for it to represent everybody. I said, 'But he's not everybody. He's white.' Sam paused for a second and said, 'Oh, yeah. I'd never thought of it like that. You're absolutely right. Okay.' He made a few calls and the Donmar had another series of posters printed but this time with a Black man on the image. While we did the run at the Donmar both sets of posters could be seen around London.

What had escaped Mendes was the realization that, in a predominantly white society, fictional characters are, more often than not, assumed to be white. This bias, unconscious or otherwise, drives the casting process in the live and recorded arts. The default remains the casting of a white actor, unless an ethnicity is specified by the writer or on casting breakdowns sent to agents. This same assumption of whiteness was silently ingrained in the audience's reaction at the Donmar because, as Reni Eddo-Lodge observes, 'Whiteness positions itself as the norm' (2018: 169). By the end of the 1990s, the practice of colourblind casting – which was Mendes' default in casting Lester as Bobby in *Company* – was becoming increasingly complex as two productions at the Birmingham Rep, directed by Bill Alexander, help to illustrate.

When Rakie Ayola played Ophelia in Alexander's production of *Hamlet* in 1998 at the Birmingham Rep, she was the only performer of colour in the cast. When Alexander revived the production in 2000, pairing it with *Twelfth Night*, Ayola reprised Ophelia and also played Viola. Shipwrecked on the coast of Illyria, Viola adopts male disguise in order to survive as a woman alone in the duchy. The plot of Shakespeare's comedy revolves around the fact that Viola also has a twin brother, Sebastian, and the play's resolution relies on the plot device of mistaken identity between brother and disguised sister. As Alexander explained to Tony Howard, that required colour-conscious casting, rather than the colourblind version he had employed for *Hamlet*:

> There is the issue of 'How do you cast Sebastian?' I mean, that has to be… that would be sort of crazy to cast a white actor in a play about identical twins, right? So, I had a bloke called Faz Singhateh play Sebastian in that and Pal [Aron] – [south] Asian actor – played Orsino.

Because of the cross-casting between the two Shakespeares, the revival of *Hamlet* in 2000 became more multiracial: Pal Aron played Ophelia's brother, Laertes; Faz Singhateh and Aaron Neil had minor roles in both productions.

Ayola's Ophelia had a white brother and father in 1998, but a south Asian brother and, once again, a white father in 2000. By then the acceptance of colourblind casting as normal practice partly made Alexander's decision possible. For performers used to creating a fictional reality, this practice can throw up questions that need to be resolved. Ayola recalls having a conversation with the 1998 Laertes, Martin Hutson, where they were asking each other, 'Shall we just decide that one of us came from somewhere else? The audience will never know, but at least we can feel better about it. Ophelia arrived when she's two months old.' That brief conversation contains the tension between the intention and reality of colourblind casting. Ayanna Thompson explains:

> The initial idea behind colorblind casting was that neither the race nor the ethnicity of an actor should prevent her or him from playing a role as long as she or he was the best actor available. … In this version of

colorblind casting, the onus of being "blind" to race is completely on the audience.

(Thompson 2006: 6)

The tension between intention and reality arises when neither actor nor audience ignores the ethnicity of the performers of colour. As much as Alexander intended his audience to be blind to race, he readily admitted that not all were:

> I don't remember anyone having a problem with *The Tempest* [in 1994, see chapter 5], although there were some snide comments in the press about, you know, 'things pick up when the white comedians come on', [as] one critic wrote, which I thought was an unbelievably racist comment. But one or two people did say [in 2000], 'Oh, how can Polonius have a Black daughter and an Asian son?'

A profile of Ayola in the *Birmingham Evening Mail* also illustrates the outright hostility that persisted toward inclusive casting practices. With a headline 'To be black in the bard and the lover of Hamlet', Fred Norris interrogated Ayola:

> And when I ask her if she ever receives strange comments when her solitary black face appears in a Shakespearean sea of white ones on stage, she fixes me squarely again and says: "Not to my face. But I know it is there. You don't even have to sense it. There are some people who constantly remind you that there were no black people around in Shakespeare's time. I could answer that in Shakespeare's time it was against the law for women to appear on stage. The parts I am now playing had to be played by men.'

(25 August 2000)

The headline, the interviewer's framing of his question and Ayola's response all show the continuing struggle for inclusion in classical theatre by performers of colour, whose continuing exclusion is most evident with the title role in *Hamlet*.

Adrian Lester, Hamlet, 2000

Between 1966 and 1999, thirty-eight performers of colour played Othello in Britain, but only two played Hamlet: Ben Kingsley in the RSC's studio theatre, The Other Place, in 1975, and Rikki Beadle-Blair in a pub theatre in London in 1986. In 2000 Adrian Lester became the third performer of colour since the mid-1800s to play Hamlet professionally in Britain.[4] Out of the major title characters of Shakespeare's tragedies, few had been played by a performer of colour in Britain by 1999 (Table 12).

Adrian Lester played Hamlet for Peter Brook, who had been away from British mainstream theatre since the 1970s. Based in Paris, the white British director was committed to creating intercultural theatre, frequently touring his productions internationally. Brook's working methods and theatrical interests are significant because he was not confined by false claims that performers from African-Caribbean backgrounds could not speak the verse, let alone play the major tragic roles in the canon.

Brook assembled a company around Lester that included a majority of international performers from African-Caribbean and south Asian backgrounds. Peter Brook streamlined Shakespeare's text, an impetus that had grown out of intercultural associations, as Adrian Lester explains:

> Peter had a very interesting idea. He wanted to do *Hamlet*, but he wanted to pare away. It was always about paring away. His images were those African statues, African sculptures where you sculpt a figure, but then you keep paring away until the thinnest line depicting a leg or the thinnest line depicting an arm is left. And they're so fragile and long, beautiful until you just about have the frame of the person and then it was left. And he wanted you to pare away the play until you just had the essential: Mother, Son, Love, God, Father, Uncle, Death.

TABLE 12 *Number of times performers of colour played male title roles in Shakespeare in Britain, 1966–1999*

Character	Actors of colour cast
Othello	38
Romeo	14
Macbeth	5
Antony	4
Hamlet	2
King Lear	1
Coriolanus	0
Titus Andronicus	0

---

[4] The African-American Ira Aldridge may have played Hamlet in Sheffield in 1856, based on one eyewitness account (Evans 2007: 175); Samuel Morgan Smith had Hamlet in his repertoire, but it is unlikely he played the part in what we would recognize today as a full production.

Brook's approach also meant that whiteness was not the dominant influence of his *Hamlet*, and therefore the cast was not required to subsume their heritage. Lester played Hamlet with his hair in dreadlocks, for example, and the production's influences were global. Lester explains:

> What we tried to construct in our production, which I thought is where Peter's genius lay, is a sense of a stage that was before time. You could imagine this taking place with pyramids in the background or a Mayan temple. You could imagine this taking place with a very powerful royal family before common history began. And then in the middle of this tragedy, I tried to repeat Shakespeare's device of placing a modern thinker, a prince with empathic responses in the middle of an old, revenge play. My mannerisms were, if you like, un-Shakespearean. I would allow myself very modern responses: shrug, use sarcasm, modern forms of mockery. I wanted to place someone you might see on the streets of our modern cities in the middle of a very old classic revenge tragedy.

Brook excized the play's politics, focusing the production on Hamlet, his dilemma and its effect on the people in his orbit. Lester discovered that playing Hamlet works without reliance on twentieth-century naturalistic performance practice:

> The audience completes the character for you. As an actor you don't have to worry about consistency or keeping a conscious, constant through line going through every scene; you just play. Every scene is a chord, notes on a scale. You take these separate notes and play them as fully and as perfectly as you can with almost a complete disregard for what is to follow, then let the audience do the rest. It was a good lesson to learn. It freed me from the prison of trying to make an overall sense of what character is, and allow the logic of who Hamlet is and what he is going through to be an unconscious amalgam of moments where we see him live under extreme stress because of his doubts. Hamlet, in order to protect himself, is incredibly versatile with his perceived character in front of each person he meets.

These revelations also had implications for working out whether Hamlet's madness is real or feigned:

> It is much more interesting to approach the character as if generalized madness isn't present. Take any normal, sane person and put them into extreme circumstances, as they try to cope they're going to start to behave in extraordinary ways. It is the way people cope with profound extremities that we perceive as madness. Objectively, you can call it what

you like, but subjectively – from the point of view of playing the character – it is a logical response to incredible circumstances. He's too lucid to be crazy. The other point to note is that his seeming madness is greatest in front of those people he feels he must hide the truth from. So, he is mad when he is with Polonius or his uncle the king; he's a little bit mad with his mom, before he starts to speak his truth with laser-like intensity [in the closet scene].

Lester received numerous plaudits for *Hamlet*, but one of Benedict Nightingale's adjectives describing his performance stands out: 'intelligent' (*Times* 24 August 2001). The critic's description is important because the word is also the antithesis of one long-standing stereotype that falsely claims African-Caribbeans lack intelligence.

As far back as 1971, Bernard Coard identified problems with standardized tests given to the children of immigrants, which saw large numbers of young people classified as 'educationally subnormal' (Hartmann and Husband 1974: 17). In *Natives: Race and Class in the Ruins of Empire*, Akala notes that nearly half a century after Coard's report was published the 'trend of underestimating black children's intelligence [still] continues right throughout schooling' (2019: 81). This important thread runs through not only education, but it also plays into the history of integrated casting with the persistent dismissal of African-Caribbeans' ability to speak verse the classical theatre equivalent.

Shakespeare's Hamlet epitomizes intelligence in the canon. Visual images of a man contemplating mortality while gazing at a skull help to depict Hamlet as a scholar and philosopher. Rodin's *The Thinker* is the sculptural equivalent of Shakespeare's Hamlet in evoking searing intellect. If Hamlet equates to Rodin's *Thinker*, the negative stereotyping of African-Caribbeans as unintelligent also explains the overwhelming reluctance to view African-Caribbean performers as potential Hamlets. Societal bias seeps into the cultural landscape: the doubt of artistic ability intertwined with the discrimination that viewed immigrants' children as intellectually 'subnormal'.

Lester may have encountered these negative perceptions in a meeting he attended shortly after his casting as Hamlet:

> [Playing Hamlet] changes what people think of you. I was at this board meeting, surrounded by middle-class theatre at its height. We were talking about various projects and what we were going to do. I said I was doing Hamlet for Peter Brook. I won't even guess what people were thinking. Obviously, I was not the image of Hamlet they had in mind. My dreads were really long then, in my face. But from that point on in the meeting it was very easy to say what I had to say and give my opinions.
>
> (*Telegraph Magazine* 11 November 2000)

The prestige of working with Peter Brook and playing Hamlet for the legendary director had produced an unsubtle shift in attitude. Lester's experience was similar to Cyril Nri's, noted in chapter 3, at the Bristol Old Vic Theatre School twenty years earlier. The common denominator between Nri winning the Best Actor prize at the National Student Drama Festival and Lester in his board meeting were the initially low expectations of both men, the result of persistent negative stereotyping.

David Oyelowo, Henry VI, 2000

Born in Britain to Nigerian parents, David Oyelowo had minimal experience of Shakespeare when he joined the RSC in 1999. One of his few prior encounters with the playwright as an actor came while at LAMDA. *The Scotsman* highly praised his performance in *Coriolanus*, which played at the Edinburgh fringe festival:

> David Oyelowo's Tullus Aufidius has grace, power, nobility, anger, passion and – strangely but most effectively – eroticism. A Black Volscian leader seems an appropriate emendation, but this performance is definitive.
>
> (20 August 1996)

Three years later, Oyelowo's sum total of Shakespeare in his first RSC season were the three lines of Decretas in *Antony and Cleopatra*. It was his work in Biyi Bendele's adaptation of *Oronooko* that brought Oyelowo to the attention of Michael Boyd. As Oyelowo recalled, 'Michael came up to me after one performance and said that he desperately wanted to work with me one day, which I thought was very flattering' (*BP* 19 September 2000). Boyd would cast Oyelowo as Henry VI, which made him the first performer of colour to play one of Shakespeare's English kings at the RSC.

Oyelowo was no naïve, young actor when Boyd tapped him for Henry VI, but well aware that actors of African-Caribbean heritage were negatively stereotyped by the industry he had joined:

> As a black actor it's a very difficult mould to break out of.... A lot of my friends in the industry have found it very difficult. They are constantly offered "drug dealers on *The Bill*". You can imagine how demoralising that is.
>
> (*DM* 19 September 2000)

Peter de Jersey independently echoed this experience in an interview around the same time: 'I looked at the showreels [of his television work] I was doing before and, in a lot of the things, I was in trouble with the police' (*The Stage* 12 October 2000). In casting Oyelowo as Henry VI, Boyd broke the colour bar *and* disrupted prevalent stereotypes.

Oyelowo playing Henry VI was a departure from depictions of violence and criminality partly because of the character's status as monarch, but also the character's demeanour: contemplative, religious and, most of all, pacifist. For Oyelowo, Henry VI was a man 'dealing as best he can with the insurmountable odds surrounding him' (2003: 15). Henry's anchor is his faith, a facet of his character that Oyelowo found compelling:

> He doesn't think in a political way. His eyes are on eternity and on being good, rather than what he can do that day to keep him on the throne. He believes in peace and goodness, and that if everyone else thought the same way things would be OK. Perhaps that is naive but it is not weak.
> (*ST* 10 December 2000)

The character is often a bystander to events and Henry VI is neither the largest part nor the driving force in any of the plays that bear his name,[5] but the symbolism of Oyelowo's casting as a king of England was not lost on the actor's father. The elder Oyelowo had emigrated from Nigeria to Britain in the 1960s, arriving when African-Caribbeans were facing overt racism from white Britons. David Oyelowo remembered the impact of the news on his father:

> I rang my father who, when he first came to this country 40 years ago, was spat on and things. His reaction was just phenomenal, and that was when I first thought this might be a big deal. He was, like [in a rich Nigerian accent] "Oh! This is a revolution. I cannot believe it. My boy?!" My father doesn't know anything about acting. If I say the RSC or the National it doesn't mean anything. But King of England he can understand.
> (*ST* 10 December 2000)

A furore, for which Oyelowo and the RSC were unprepared, followed Oyelowo's casting: 'I can only think of it as another part', Oyelowo told the *Coventry Evening Telegraph*, 'I can't understand the kerfuffle. Black actors have played Shakespeare before and I was a bit shocked that people would question the casting' (29 November 2000).

The controversy surrounding Oyelowo's appearance as Henry VI was reminiscent of the backlash in the 1980s, as performers of colour made inroads into classical theatre. One Oxford don, quoted anonymously, objected to Oyelowo's presence outright because of the actor's

---

[5] The character of Henry VI is the second largest part in *Henry VI, Part Two*, but in the other two plays of the trilogy he is not even the third largest role. The three largest parts, and the leading parts as defined here, are: Talbot, Joan la Pucelle, Duke of York (*1 Henry VI*); Duke of York, Henry VI, Duke of Gloucester (*2 Henry VI*); Edward IV, Earl of Warwick, Duke of Gloucester (*3 Henry VI*).

ethnicity: 'Moves like this leave us open to ridicule. King Henry VI wasn't black and should not be cast as such' (qtd in *STimes* 24 September 2000). Robert Gore-Langton took the opportunity to suggest that 'the informal ban on white actors playing [Othello should be] lifted' (*Sunday Express* 24 September 2000). Other critics reacted against the backlash, including *The Times*' Jeremy Kingston, a shrug evident in his comment: 'honestly, what's the big deal?' (19 September 2000). As a few performers of colour were beginning to reach the pinnacle of the profession, regularly playing leads and title characters in Shakespeare, resistance to progress was once again vociferously emerging.

Paterson Joseph recalls a sense of disbelief that, after the clear breakthroughs of the 1980s and 1990s (including his own promotion from understudying Ralph Fiennes to playing Troilus at the RSC), a performer of colour playing a leading role still had to be defended:

> We were expecting a bit of controversy [when Oyelowo was cast as Henry VI], but I don't think the sort of level of furore surrounding him was expected. Because, when I played Troilus, there was an article in the *Standard*, I think it was by Milton Shulman, and I was interviewed for the [television] news, so it was like a big deal. But that was 1991. I didn't think that, ten years later, it would have been as big a controversy to have a Black guy play a lead. But it wasn't about that; it was about the English king. It was about him playing the English king. And that was where it became purely an argument about who belongs and who has the right to impersonate historical characters, even in fiction.

The battle over who belongs continues to play out in contemporary Britain and, as a consequence, Shakespeare's histories remain the least representative Shakespearean genre. In the twenty years since Oyelowo played Henry VI at the RSC, only four other performers of colour have played one of Shakespeare's English kings.[6]

Romeo and Juliet, Mu-Lan, 2001

British east Asians are not so much excluded as practically invisible in Shakespeare. Between 1976, when David Yip became the first east Asian to perform in a Shakespeare play in Britain, and 2000, only twelve others were cast in a Shakespeare role. Many of these appearances were small parts in touring productions, playing characters already established as part of the

---

[6] They are: Adrian Lester as Henry V (NT, 2003); Chuk Iwuji in the 2006 revival of Boyd's *Henry VI* trilogy (RSC); Adjoa Andoh as Richard II (Shakespeare's Globe, Sam Wanamaker Playhouse, 2019); Sarah Amankwah as Henry V (Shakespeare's Globe, 2019).

'Black canon', including Hélène Patarot as Charmian in Moving Theatre's *Antony and Cleopatra*. Paul Courtenay Hyu had been one of the few British east Asians to play a substantial Shakespeare part between 1976 and 2000: Lorenzo and the Prince of Morocco in Jamie Garven's production of *The Merchant of Venice* (chapter 5).

British east Asians reached another significant milestone in Shakespeare after Hyu became artistic director of Mu-Lan Theatre, a company committed to providing a voice for the British east Asian community. In 2001 Mu-Lan co-produced *Romeo and Juliet* with the Haymarket Theatre in Basingstoke, the first Shakespeare play to have a majority east Asian cast. At the season press launch, Hyu spoke directly to the crux of what was facing British east Asians in the live and recorded arts: 'This is a unique production. For far too long, Chinese actors have been cast in stereotyped roles. This is their chance to demonstrate their talent in one of the finest plays in the English language' (*Southern Daily Echo* 13 July 2001). Hyu and his co-director, the Haymarket's white artistic director Alasdair Ramsay, used 1930s Shanghai as the production's backdrop. In this locale, Romeo's family were British expatriates, while Juliet's were Chinese nationals with the Montagues and Capulets rival opium merchants.

When a marginalized community puts its head above the parapet for the first time, it usually meets resistance. 'We got complaint letters before we opened', Daniel York Loh, who played Mercutio, recalls. '"My husband and I very much enjoy Shakespeare. Traditionally the way it should be done, certainly not Chinese,"' was one piece of irate correspondence he was shown. On the whole, however, the production was well received, including by schoolchildren that Loh and the cast encountered at a local takeaway. 'There were these kids in there, white kids, who were just, they were so nice to us. They were in awe, they were like "Wow, you lot, oh my god!"'

Given the lack of classical experience within the company, some critics made the inevitable complaints about the company's 'verse speaking'. Objections to Bronwyn Mei Lim, who played Juliet, surfaced in two publications: 'In catching Juliet's urgency, she sometimes hurries and flattens the script' (*Reviewsgate* 18 October 2001) and 'Simon Grieff and Bronwyn Mei Lim make an appealing pair of lovers, although Mei Lim sometimes hurries her lines too much in her emotional scenes' (*Berkshire Live* 24 October 2001). Criticism about 'verse speaking' has been levelled at performers of colour since at least 1963, when critics found fault with Errol John's Othello at the Old Vic (see Introduction). In reality, actors who have been consistently denied opportunities to regularly practise their craft are often unfavourably compared to their white counterparts. Performers with limited classical experience are also more likely to be reliant on a director than their more experienced counterparts. Loh felt Lim was an excellent actress and found her Juliet compelling, but Ramsay also had his cast 'speaking at this ridiculous lick', as Loh describes it, which undoubtedly contributed to Lim's negative reviews as Juliet.

The issue of pace also brings up an important disparity in the ways people of colour are treated compared to established and predominantly white classical actors. The ability to make use of techniques such as pauses is one such notable difference, as Loh observes:

> When you watch Simon Russell Beale or Antony Sher, they're taking their time. They're given that platform. They're allowed. They're put up there. We're [the audience] going to be here for three hours and it's absolutely fine. Whereas we [performers of colour] are always told, 'No, you've got a [time] limit. Cut it down. Cut it down.'

Loh also feels Mu-Lan's *Romeo* came too early to have a lasting impact for British east Asian Shakespeareans:

> It's a shame, really. I think if it had been on now [2018], it would be quite ground-breaking. It would get a lot of coverage on social media and stuff. There was no social media or anything then. It was literally just the print news and local press. It did go down well and it sold quite well. It was quite successful. It's a shame it couldn't have been done a bit better and done more performances. I really enjoyed it.

For British east Asians, Shakespeare continues to be the 'closed shop' that Norman Beaton described back in 1979.

Adrian Lester, Henry V, 2003

Adrian Lester became the first performer of colour to play Henry V in Britain, when he took to the National Theatre's Olivier stage in 2003. The production was Nicholas Hytner's inaugural one as the National's artistic director, a post first held by Laurence Olivier, whose Second World War-era film of *Henry V* defined the play for a generation. Hytner's multiracial cast challenged the idea of an all-white national identity, but race was not the major focus for either director or leading actor. Lester recalls:

> I didn't think about it politically or in terms of race, I just wanted to play the part. And Henry V is a great part. I did think: *Why me? Why me play him?* I just couldn't imagine myself as Henry V. Nick wanted to do a modern production and, just like in *Othello* [in 2013], he put me in khaki combat gear with automatic weapons. I didn't think about it in political terms. I thought about getting on with the role. I didn't fully politicize my artistic decisions then, I just went: I want to try and be the best actor I can be, which means I take on these difficult roles if I have the opportunity.

Although Hytner had been planning the production since 2002, it was inevitably defined by current events: the invasion of Iraq. As 2002 waned and rehearsals drew closer, events began to overtake the planning, as Lester recounts:

> We were preparing to rehearse the play as tensions were mounting and Blair, Bush and the coalition forces were prepared to go to war and invade Iraq. We didn't know if it was going to be a full-scale invasion. Eventually we found ourselves performing the play at a time of war.

Britain and America invaded Iraq in March 2003, three days before rehearsals for *Henry V* began. That indelibly shaped the production and its reception.

Hytner describes Shakespeare's opening scene as 'a council meeting' in which Henry 'needs rock-solid legal justification for the invasion of France' (2017: 54). The modern-dress staging opened with a conflated 1.1 and 1.2, set in the Cabinet Room at 10 Downing Street. For Lester, Henry is 'a great politician' and this moment was 'a pure political act':

> He's basically saying to the church: 'You back my campaign to go into France and get their land and get their money, by right of this ruling. If you don't back it, or fail to make the case, I'll take all the lands that you own.' That was Henry's challenge to them, 'This Cabinet meeting is your chance to save the Church because, if you don't convince these people that we have a rightful claim to the throne of France, I will take everything that you have.'

Hytner saw *Henry V* as a malleable play, with its 'belligerent patriotism coexist[ing] with its insistence on the bloody consequences of armed conflict' (2017: 53). The war had personal costs for the king and Lester's Henry felt 'a constant tension between the heroic and noble King Henry and the destructiveness of the war he wages'. This was a monarch who:

> is bloody minded in his service of the people. The people needed more land, more money, so he had to find a way to get it for them. If the people hate him for it, fine, he may even hate himself, but he'll still do what he feels is his duty and take what his country needs. He serves. Any conscience he may have about serving envelops him in that dark night of the soul when he wanders around his camp, in the dark, talking to his men as a common soldier [4.1]. For that moment I put my hood up. There's no pomp, no deference, the other soldiers were looking at me like, 'Who are you?'

On the eve of the Battle of Agincourt, Henry walks through the English camp unrecognized. Having other performers of colour around Henry in the British army was necessary for this scene because, as Lester explains, 'For Henry to visually blend into the crowd, you have to have other Black soldiers.'

Hytner reflected multiracial Britain in his casting, the first director to do so in one of Shakespeare's history plays. His *Henry V* had a cast of twenty-seven actors, six of whom were performers of colour: Lester, Jude Akuwudike, Cecelia Noble, Faz Singhateh, Rohan Siva and Mark Springer. By contrast, Michael Boyd's *Henry VI* company at the RSC in 2000 had three performers of colour, including David Oyelowo, in a cast of twenty-nine adult actors. This makes for a stark difference in percentage terms: white performers comprised 90 per cent of actors cast in Boyd's productions and 78 per cent of Hytner's for *Henry V*. For all the press attention showered on Oyelowo's breakthrough as an English king, Boyd's productions were far less inclusive across the board.

The multicultural society portrayed in Hytner's *Henry V* was closer to the reality of contemporary Britain. Performers of colour played characters from all levels of society, from royalty to nobles to Henry's tavern companions. Cecelia Noble's double of the Hostess (Mistress Quickly) and the French Queen Isabel, along with the south Asian performer Rohan Siva's appearances as Captain Jamy and the French herald Montjoy perhaps best embody this broad spread across society. Hytner's achievement was in depicting contemporary *and* multicultural Britain on the Shakespearean stage, but staging a history play with a multiracial cast also made a statement about who has the right to tell the nation's stories.

The peak of progress?

Hytner's *Henry V* was one of the major milestones in integrated casting in British Shakespeare, but few have followed it. On the surface, the years between 1997 and 2003 were extraordinary, signalling that equality had arrived in classical theatre by way of a number of high-profile castings. The two main national companies had each, at long last, hired African-Caribbeans to play Othello. A major production of *Hamlet* had an African-Caribbean as the lead; and the National and the RSC had cast African-Caribbeans to play two of Shakespeare's English kings: Henry V and Henry VI, respectively. Nicholas Hytner paid tribute to this unequivocal cultural change: '25 years ago it would have been unlikely that the leading heroic actor of our day was black. It says something about what has happened to the country' (*DT* 24 January 2003).

Many in the press viewed the casting of two African-Caribbeans, both British-born, to play two of Shakespeare's English kings as a turning point. David Lister wrote in *The Independent* that 'the rules of casting have been rewritten, not at a few fringe venues, but at some of our biggest institutions' (5 July 2003). Similarly, in reporting the casting of Lester as Henry V, Michael Billington observed this cultural shift by noting that a statement made by Jatinder Verma, Tara Arts' artistic director, a decade earlier – 'British theatre is promoting a kind of myth that does not correspond to people's experience [of a multiracial society] as they walk down the street' – was no longer accurate. For Billington, this meant the trope of '"Black actor plays Shakespeare king" [had] ceased to be news' (*Guardian* 4 December 2002).

While directors and some in the media celebrated first David Oyelowo and then Adrian Lester as Black English kings, they promulgated a complacency that did not reflect reality. Progress had peaked: that would become increasingly apparent as the twenty-first century continued. The glass ceiling began to re-emerge and old stereotypes crept back to prominence on to the British Shakespearean stage.

7

Progress postponed, 2004–2011

'I tried to put you up for a role in a Shakespearean play', Nicholas Bailey's agent told him in 2003, 'because you've done a lot of Shakespeare. You love Shakespeare. I think you'd be tremendous for this role.' When she had contacted the production's casting director about the part, an awkward pause came from the other end of the telephone line. The response would not have been out of place in the 1970s: 'We didn't see that character as Black.' This was not an isolated incident, as an anecdote from 2004 attests (Joseph 2018: 78):

> [Samantha Lawson] recalled being told by young, white peers that she should not really be playing a Scandinavian witch in Philip Pullman's *His Dark Materials* as she was black. Unless, of course, they were doing a 'thing' where all the witches would be black. 'Juliet' was also out-of-bounds for Samantha, according to these same contemporaries of hers.

Integrated casting was, by then, part of the fabric of British Shakespeare, but the glass ceiling for performers of colour remained firmly in place.

By the turn of the century, classical theatre was no longer the 'closed shop' Norman Beaton had described in 1979 (chapter 2). As we have seen, performers of colour were regularly included in productions of Shakespeare, but equity had not been achieved. In the first decade of the twenty-first century, progress in the integration of Shakespeare was either stalled or, by some measurements, had gone backwards. No longer about inclusion, the battles were increasingly about the continued lack of access to Shakespeare's leading roles. Discrimination and exclusion began to take on more subtle shapes, as performers of colour were placed in an increasingly narrow frame.

The inroads performers of colour had made in the 1980s and 1990s obscured a basic fact: the bulk of inclusion on the Shakespearean stage occurred within a narrow section of the canon. Table 13 reveals a consistency in the plays with the greatest level of inclusion, measured by the total number of roles cast in productions of each play, with *A Midsummer Night's Dream* and *Romeo and Juliet* regularly leading the casting league table (to borrow football terminology). Both plays had been among the first to be integrated in 1982 and they still dominated inclusion practices, in terms of the sheer volume of roles played by performers of colour, in the 2000s. The appearance of *Hamlet* and *Antony and Cleopatra* as one of the top five plays, per number of roles cast, in the period between 1997 and 2003, and their disappearance after 2004, is one illustration of how inclusion had expanded and then retreated.

The levels of integration in productions of two tragedies – *Romeo and Juliet* and *Hamlet* – across the 1990s and 2000s will help to show the complex nature of inclusion in – or, more accurately, the continued exclusion of performers of colour from – British Shakespeare (Table 14). In the 1990s, at least one performer of colour was cast in 65 per cent of all productions of *Romeo and Juliet* but in only 50 per cent of the *Hamlet*s. In the 2000s, productions of *Romeo* became more integrated, while those of *Hamlet* became less.

This marked difference in inclusion across the two tragedies is a microcosm of the integration of British Shakespeare, as performers of colour continued to be included in particular plays in the canon (*Romeo*) while

TABLE 13 *Plays ranked by total number of roles played by performers of colour*

1988–1996		1997–2003		2004–2011	
Play	Roles cast	Play	Roles cast	Play	Roles cast
Macbeth	76	*Dream*	82	*Twelfth Night*	79
Romeo	74	*Romeo*	75	*Macbeth*	68
Dream	54	*Antony*	37	*Dream*	64
Twelfth Night	51	*As You*	37	*Romeo*	57
Tempest	39	*Hamlet*	37	*As You*	55

TABLE 14 *Integrated vs all-white productions in the 1990s and 2000s*

Decade	Number of productions (% of all productions)			
	Hamlet		Romeo and Juliet	
	Integrated	All-white	Integrated	All-white
1990s	15 (50 %)	15 (50 %)	22 (65 %)	12 (35 %)
2000s	10 (48 %)	11 (52 %)	36 (80 %)	9 (20 %)

TABLE 15 *Total leading roles cast, by genre, 1988–2011*

Genre	Leading roles		
	1988–1997	1998–2003	2004–2011
Comedies	56	46	75
Tragedies	79	35	60
Histories	1	3	7

being excluded from others (*Hamlet*). If classical theatre had continued its trend towards greater inclusivity, *Hamlet* should have become more inclusive in the 2000s. Instead, as *Romeo* became 15 per cent more inclusive in the 2000s across all productions of the play, the overall inclusivity of productions of *Hamlet* declined by 2 per cent.

Additionally, Table 15 shows a realignment in the roles available to performers of colour between 1988 and 2011, by genre. The total number of leading roles, defined here as a play's three largest parts, played by performers of colour across time and by genre are shown in this table.

Table 15 starkly shows the shift in opportunities for actors from African-Caribbean, south Asian and east Asian heritages in leading roles. Between 1988 and 1997, performers of colour were more likely to be cast in a leading role in a tragedy than a comedy; that metric had flipped by the period between 2004 and 2011. The shift was subtle, but nevertheless collectively amounts to the segregation of performers of colour at the light-entertainment end of the Shakespearean canon, and their exclusion from the more prestigious tragedies.

'There's a few more parts we could play, you know'

Patrick Robinson's first encounter with *Macbeth*, while he was at LAMDA, ignited his passion for the play: 'I was like Wow! What a brilliant piece! And it's been my favourite ever since.' His first professional job at the RSC in 1986, as Seyton in Adrian Noble's production, cemented his admiration for it:

> I always remember watching Jonathan Pryce play [Macbeth] and I'd go, 'Wow!' The part I played was Seyton, their servant. Seyton was the right-hand man for Macbeth throughout the whole thing. So I've watched him do so many scenes, he and Sinead Cusack who was playing Lady Macbeth, like wow! That was my favourite and best show [that year], one of the best shows of that season to me. And it was great because the

way Jonathan treated me was [as an] equal as an actor. That was when I kind of thought: *You're a big star to me because I've seen your films, man, and I think you're brilliant and here I am working with you and you're saying, 'Pat what do you think?'*

Five productions of *Macbeth*, from 1986 to 2018, span Patrick Robinson's acting career, comprising nearly a third (29 per cent) of his total Shakespearean work. As Table 16 shows, Robinson hit the glass ceiling with *Macbeth* after playing Banquo in 2004 for Out of Joint; after that production, he reprised roles he had already played: Macbeth and Banquo.

The subtlety of inequality in twenty-first century British Shakespeare is partly illustrated by *where* leading roles are played. Robinson played Macbeth on a tour of America and for five nights in Shrewsbury, while he played Banquo for a major touring company and at the National Theatre. Robinson is not alone in this experience as male performers of colour are more likely to play Banquo than Macbeth at a ratio of slightly less than 2:1, according to data in the British Black and Asian Shakespeare Performance Database. *Where* performers of colour play both roles is important because eight of the thirty-one performers of colour have played Banquo on the main stages of the RSC, National Theatre and Shakespeare's Globe; only one has played Macbeth on those same stages (Ray Fearon, Shakespeare's Globe, 2016).

Macbeth is not the only Shakespeare play in which Patrick Robinson has appeared more than once. His second season at the RSC in 1988 included parts in *Much Ado About Nothing* and *King John*. Between 1986 and 1989 Robinson had spent a total of four years at the RSC, appearing in two two-year season cycles, but then, he says, there was 'nothing for?... Well this is the late 80s until 2006 [before another season at the RSC], and I get [cast in] the same two shows. Then you kind of go, "Eh?! Oh yeah, *King John* and *Much Ado.*"'

The parts had improved from the early days in Patrick Robinson's career, but the stereotyping was familiar in his casting in the 2006 production of *Much Ado*, in which he played Don Pedro. Kenneth Branagh's hiring of the

TABLE 16 *Patrick Robinson's roles in* Macbeth, *1986–2018*

Role	Company, year
Seyton	RSC, 1986
Macbeth	Haworth Shakespeare Festival, 1995 [tour]
Banquo, Siward	Out of Joint, 2004 [tour]
Macbeth	Theatre Severn, Shrewsbury, 2017
Banquo	National Theatre, 2018 [tour]

African-American actor Denzel Washington as Don Pedro for his 1993 film looms large for Don Pedro's place in the Shakespearean 'Black canon'. It was after the film's release that performers of colour began to play Don Pedro regularly. Robinson referenced Branagh's *Much Ado* film when speaking about his own casting as Don Pedro:

> I figured that Marianne Elliott was seeing that as an image. But I thought: *They're casting Don Pedro as a brother? Whoa!* Because I remember being in it [in 1988]. I played Conrade, one of Don John's villains.

Robinson describes Don Pedro as 'a very cool guy, but very lonely guy' who was also 'the outsider. That's very easy for me to play. I play a lot of outsiders.'

Although an outsider, Don Pedro has a unique position in *Much Ado*. As the Prince of Aragon, he is the character with the highest status. The action, however, revolves around Benedick (largest role in the play), which reduces Don Pedro (the third-largest part) to the position of sidekick. As Reni Eddo-Lodge (2018: 139–40) observes, in fictional representations there remains:

> a real struggle to identify with black humanity in any conceivable way.... Seeing non-white characters relegated to sidekick or token status has been routine for so long that, for some, attempting to try and relate to black skin in a main character is a completely alien concept.

Defined by this outsider status, as well as five productions of *Macbeth* and two each of *Much Ado* and *King John*, Patrick Robinson's Shakespeare career illustrates the mechanics of the glass ceiling. The full Shakespearean canon is rarely on offer to classical performers of colour. As Patrick Robinson says, 'thirty-seven plays, man. There's a few more parts we could play, you know. Just give us a chance. We can do it.'

Tragic heroes and the Shakespearean glass ceiling, 2004–2011

A 2011 Equality and Human Rights Commission (EHRC) report, *How Fair is Britain?*, found that African-Caribbean men were employed in managerial positions at half the rate of their male counterparts (2011: 422). With equivalency between casting (e.g. jobs) and the high-level status tragic leads (e.g. managerial positions), British Shakespeare mirrors this systemic discrimination in its casting patterns. Table 17 shows how few performers of colour have made it into the title roles of the tragedies *Hamlet*, *Macbeth* and *King Lear* since 1966, despite regular inclusion in Shakespeare productions since the early 1980s.

TABLE 17 *Roles ranked by total times played by performers of colour in Britain, 1966–2011*

Character	1966–2011
Othello	66
Macbeth	8
Hamlet	4
King Lear	4

The EHRC report also identified a phenomenon it calls 'occupational segregation', in which 'different groups of people tend to do different kinds of jobs' (382), with ethnic minorities funnelled into professions such as health care (women of African-Caribbean heritage) or transport drivers (men of Pakistani heritage). The Shakespearean equivalents of occupational segregation include the funnelling of performers of colour into *Romeo and Juliet* rather than *Hamlet*, as we saw earlier in this chapter. Table 17 also shows another form of Shakespearean occupational segregation: the title role of *Othello*.

Othello is a success story in terms of integrated casting (chapter 2), but the lopsided differences in casting between Othello and other major title roles indicates Shakespearean occupational segregation when it comes to the prestigious title roles of Shakespeare's tragedies. This exclusion goes to the heart of what roles are still considered to be the 'Black parts' of the Shakespearean canon, a view exhibited in the first sentences of this chapter. These figures also indicate a continuing inability of decision makers – casting directors, directors, executives – to envision performers of colour as Hamlet, Macbeth or King Lear. Hugh Quarshie recalls a conversation he had at the RSC in 1995 that encapsulates this lack of imagination (*STimes* 24 May 2015):

> I once played Mark Antony for Peter Hall and in the wings he came up to me and said, 'I think you're ready to play Othello.' He meant it as a compliment, and I took it as such. But I would have taken it as a greater compliment if he had said, 'I think you're ready to play Macbeth.'

When Chiwetel Ejiofor played Othello at the Donmar Warehouse in 2007, journalist Stuart Husband asked: 'As a black actor, [do you] find Othello lurking in the back of [your] mind, like K2 out there, waiting to be conquered?' (*DT* 11 November 2007). The question seems innocuous, but it indicates the ways in which performers of colour are limited by a wider culture that cannot see past skin colour. Husband's choice to describe Othello as 'K2' – the second highest mountain on Earth – rather than the pinnacle of mountaineering achievement, Mount Everest, also speaks to a perceived lesser status for Othello. White actors are given the space to dream about playing Hamlet, Macbeth or Lear, while the ambitions of their African-Caribbean colleagues are assumed to begin and end with Othello, an inferior peak in the classical canon to the Everests of Hamlet, Lear and Macbeth. Lucian Msamati provides his perspective to these narrow opportunities: 'I continue to resent the notion that the height of my ambition or achievement as an actor of a particular persuasion is to one day play the Moor' (*STimes* 24 May 2015).

Cross-cultural casting

Dominic Cooke staged *Pericles* and *The Winter's Tale* at the RSC in 2006 with a company of twenty-three actors, ten of whom were performers of colour. *Winter's Tale* was arguably the 'white' production of the pair, with semiotics that signified England. Charles Spencer described its locale as an 'austere, monochrome 1950s before bursting into the psychedelic colours of the hippie-dippy '60s during the sheep-shearing in Bohemia' (*DT* 17 November 2006). *Winter's Tale* was also led by white performers: Anton Lesser (Leontes), Kate Fleetwood (Hermione) and Linda Bassett (Paulina). Only one of the play's three largest parts (e.g. leading roles) was played by a performer of colour, the African-American Joseph Mydell, cast as Camillo. *Winter's Tale* was a classic example of colourblind casting in which 'the races, ethnicities, and colors of the actors were not semiotically relevant' (Thompson 2008: 2).

Pericles, by contrast, was the 'Black' production of the pair. The early scenes were situated in east Africa, signified by costume and a percussion-infused musical score. As Dominic Cooke describes it:

> We set our production against a contemporary background of sex trafficking. Antioch was based on Somalia. We chose Somalia as it is a very unstable country, run by feudal warlords, which felt right for the ruthless unpredictability of Antiochus and his court. Then we made a journey north, through North Africa, across the Mediterranean to Greece. Mytilene was like present-day London, a seedy Soho or King's Cross [districts known for prostitution].
>
> (Cooke 2012: 147)

Cooke's concept was problematically rooted in negative portrayals of Africa and African-Caribbeans in the media: conflict and prostitution.

Pericles fell into the cross-cultural model of integrated casting, where 'the entire world of the play is translated to a different culture and location' (Thompson 2011: 76). As the story shifted from Antioch and Tyre to Pentapolis and Mytilene, west and then north, whiteness became more prominent. Location and chosen setting dictated casting, and the

African-Caribbeans in the company – Lucian Msamati (Pericles), Joseph Mydell (Gower) and Ony Uhiara (Marina) – played the three leading roles in *Pericles*. The two differing approaches to integrated casting, colourblind (*Winter's Tale*) and cross-cultural (*Pericles*), also illustrates the subtle ways exclusion persists in twenty-first century British Shakespeare.

Winter's Tale, with its colourblind casting pattern, was largely exclusionary, keeping its performers of colour on the periphery of the story. Joseph Mydell explains that, as a Black man, parts are often 'limited to only trying to play my blackness, which is usually in relation to someone's whiteness, which is so boring because then you are just reacting' (qtd in Thompson 2008: 5). Maynard Eziashi, the British-born actor of Nigerian heritage who played Dion in *Winter's Tale*, explained: 'Apart from Camillo and Antigonus, the main characters, the main thrust, were white. So most of the black actors in that play were not helping with the exposition: They were just there. There were only really two black actors who were storytellers. So everyone else were just fillers' (qtd in Thompson 2008: 5).

Pericles, rather than *Winter's Tale*, provided opportunities for the performers of colour in the twenty-three-strong company to play the parts Cyril Nri calls 'the intellectual kernel of the piece'. The problem was that, before rehearsals began, few cast members knew that *Pericles* would be partially set in Africa. Maynard Eziashi explains:

> It was only on the first day that I realized, "Ooh, there are a lot of black actors." And I thought, "That is very interesting." Having heard of Dominic Cooke but not really knowing him, I thought, "Well, he is very egalitarian. Go, Dominic, go." I was really pleased. Then after about the third day, he said, "Right, the setting for *Pericles* is going to be in Africa." And I was like, "I see, Okay, I get it now. Alright, fine. Fair enough, fair enough.... I see what my role is. It is to be an African."
>
> (qtd in Thompson 2008: 3–4)

The idea that the job was to 'be an African' is key to the functioning of institutional racism in the early twenty-first century, not just at the RSC but across the industry.

In 1981, Michael Rudman had staged *Measure for Measure* at the National Theatre to give opportunities to performers of colour that they otherwise lacked. Rudman's *Measure for Measure* was problematic at the time, with both Rudolph Walker and Norman Beaton registering varying degrees of unease with the concept (chapter 3). Seemingly the only way Rudman could have a largely African-Caribbean cast was by relocating the action to the Caribbean. It was a setting in which a white audience would not find African-Caribbean characters out of place. A quarter of a century later, for all the individual productions that had pushed the boundaries of integrated casting, Dominic Cooke's *Pericles* illustrates how the thinking about race in Shakespeare in Britain was, at best, stagnating or, at worst, regressing.

As Ayanna Thompson observes, in Cooke's *Pericles* the performers' skin colour, combined with the adoption of African dress and accents, did the semiotic work of setting the location for the audience (2008: 3). Through his theatrical conceit for *Pericles* Cooke, like Rudman before him, was signalling that his actors were not British. The marginalization of the African-Caribbeans in *Winter's Tale* to its minor parts compounded associations of 'blackness' with foreignness as they were not provided with equal opportunities in both productions. Cross-cultural productions in twenty-first century Shakespeare continued to segregate British performers of colour from their white contemporaries.

'I think I need you to do an accent'

The start to Paul Bazely's career (chapter 5) held the promise of breakthroughs for the mixed-race actor of south Asian descent. He joined the National Theatre in 1992 for the US tour of Richard Eyre's production of *Richard III* with Ian McKellen:

> [*Richard III*] was my first ever job at the National. I was twenty-five. I couldn't believe I was there. It was a massive room with Terence Rigby and Ian [McKellen] and Charlotte Cornwell and all these amazing actors and I just thought: *Brilliant!* But I knew also that I really wanted to go back and do more.

Back in the United Kingdom, the reality of his prospects in classical theatre at the National Theatre gradually became clear:

> After that tour [of *Richard III*], a lot of my fellow actors were going back [to the NT] and I remember [the National] got me in for the Caryl Churchill play *The Skriker*. For a really tiny part, smaller than the part I played in the Shakespeare. I started to think: *Oh. Is this kind of show we're [performers of colour] allowed to be in?* Because *Skriker* was, you know, really audacious and modern and I just thought, *Am I not going to be called in for the Chekovs and the Ibsens?* And I wasn't. I wasn't.

Several years later, Bazely returned to the National for the stage adaptation of a story by a well-known British Indian novelist:

> The next time I worked [at the National] was years later, in a Salman Rushdie production, *Haroun and the Sea of Stories* [in 1998]. All Asian. I hadn't even really got any auditions there during that period. See, what

was interesting was at the beginning [of my career] I thought: *I'll play all sorts of different ethnicities because I'm very hard to place*, but as soon as I [got] one of my first roles I ever played, with Tom Wilkinson in the [BBC] series called *Resnick*, where I played DC Patel, I never went up for anything other than Asian parts for probably twenty years from that moment. Because after that, I couldn't [be] seen [by casting directors as] Italian or Greek or whatever. At the National I was just thinking: *I'm just going to crash it*. And in a way I wanted to be in the shows that were the 'white' plays. And I still to this day don't want to be in just ['Asian' plays]. Don't just get us all in and put us in one show that's nice and colourful [like *Haroun*]. Get us in for everything.

At the turn of the millennium, Bazely recalls asking one eminent Shakespearean director at the National Theatre, '"When am I going to be in the Chekovs here?" and he said, "You're not." So I could see that the culture hadn't really changed.'

Bazely cites two productions that changed the course of his career: the original production of *East is East* and a West End production of *Twelfth Night* in 2004. The latter was the brainchild of the white actor Stephen Beresford, who had played Sir Andrew Aguecheek three years earlier at the Liverpool Playhouse. That production had a modern setting in which, Beresford recalled: 'We wore sharp Italian suits and moved in front of a cool blue backdrop. It was crisp and stylish; we looked like Arsenal being photographed by Mario Testino' (*Times* 14 August 2004). Beresford felt that setting was 'fine for the first few scenes, and then some poor bastard has to come on with bells saying 'I'm Feste'. And I find that incongruous' (*Time Out* 11 August 2004). For his directorial debut, Beresford decided on modern India as a location in which Shakespeare's Elizabethan comedy could realistically operate.

Aware of the Indian setting, Paul Bazely tentatively auditioned for Beresford's *Twelfth Night*:

The first thing I said was, 'Why do you want to do the show?' and [Beresford] said it was a great play. He said, 'I was trying to think of an environment where women could reasonably wear veils, where you could have a kind of holy man just wander into our house and play the guitar and possibly cross-dress.' He went through all these things and I just thought: *You know what, that's really, really modern-day India. You could still do all of that*. And I thought, *God, he's really thought this through*.

Beresford assembled a cast that was predominantly British south Asian, including Bazely (Aguecheek), Kulvinder Ghir (Feste), Paul Bhattacharjee (Malvolio), Raza Jaffrey (Orsino) and Shereen Martin (Viola). He also brought two performers from India to London to join the cast: rising Indian film star Neha Dubhey (Olivia) and an actor discovered by open audition in Delhi, Raghaav Channana (Sebastian). The production opened to sounds of a sitar and the monsoon rain beating down on cream-coloured tenement buildings.

Feste (Kulvinder Ghir) was, as the programme states, modelled on a type of Baul singer, a Bengali traditional minstrel. For 'Come away death' (2.4.51–66), Feste 'covered his head with cloth, crouched on the ground, rocking back and forth, keening', actions that 'powerfully showed the mortal subject matter of the song' (Rogers 2005: 54). Ghir remembers thriving on the discovery of analogies between Shakespeare's Elizabethan jester and contemporary Indian counterparts: 'We based [Feste] as a street dancer who dresses up as a woman. That's how he learnt, he makes his living as a hijra and then changes himself into a swami, a holy man.' While some critics found the Indian references in Ghir's performance grating, John Gross praised its mixture of English and Indian cultures, observing that Ghir's 'spirited Feste somehow manages to weave Elizabethan wordplay and Bengali folk traditions into a seamless web' (*ST* 5 September 2004).

Paul Bazely played Sir Andrew Aguecheek as a westernized man. Dressed in tan slacks and a cream shirt, he did not fit comfortably in Indian culture and his line 'I am a great eater of beef' (1.3.85) only served to emphasize his estrangement from Hindu society (Rogers 2005: 54). The evolution of Bazely's characterization of Aguecheek also speaks volumes about the growing tension between British-born performers of colour and the cross-cultural settings in which they were being placed more frequently:

In the audition I played [Aguecheek] as a very posh, silly boy and Stephen loved it and wanted me straight away to do that. But once we were in rehearsals he had to have a difficult conversation with me to say, 'I think I need you to do an accent.' Because some of the actors were actually from India. He'd got them in. And then someone like Paul Bhattacharjee was doing an accent, Kulvinder Ghir was doing an accent, so [Beresford], I think, had decided, 'It's modern day India, so we've got to do an accent.' And I'm always a bit like, 'Well if you were doing a modern day Chekov, would you have me do a Russian accent? I don't think so.' So I was like, 'Well I don't know if I want to do this.' But then I looked around the room and I thought: *Actually it would be quite weird if I was the [only one with a British accent]*. But I did a posh Indian accent. So I did him like he'd been to Oxford. Because he was just rolling in it. I mean, he was not clever enough to go to Oxford, but he was so rich that his dad would build a wing or whatever [to buy his place at university]. And then he'd come back [to India]. And that worked for me. But yeah, that was, I remember that was a slight moment of contention. But I knew what he was trying to do and you know he found the difference. He's a white person and he had a room full of Asians. It was really exciting what he did, I thought. So Stephen certainly wasn't an *auteur* about accents.

FIGURE 9 *Kulvinder Ghir as Feste.* Twelfth Night, *Albery Theatre, London, 2004. Photo by Photoshot/Getty Images.*

Beresford's setting for *Twelfth Night* was another in the growing list of productions that used cross-cultural casting as a way to diversify British Shakespeare. Its setting of modern Delhi and the choice to use Indian dialects positioned his cast as other, which was the crux of Bazely's initial objections. Beresford's *Twelfth Night* was also that rarest of creatures, a West End production featuring a south Asian cast playing Shakespeare. The production was well received and Bazely recalls that he 'got great reviews for playing Aguecheek in that. Even then I was thinking: *I wonder if I'm going to get asked now to go back and do more [Shakespeare] at the National.*' Stephen Beresford's 2004 West End production of *Twelfth Night* was, at the time of writing, the last production of Shakespeare in which Bazely has been cast.

Maids and prostitutes, stereotyping Lucetta and Bianca

For all the progress that had occurred since the 1980s, the casting of performers of colour in productions of Shakespeare continues to rely on stereotypes. As early as 1929, 'most Black actors landed their first film role by playing maids or servants' (O'Hara 2021: 65). By 1950 that Hollywood film trope had been translated into a British theatrical idiom that was so ingrained the first person of colour to train at LAMDA, Pauline Henriques, recalled, 'it was very hard breaking into the theatre, and I found myself playing a variety of American coloured maids' (qtd in Pines 1992: 26). The performance history of Shakespeare's early comedy, *Two Gentlemen of Verona*, provides a microcosm of the journey from overt stereotyping in the 1970s and 1980s to the flawed inclusivity of the 1990s and, finally, a return to overt stereotyping in the 2000s.

Alton Kumalo became the first performer of colour to appear in a stage production of *Two Gentlemen of Verona* in 1969, playing Speed at the RSC. Although it is a substantial part – the sixth largest – Speed is the servant of Valentine, one of the two gentlemen of the title. In earlier chapters we saw Kumalo had objected to the RSC's casting of him in a string of servant roles. There are, in fact, two servants in *Two Gentlemen*, Speed and Lucetta, the main female character's maid. Such is the pervasiveness of the typecasting of performers of colour as servants that, out of the twelve productions of *Two Gentlemen* with inclusive casting, 50 per cent of them (six) have cast a performer of African-Caribbean heritage as one of its two servants. Lucetta is also the role in *Two Gentlemen of Verona* that has been most frequently played by performers of colour.

The shift in the representation of Lucetta on stage from the more progressive 1990s to the 2000s is another key to comprehending the state of integrated casting in Britain by the millennium. In 1991 Josette Bushell-Mingo became the first woman of colour to play Lucetta in Britain, for David Thacker at the RSC. She was also the only performer of colour in the RSC that season. As Thacker remembers, 'I stood the first day at Stratford with Josette standing next to me and she said, "I'm the only Black woman in the room."' It was a fact that did not go unnoticed by Alby James, then artistic director of Temba, who observed: 'Only one black actor has been cast in the new RSC season' (*Observer* 21 April 1991). Without Thacker's *Two Gentlemen of Verona*, Bushell-Mingo would have spent the season without appearing in any Shakespeare (like Sophie Okonedo, in fact, did in 1992, who did not play a Shakespeare role during her sole RSC season); Bushell-Mingo's absence from the RST stage also meant that the RSC's main house Shakespeares had all-white casts in 1991. It is against this wider backdrop that Bushell-Mingo's only Shakespeare part was that of a maid, Lucetta.

Thacker's *Two Gents* was set in the 1930s in England and the south of France, the Verona and Milan of Shakespeare's original locations. Visually Thacker and his designer, Sheelagh Keegan, opted for the glamour of the era through detailed reconstructions of the 1930s material world. This was one of wealth and leisure and the characters were depicted attending balls, playing tennis and drinking cocktails. The representation of Lucetta in this elegant environment is crucial to understanding the ways in which overt stereotypes were minimized in Thacker's production. Lucetta appears in two scenes, both in a duologue with her mistress, Julia. That relationship between Bushell-Mingo's Lucetta and the white actress Clare Holman's Julia was fundamentally affected by the casting of what Bushell-Mingo remarked was 'another black maid'. As she notes, 'the director did become very conscious that I was a black actress playing the maid' (qtd in Yin 1992: 143). The production partially defused that stereotype through its portrayal of Lucetta.

In Thacker's production Lucetta and Julia were depicted as equals, both in terms of representation by costume and in the characters' interactions. In their first appearance both women were dressed in formal evening gowns, Julia in black from head-to-toe while Lucetta was adorned in purple velvet. As the lights went up, they ran out into Julia's garden during the musical interlude, briefly posing with their arms above their heads, giggling and having fun. Referring to the dance card hanging from her wrist Julia asked of Lucetta which of her suitors 'In thy opinion... is worthiest love?' (1.2.6). The overall impression from the setting and costumes was that the women had come out to the garden for a gossip during a ball. Their second scene continued to build a picture of two friends idling away the time. As the lights went up, Bushell-Mingo's Lucetta was sprawled stomach-down on a tartan rug, idly swinging her legs behind her and perusing a magazine; Julia stood barefoot near the bench. Lucetta was wearing a trouser ensemble and Julia a cream and blue floral summer dress; each had discarded her shoes. The bright lights, leisure activities, rug and the lack of footwear all denoted a hot summer day. These signifiers, combined with those from the earlier evening scene, reinforced the picture of an upper-class, leisured lifestyle and two women who are both friends and equals in status. While Thacker's 1991 production of *Two Gentlemen of Verona* had cast the only performer of colour at the RSC that year as a servant, the stereotypes were consciously broken by director, designer and cast.[1]

While not a carbon copy of Thacker's production, the similarities between his and Fiona Buffini's 2004 production for the RSC with their 1930s settings provide a stark contrast in their depictions of Lucetta. The relationship between Brigid Zengeni's Lucetta and the white actress Vanessa

---

[1] In 1992 Josette Bushell-Mingo, who had been understudying the white actress Saskia Reeves, took over the role of Silvia, the daughter of the Duke of Milan, for the London run of *Two Gents* at the Barbican Theatre.

Ackerman's Julia was that of servant to mistress, both in actions and costume. In their first scene Julia lay idly on a *chaise longue* in her untidy room as Lucetta stood in the background, picking up the clothes Julia had discarded from off the floor. Ackerman's Julia also showed her superior status by dismissively and shrilly chastizing Lucetta during their conversation. The class distinctions were even more visible in their costumes: Julia wore a floral print dress, while Zengeni's Lucetta was dressed in a stereotypical black-and-white maid's uniform. As I observe elsewhere, within Zengeni's costume 'all the imagery of white supremacy and Black subjugation was problematically on view' (Rogers 2013: 426).

'That's all we ever are, prostitutes or princesses from Africa', Cathy Tyson lamented to a *Guardian* journalist in 1986. The statement was so eye-catching, the paper's sub-editor chose it for the headline of the printed article. Tyson was then in rehearsals for the RSC's production of *Mephisto* and was relaying a discussion with her director about her character's backstory. Tyson was told, 'Well, she's probably been an African princess, my dear.' At the same time, Tyson was also publicizing her breakthrough film, Neil Jordan's *Mona Lisa*, in which she played Simone, a prostitute (*Guardian* 3 September 1986). This stereotype of women of colour as prostitutes can also be found in the casting of Shakespeare characters from Mistress Overdone in *Measure for Measure* to Bianca in *Othello*: roles, like Lucetta, frequently played by women of colour. As with Lucetta, the reason why Bianca would be seen, stereotypically, as a 'Black' character is not difficult to unearth: it is present in Shakespeare's language.

Bianca first appears in Act 3, calling out to Othello's disgraced lieutenant, 'Save you, friend Cassio!' (3.4.169). Cassio returns her greeting in a similarly affectionate vein, telling her she is 'my most fair Bianca' and 'sweet love' in the space of two lines (3.4.170–1). The descriptions of Bianca by both Iago and Cassio in a later scene provide clues for the origins of the stereotypical casting of Bianca in classical theatre. In an aside to the audience, Iago describes Bianca as:

> A housewife that by selling her desires
> Buys herself bread and clothes: it is a creature
> That dotes on Cassio – as 'tis the strumpet's plague.
>
> (4.1.95–7)

The brutal language shows that Iago views Bianca as a prostitute who barters sex with Cassio for food and apparel. Cassio confirms Iago's opinion by referring to himself as Bianca's 'customer' (4.1.120). By far the most racially charged element of Shakespeare's language, however, is Cassio's epithet for Bianca: 'monkey' (4.1.128). When Bianca is played by a woman of African-Caribbean descent, that slur adds an overtly racist layer to the proceedings.

Martina Laird played Bianca in Michael Grandage's 2007 production of *Othello* at the Donmar Warehouse with Chiwetel Ejiofor and the white actor Ewan McGregor as Othello and Iago. Laird viewed Bianca, within the context of the production, as an immigrant to Cyprus. She explains:

> They [the Venetian army, led by Othello] have travelled to Cyprus, away from Venice and the idea [was] that [Grandage's Cyprus was] a port. So I was allowed, or encouraged, to have Bianca be Trinidadian. Or to use my own accent anyway.

Laird found Bianca to be a multifaceted character, not the stereotype that Shakespeare's language – and her casting – implies:

> The point with Bianca is she's really in love with Cassio. She's a woman of no means, trapped in a port city and, in our version, somewhere that she's not even from. With no way of getting by.

Bianca's journey through the play is inextricably linked to Cassio's, as both are pawns in Iago's deadly machinations. The passing of Desdemona's handkerchief from Iago's wife to Iago, who then gave it to Cassio who, in turn, presented it to Bianca set off a chain of events that rocked Bianca's fragile foundations to the core. Laird explains:

> To me, Bianca's story was immense. That kind of tempestuousness of her taking the handkerchief and then coming back and going, 'I've thought about it. No, fuck you and your handkerchief! What is this?' That's her own self-doubt. That's her going, 'No, no, you bastard! You're not actually treating me right!' But we see women who stand up for themselves and who get angry as one dimensional. But there's a reason she responds like that. The hurt is what I was playing. The absolute hurt of this woman. Because anger, as we know, is a secondary emotion. It comes out of something else, out of another emotion. It's not a shallowness of character, it's another layer of her survival. And I think that it's very easy to just see her as whichever cliché, whichever it is, whether it's the tart with the heart [of gold] or the loudmouthed, what's the word? That they love to use for Black actresses? Or Black women characters? 'Feisty.' It's like the number-one word, I think, in the character breakdowns [sent from casting directors to agents when describing a character designated as a Black woman]. And I think that that's an error. That's just shallow and it's easy to go beyond that. Bianca is a woman with no options, looking after herself, and she can't afford to be a lady like Desdemona with all [her wealth and privilege]. But look what happens to her, for Christ's sake. At least Bianca's alive at the end of the thing. She might be imprisoned, but she's alive.

The decision for Laird to play Bianca with her Trinidadian accent also reinforced negative stereotypes, as broadcaster and writer Rosie Boycott's diary week illustrates. Having praised the two film stars who led the cast,

Ejiofor and McGregor, Boycott turned her fire on Laird in the minor part of Bianca:

> The same, however, could not be said of Martina Laird, who appears late on, playing Cassio's lover, Bianca. She was clearly Comfort Jones, the feisty paramedic from [the BBC's popular continuing drama] *Casualty*, only thinly disguised by the substitution of a colourful robe for her usual NHS uniform. I freely admit to being a fan of *Casualty* and Comfort is always good in a crisis when someone's jumped off a building or been stabbed by their stepfather. But however hard she flirted with Cassio, I couldn't shake the notion out of my mind that she was suddenly going to whip out the bandages and give him a cardiac massage'
> (*Observer* 9 December 2007)

Boycott's reference to Bianca as Cassio's 'lover', instead of using the derogatory language Shakespeare provides, is perhaps the only positive element to her prose. That 'prostitute' was not Boycott's go-to noun testifies to Laird's skill in presenting an alternative view of the character. Boycott's inability to see Laird as anything other than a Trinidadian health care worker, however, speaks to the ways British culture limits the people of colour in its midst. Laird puts it this way:

> Until you diversify the experience of theatre, you're not truly diversifying. Because at the end of the day, the space is still the same. It's run by white institutions. It's a battle. The industry is run according to white sensibility and priorities, etc. Historically. So you can have me on stage doing a Trinidadian-voiced Bianca, but you've got Rosie Boycott sitting in the audience going, 'Well, I can't see her as anything other than the last Trinidadian I saw her play [e.g. Comfort Jones in *Casualty*].' The limitations are put on you.

Stereotypes are powerful tools in the arsenal of gatekeepers, whether used wittingly or not.

A new dawn

Ashley Zhangazha graduated from the Guildhall School of Music and Drama in 2010 with ambitions to play Shakespearean leads. He sensed, at the time, that his opportunities might be limited:

> I couldn't say 100 per cent that I was sure I would achieve what I wanted to. Not because I didn't feel I had the talent to do it, but just because these opportunities are few and far between.

Zhangazha's first job after leaving Guildhall was in Michael Grandage's production of *Danton's Death* at the National Theatre. It led to his second.

When Grandage cast Zhangazha as the King of France in his 2010 production of *King Lear* at the Donmar Warehouse, new conversations about inequality were yet to begin in the British live and recorded arts. Zhangazha recalls:

> Where we've got to now [in 2019] with theatre, you know, in terms of casting, [there are] lots of conversations happening. But at that time [in 2010], even though it was an early job, it was a big thing to be cast in this part. There wasn't a lot of [integrated casting] happening.

Although the King of France remains the part in *King Lear* most frequently played by actors of colour, the data bear out Zhangazha's recollections. Before Grandage cast Zhangazha, only one African-Caribbean had played France between 2000 and 2010, while seven had done so in the 1990s. These had included Clarence Smith, who had been heckled by an audience member while on stage playing the French monarch (chapter 5).

Along with Zhangazha, Grandage hired a woman of colour to play Cordelia in *Lear*: another recent drama-school graduate, the RADA-trained Pippa Bennett-Warner. Although performers of colour have subsequently played Cordelia remarkably frequently, in 2010 Bennett-Warner was only the fourth to play the part in Britain. Their presence in Grandage's *Lear* clearly unsettled some audience members. Zhangazha recalls one example of overt racism that greeted their performances:

> I remember Michael telling me and Pippa that he received a letter from an audience member saying, 'I really enjoyed the production, but I didn't understand why you had a Black King of France and a Black Cordelia.' Michael wrote back and said, 'I cast these actors because they're fantastic young actors and they were the best for the part.' This is ten years ago and many actors, as I'm sure you've spoken to, have talked about this happening way before my time.

This correspondence illustrates how little had changed in the twenty years since Clarence Smith had been shouted at from the auditorium of the Royal Shakespeare Theatre.

Two snapshots from 2011 perhaps best illustrate the progressive and regressive state of integrated casting at the time. First, Rupert Goold staged a production of *The Merchant of Venice* at the Royal Shakespeare Company. In the blackout during the scene change between Venice and Belmont, actors in the circle hooted monkey noises and flung yellow banana peels onto the stage. These racist gestures were aimed at the Prince of Morocco, played by an actor of African-Caribbean descent.[2] The performance mirrored,

---

[2] The actor originally cast as the Prince of Morocco left the production during previews.

however briefly, an image that was more commonly seen in English football grounds, a disturbing feature of the racist abuse of the 1970s and 1980s where spectators hurled, literally, bananas at African-Caribbean players. Like Brigid Zengeni's maid's uniform in Fiona Buffini's *Two Gentlemen of Verona*, this moment in Goold's *Merchant* was symptomatic of how far British theatre had lapsed in terms of portrayals of people of colour in its reinforcement by replication, wittingly or not, of overt racism.

Michael Grandage's next Shakespeare production at the Donmar Warehouse after *King Lear* illustrates the more progressive outlook. At the end of 2011, he staged *Richard II* with the white actor Eddie Redmayne in the title role. The importance of Grandage's decision to bring back Ashley Zhangazha and Pippa Bennett-Warner for *Richard II* cannot be underestimated. Representation of performers of colour in Shakespeare's history plays remains negligible, so their casting would always have been noteworthy. Grandage, however, cast both in roles with status: Bennett-Warner became the first performer of colour to play Queen Isabel in *Richard II* on a British stage[3] and Zhangazha doubled as Aumerle, a nobleman who has the ear of the monarch, and the Groom. Aumerle and Queen Isabel are the seventh- and eighth-largest roles in the play, respectively. The size of these roles in *Richard II* also made Grandage's casting of Bennett-Warner and Zhangazha progressive. At the time of Grandage's production in 2010 only two performers of colour – both of south Asian descent, Abraham Sofaer (1943) and Sam Dastor (1979) – had played roles larger than the Queen and Aumerle in British stage productions.

Grandage's *Richard II* stands at another turning point in the history of integrated casting, foreshadowing the renewed progress that would follow. Table 18 illustrates that progress through *Richard II*, as performers of colour would first play all the remaining roles larger than Aumerle in 2019.

TABLE 18 *First casting of a performer of colour in the six largest roles of* Richard II

Date, venue	Rank and character	Performer
2019, Shakespeare's Globe	1. Richard II	Adjoa Andoh
1943, Shakespeare Memorial Theatre	2. Bolingbroke	Abraham Sofaer
2019, Shakespeare's Globe	3. Duke of York	Shobna Gulati
2018, Almeida Theatre	4. John of Gaunt	Joseph Mydell
2019, Shakespeare's Globe	5. Northumberland	Indra Ové
1979, St. George's Theatre	6. Mowbray	Sam Dastor

---

[3] Sophie Okonedo played Queen Isabel in a radio production of *Richard II* for the BBC in 2000.

The significance of the change in classical theatre since he left Guildhall has particular resonance for Zhangazha:

> In the nearly ten years that I've been out [of drama school], there has been a massive change. When I was at drama school I could never have imagined that the RSC, six years later, would cast a Black actor as Hamlet.

8

Shakespeare from multiculturalism to Brexit, 2012–2018

Gregory Doran's 2012 production of *Julius Caesar*, set in Africa, was the first RSC Shakespeare production to assemble a cast composed of performers of African-Caribbean heritage. Marcus Griffiths, then a recent drama school graduate, was cast in Doran's production, realizing in retrospect the production's historical import:

> I was a twenty-two-year-old young, Black actor, just out of Guildhall. Barely [out] a year and had about two jobs under my belt. I'd been at the Globe and I'd done a bit of TV. But I didn't quite understand the significance of what it meant to put twenty-two Black actors in a room together. You know, because usually when you're a Black actor – and it is the case, and I'm sure all will attest – you're used to being the minority in the room.

Gregory Doran's *Julius Caesar* included some of Britain's best classical performers, many of whom were Shakespearean pioneers themselves, including Paterson Joseph (Brutus), Ray Fearon (Mark Antony), Jeffery Kissoon (Julius Caesar), Adjoa Andoh (Portia), Ewart James Walters (Caius Ligarius) and Cyril Nri (Cassius).

Julius Caesar was Cyril Nri's first Shakespeare production at the RSC since 1983, when he had played Brutus' servant Lucius, along with a string of other servant roles (chapter 3). The white Welsh actor Emrys James played Cassius in Ron Daniels' 1983 production. James' skill had captivated the young Nri, who, like many apprentice performers before and after, learned their craft by watching his more experienced colleagues:

> [Emrys James] was the only man who has convincingly died of a broken heart, which he did in [Philip Massinger's] *A New Way to Pay Old Debts*, on stage and was just stunning. [When] I watched him play Cassius I thought: *I want to do that.*

Nri also remembers having artistic battles with the white director John Barton during that season, which he partly ascribes to the 'arrogance of youth':

> We're having these arguments about where you put the pause and whatever else: 'You are John Barton, but I want to say it this way because I want to have all this – my Nigerian/Shepherd's Bush/posh/Black/whatever heritage – in it and that doesn't fit with your pause there, so I'm going to pause here.'

Nri's second encounter with *Julius Caesar* in the late 1980s had parallels with Doran's approach to the play. As Nri remembers:

> When I went back to Nigeria in early '88, or late '87, deciding I'm not going to do this [continue his acting career in Britain] anymore, I had wanted to do *Julius Caesar*. I'd wanted to set it in Nigeria. I'd wanted to set it there because the [two opposing leaders of the Nigerian Civil War] [Yakubu] Gowon [and C. Odumegwu] Ojukwu were of different tribes, but they both went to the same schools. Essentially they were the elite, the upper class, they went to military school; these families ran Nigeria. I was a Nigerian Biafran refugee. Ojukwu [leader of the breakaway republic of Biafra] used to appear in our city with my father. My father was a civil engineer [who] set up radio stations in Biafra. As an Ibo, Ojukwu used to come to the house. I used to have to serve him kola nuts and stuff and the thing about the Nigerian Biafran War, civil war, is that at the end of the day all these men – I was very aware that Gowon went to study politics in Britain after the war, after he had led the country, after three million dead, you know – and yet these guys all went to the same schools. I remember thinking: *I want to do this play set in Nigeria with a military leader that takes over and they have a coup because he's getting above himself.* And I remember being told at the time: 'If you do that, they will kill you. You will not get away with doing that in Nigeria because these people are not playing.'

When Nri returned to the RSC thirty years later, he was able to utilize his Nigerian heritage while playing the leading role that had long captivated him:

> It was just a joy to be privileged enough to be able to go: 'Oh wow, I started here and I looked at that man [Emrys James] and thought: *That's*

what I would like to play. Because it's complex and its difficult.' Brutus is extremely complex and difficult as well, but for some reason, I was drawn towards Cassius and the chance to play that. So thirty years on, coming [back] to the RSC and here I am playing Cassius, the part that I wanted to play [since 1983]. The part that I look at and go: 'Oh, yeah, that's interesting!' Then doing it in an all-Black company and getting to play out what, in 1988, I had thought [about the play]. Just fantastic.

When Cyril Nri stepped onto the stage at the RSC in 2012, he became the first performer of colour to play Cassius at the RSC, and only the third to have played the role in Britain.[1]

Julius Caesar and *Much Ado About Nothing*, RSC, 2012

'Shakespeare is no longer English property', stated the RSC's artistic director Michael Boyd in a press release announcing the World Shakespeare Festival (WSF). A key component of the London 2012 Olympic Games' Cultural Olympiad, the WSF was an international celebration of Shakespeare. More than seventy productions were performed in theatres or televised between April and September 2012, many staged in foreign languages by international companies.

The RSC contributed a dozen productions to the WSF; Shakespeare's Globe hosted an international festival, Globe-to-Globe, and produced one in-house Shakespeare, while the National Theatre, Almeida Theatre and National Theatre Wales also contributed one each. While the World Shakespeare Festival basked in its all-encompassing internationalism, most home-grown productions were replicating discriminatory casting patterns. By 2012 inclusion in British theatre meant that the casts of Shakespeare productions generally consisted of 10–20 per cent performers of colour and 80–90 per cent white actors. What the lost decade of progress in the 2000s (chapter 7) had meant was a glass ceiling that remained firmly in place, including in most British productions in the WSF. Alfred Enoch was the lone performer of colour in Nicholas Hytner's production of *Timon of Athens* at the National Theatre, playing Philotus, for example. At the RSC its worst instincts were apparent in the 'Shipwreck' trilogy as David Farr cast Ankur Bahl as Curio in *Twelfth Night*, a role that had been systematically handed down to African-Caribbeans between 1967 and 1983, from Alton Kumalo to Cyril Nri.

---

[1] Peter Straker played Cassius for Roger Rees at the Bristol Old Vic in 1987; Howard Saddler appeared in Moving Theatre Company's 1996 tour of *Julius Caesar*.

Along with Ankur Bahl, Cecilia Noble and Solomon Israel completed the trio of performers of colour who appeared in the RSC's main summer season on the RST stage.[2] With the exception of Israel as Ferdinand in *The Tempest*, all played supernumeraries or parts that conformed to stereotypes that had been apparent since the late 1960s, including Bahl's appearance as the servant Curio (Table 19). This pattern was particularly egregious with Noble's casting, an experienced actress who had made her Shakespeare debut playing Miranda in *The Tempest* for Cheek By Jowl in 1988. Noble's only prominent role in the season was Maria, the Countess Olivia's servant, in *Twelfth Night*, which remains the most frequently cast role of the play for performers of colour in Britain.

Out of the British-made productions for the WSF, across all venues, only Gregory Doran's *Julius Caesar* and Iqbal Khan's *Much Ado About Nothing* had British performers of colour playing leading roles. They were also the first RSC productions to have casts composed entirely of performers of colour, African-Caribbean for *Caesar* and south Asian for *Much Ado*, set in Africa and Delhi, respectively. Their presence in the season is redolent of the trend, discussed in the previous chapter, of segregating performers of colour into cross-cultural productions.

Michael Boyd had already tapped Meera Syal to play Beatrice when Iqbal Khan was approached as a potential director for *Much Ado About Nothing*. The actress was well known to British television audiences for her appearances in popular comedies depicting the British south Asian experience, *Goodness Gracious Me* and *The Kumars at No. 42*. With *Much Ado* pencilled in for the WSF, Iqbal Khan recalls how Boyd gently guided the production towards an Asian framing for the play:

Now, he didn't say Indian. It could have been [set] here [in Britain]. Now, my response to him was: 'Is this a condition of employment?' and he

TABLE 19 *Performers of colour appearing in the 'Shipwreck Trilogy', Royal Shakespeare Theatre, 2012*

	Comedy of Errors	The Tempest	Twelfth Night
Ankur Bahl	Messenger	Spirit	Curio
Cecilia Noble	Amelia	Juno	Maria
Solomon Israel	Officer	Ferdinand	Security Guard

---

[2] *Julius Caesar* and *Much Ado* were both situated outside the RSC's main 2012 season, as their casts did not overlap. In addition, *Caesar* replaced the 'Shipwreck Trilogy' in the main house for six weeks and *Much Ado* played in the Courtyard Theatre, which had originally been used as a temporary theatre while the RST was rebuilt between 2007 and 2010.

went, 'No, you do what you want to do.' So that reassured me and then I thought about it. But I was very, very wary of doing the exotic thing with it.

Iqbal Khan rooted his *Much Ado* in modern Delhi, which he visited with his designer, Tom Piper, and producer, Kevin Fitzmaurice:

> When I thought about modern Delhi and I thought about the complexity of women's place in that world, I found that a compelling environment for the play. A lot of the codes of that world that are to do with caste, to do with money, and to do with gender. I got more and more excited and, this is very unusual for me, actually setting up a very real context for the world of the play. And Delhi with all its noise and joy and simmering violence, all of that, the contradictions to do with a woman's position in that world. They [the women in modern Delhi] can be entrepreneurial, but there's also a sense of duty that is present, the sense that the ancestors, the ancient, is always present and yet [Delhi is] very much in the vanguard of the new. A sense of the religious, the divine of that world, again spiritual, it's very close to the surface. So that seemed to me a very, very rich setting for the piece.

Gregory Doran's route to his African setting for *Julius Caesar* began partly with an assertion by the Black South African actor and civil rights activist, John Kani, that *Caesar* is 'Shakespeare's African play' (*DT* 31 May 2012). The creation of the stage world was a collective process, however, led by the practitioners of colour Doran had assembled. Marcus Griffiths calls rehearsals a 'crash course' in African history, which shaped the production:

> I was a fly on the wall. We would have an open forum [and] people would tell their stories. Cyril [Nri]'s family, for instance, fled the Biafran War in Nigeria to come to England. Ivanno [Jeremiah]'s mum fled Uganda when there was the civil war to come to England with him. These stories are being shared and I was sitting round like: *Okay, there's a lot of rich material here.* Hearing the African stories coming out of my cast members, [I knew we were] not only pushing the Black envelope, but we were also about to tell an African story. We were going to own Shakespeare for our own culture.

The world of Doran's *Julius Caesar* was an amalgamation of these multiple histories, based on experiences the performers brought into the rehearsal room. Cyril Nri explains:

> We were not in some amorphous African country. It was about deciding we are going to have this country which is closer to east Africa. But it's

not Kenya, it's not Uganda, it's not Nigeria. It borrows from all these countries around it, but it isn't any of those countries, so it doesn't suffer from the politics of that particular country. It is *this* particular country. It is *our* Rome, which is not in Italy. It's a Rome somewhere in that mid-Africa section, closer towards the east.

Nigerian-born, British-raised Theo Ogundipe, who played the Soothsayer, explains how this amalgamation of cultures worked in crafting his performance:

I had this part that is seen as quite a small role and I was just given free licence to play. It was literally like: this is your position in society, the truth-teller, the foreseer, the prophet almost. That character basically [Soothsayer] was an amalgamation of different African tribes from different countries and [an] expression of different rituals that different tribes have and what they were for. Greg brought a bunch of books [about] African tribes, different African tribes. Whether they were photographer's books or whether they were just books describing the history and daily life of where they were from. One of the tribes that we looked at was the Nuba tribe, which is where the ash on the [Soothsayer's] skin came from. And [we were also] finding ways to assist the narrative [by using these rituals]. For example, Adjoa Andoh told us once in rehearsal that in her father's culture, in Ghana, libations are poured in remembrance and respect for the dead. When she was telling that story, that was something Adjoa offered: what if the Soothsayer pours a libation for Caesar? [It was] another kind of cultural ritual thread we were able to use.

Iqbal Khan's framework for modern Delhi was more precisely located, but arose from similar impulses to use the location to create a world for the play. Tom Piper's set was based on material gathered from the research trip to Delhi. It was dominated by a re-creation of the *hivali* in Old Delhi, a two-storied structure with latticed windows and heavy, carved wooden doors. Electric cables, ropes and lightbulbs were wrapped around a tree, evoking the chaos of the modern city founded on an ancient one.

India's capital city had changed rapidly since the 1990s and Khan's production captured the rupture between traditional gender norms (Leonato and Hero) and the traits displayed by Meera Syal's Beatrice, an example of the 'young, professional women' who were, as Rana Dasgupta observes in *Capital: A Portrait of Twenty-first Century Delhi*, 'the icons of the new India' (2014: 134). Costumes signified these differences, as Beatrice wore her brown pinstripe pencil skirt suit inside Leonato's house, while Hero changed from jeans into an aqua-and-yellow print kurta when she returned home from shopping.

The crucial difference between *Julius Caesar* and *Much Ado* and previous productions that used foreign settings was the casts' ownership in creating their on-stage environments. Iqbal Khan explains:

> I think who makes those decisions, how invested the people in that room feel in creating the world is a big question and for me it's very important that almost all of what we created is in some ways responsive to the people we have in the room.

For both productions it was decided that the characters would speak in dialects that reflected the settings, rather than RP or a British regional accent. Paterson Joseph initiated the adoption of an east African accent for the world of *Julius Caesar*. Joseph writes persuasively of a cultural shift in the Shakespearean landscape that has allowed regional accents on the stage (Joseph 2018: 52–3). His argument in favour of the east African dialect's suitability to Shakespeare was another example of performers able to explore their heritage in an amalgamation of British theatrical tradition with east African culture:

> The accent is lyrical and gentle, with consonants that are crisp and clear. Rhymically, it mirrors well the iambic pentameter, the prevailing de *dum* de *dum* de *dum* de *dum* de *dum* rhythm, alternating feminine (weak) and masculine (strong) stressed syllables, so prevalent in Shakespeare's writing.
>
> (2018: 53)

For *Much Ado*, Iqbal Khan similarly discovered Indian dialects also fit snugly into Shakespeare's rhythms:

> We had a conversation about names and whether we should change, particularly if it's so obviously Delhi or a version of Delhi. You know, should we call it Delhi or should we keep it with Messina? And actually, Mess-een-ah, we did the Indian dialect thing with it. It actually sounded very much like a place that could be in India and a lot of the names sounded [like Indian names]. So we didn't adjust, it didn't require [it]. It changes the music of the noun, it sort of seems to change the noun and I think that's quite profound actually. That so much of the meaning of a word is, it adheres in the euphony of the word, the music of the word.

Julius Caesar and *Much Ado* were both successful productions and received positive reviews, but some cast members also had a sense that their work was undervalued. Cyril Nri explains:

> The expectations [for people of colour] are low. Of the main cast I would say the main seven or eight of us have been doing this for years and are

actually quite good at it, you know. The other thing was [*Julius Caesar*], sadly, surprised the RSC. It surprised Stratford, when we were in Stratford, the take-off of the show. Because I think that what they had done was they had – and I've said it before – they had ticked a lot of boxes.

The continued stereotyping of performers of colour in the RSC's more traditional work – as servants, attendants or outsiders – over the next few seasons bears out Nri's assertion that the RSC was ticking diversity boxes with *Julius Caesar* and *Much Ado*. The two productions, however, were also harbingers of a renewed shift towards greater equality that would be evident by the end of the decade.

Othello

Kim F. Hall observes, '*Othello* so often becomes a vehicle for articulating an era's racial concerns' (2003: 360), which is nowhere more apparent than in British productions of *Othello*. This book first encountered *Othello* with Rudolph Walker's 1966 portrayal at the Malvern Festival Theatre; for Walker:

> Playing Othello became very personal. It became very personal as a Black man in this society. It helped me to understand the society in which I was living and the challenges that are going to be placed before me.

Walker has lived through a societal sea change that began with the dominant sentiment of, as he observes, an era where the feeling was that 'Blacks shouldn't play [Shakespeare] at all' to now, when audiences are willing to 'queue up to see a National Theatre production of Hugh Quarshie or whoever' playing Othello.

Rudolph Walker's *Othello* was part of an era rooted in the tradition of Paul Robeson's activism. The African-American, who played Othello at the Savoy Theatre in London nearly forty years before Walker at Malvern, had 'made *Othello* a political symbol' of oppression (Howard 2010: 95). For nearly four decades after Walker's first Othello in 1966, productions of the play depicted the title character as the sole Black man in a white world. As the overt racism Robeson faced dissolved into more subtle forms of discrimination, questions began to arise about Shakespeare's depiction of his famous character.

As Ayanna Thompson argues, the 'way *Othello* currently exists on the page is a white man's view of a fantasy of a black man' (2017: 55). For an actor in twenty-first century Britain, the challenges of playing the character are partly technical, caused by the writer himself. Hugh Quarshie feels Shakespeare 'isn't that interested in Othello's psychology' and he prioritizes Iago, whose 'soliloquies enable him to engage directly with an audience in the way Othello's soliloquies don't' (2015). Similarly, Adrian Lester observes:

> The actor playing Othello is tearing himself in half to sustain the play, to make the narrative work and, by default, to give huge, deeply emotional responses to Iago's tiny, manipulative actions. This, alongside the fact that Iago is the only character who addresses the audience directly, results in the character of Iago looking and feeling very powerful on that stage. Whereas the lion's share of the sheer weight of emotion and powerfully held beliefs rest on the shoulders of the actor playing Othello.

In strengthening Iago, Shakespeare underwrote Othello and used his ethnicity as shorthand 'to account for Othello's actions and the reactions of other characters to him' (Quarshie 1999: 14). Scholars have also fallen back on centuries-old stereotypes to explain Othello's behaviour; for example, Norman Sanders asserted in his introduction to the New Cambridge Shakespeare edition of the play that Othello 'relapse[s] into barbarism' (1984: 47). Counteracting the 'racist conventions [that] have persisted for so long' (Quarshie 1999: 20) now falls to actors and directors. In the twenty-first century, productions are increasingly exploring contemporary racial politics through integrated casting.

Preparing for the 2013 production of *Othello* at the National, Adrian Lester recalls an early conversation with his director, Nicholas Hytner, in which he argued for breaking the tradition of Othello as the only person of colour on the stage:

> I remember saying, 'We have to take away from the audience the very, very obvious response, which is: "He's doing that because he's Black" or "That's what Black people are like." So we can't isolate [Othello] on stage.' Now, many people say: 'Oh Othello should be isolated because that's the problem.' I respect their opinions but I can't help feeling like that allows us to make Othello a racial example rather than a unique individual. When he slaps Desdemona or when he sinks into his despair there have to be Black characters on stage appalled at his actions. I said, 'If you do that, for the audience, then it's not about his colour, it's about his actions.' For me – and for our version – this understanding was absolutely necessary.

So that Lester's Othello was not the only person of colour on the stage, Nicholas Hytner included two other African-Caribbean men and two south Asian men in the cast. All were present in Act 4, scene 1, part of a multiracial army on parade that had assembled to greet Lodovico on his arrival from Venice. Othello, believing Desdemona unfaithful, publicly slaps her during the course of this scene. When Desdemona fell to the ground in Hytner's production, the soldier-onlookers instinctively broke formation and went en masse – regardless of colour – to her assistance. A commanding gesture from Lester's Othello swiftly ordered them back to attention. The reactions of the four performers of colour, who comprised 40 per cent of the army ranks on stage, were an extratextual signal that Othello's action was not representative of all people of colour.

Hytner's casting of an actor of south Asian descent, Joplin Sibtain, to play Montano, the governor of Cyprus, also allowed for a corrective of stereotypes. After discovering Desdemona murdered in her bed, Emilia flung open the door to the room and shouted into the night, 'My mistress lies murdered in her bed' (5.2.181). On this cue, Sibtain's Montano and Scott Karim's Officer peered in, looking at each other in alarm. The choice of Joplin Sibtain as Montano also meant that his condemnation of Desdemona's murder, 'O monstrous act!' (5.2.186), was not spoken by a white man, but by Othello's fellow person of colour.

When Iqbal Khan directed *Othello* two years later at the RSC in 2015, his casting choices interrogated contemporary racial politics. The aspect of the production that brought the most attention was the choice of Zimbabwean-born Lucian Msamati to play Iago opposite Hugh Quarshie's Othello. Msamati was not the first African-Caribbean to play Iago, but he was the first to do so for a major Shakespeare company. Some media outlets framed the casting of Msamati as a publicity stunt: a 'twist' in the words of London's *Evening Standard* (3 September 2014). For Khan, however, 'having a Black Iago' was 'about exploring [the racial dynamics of *Othello*] in a more nuanced way'.

Shakespeare's play begins in the imperial capital of Venice, which Khan portrayed as a dominant white society:

> I wanted to create a world where – in Venice particularly – the executive is still white. I didn't want to make the point that it was white and male, so we had a female Duke. But I did want to make the point that in this state – as is the case in our modern world – the executive is still very, very white and white from a certain background. Yes, it's dominated by white men and certain women might be let through, but those women still have a certain profile.

Khan's production explored contemporary class and racial biases through the characters of Msamati's Iago and Cassio, played by the white actor Jacob Fortune-Lloyd. Before the play opens, Othello has promoted the privately educated Cassio, his deputy, to lieutenant over the head of the working-class Iago. For Msamati, class dynamics were an important building block for his character:

> He has been done over by his best friend [Othello]. He says, within three of his lines, 'You chose him over me. We have shed blood together all over the world and when [the chance for promotion] came, and I did everything, I got my three referees.... But you didn't even listen to them. You didn't even listen. You'd already made up your mind that you were

going to [hire] Mr Public Schoolboy who is just fresh out of Sandhurst and now you're expecting me to love you? I am going to take you down because you have broken the code.' It's very clear: 'I shed blood with you [Othello] and you chose [Cassio] over me.'

Msamati describes Cassio, the graduate, being fast-tracked into a position of power because of his elite education, while the hard-working Black man is denied promotion. In the exploration of race and power in Khan's production of *Othello*, this dynamic between the white Cassio and Black Iago was pivotal.

'There is a certain policing that happens around race', reflects Iqbal Khan, explaining he had wanted to explore 'these really dangerous pockets of resentment to do with the policing of instincts, the policing of vocabulary'. The scene in which a drunken Cassio loses his 'reputation' (2.3.254) was one part of the story which yielded a nuanced exploration of race and class. Khan's starting point was Lucian Msamati's Iago:

> I asked Lucian to bring in a song [to rehearsal]. Didn't tell anybody else this song was going to happen. It's a Zimbabwean song and he sang it in his own tongue. So the music was playing, there was a boom box and a mic there. Lucian just started singing on the mic a capella this wonderful song and it just eventually silenced the room.

What few knew was Msamati's chosen song was Zimbabwean, according to the production's composer and music director, Akintayo Akinbode: 'It means, my mother and father, if I die, if I don't come back, then I die for us all over the country. It's a Zimbabwean liberation song.'

Cassio's reaction pivoted from incredulity that the party had been stopped by Iago's musical lament to nervous laughter, all the while gauging the reaction of those around him. Khan describes this moment of discovery in rehearsal:

> There was a silent, violent thing that happened in the room and those that were with Cassio, and had felt isolated, suddenly felt like a little hiccup of laugh released.

Cassio's response to Iago's lament was to place an empty beer bottle on Iago's head and snigger before clapping, sarcastically. In a bid to reassert rank, Cassio then launched into a stanza from Shaggy's 'Boombastic'.

The director described the improvization: 'Everybody looked to Lucian and how he would respond [to Cassio]. He laughed and [Iago] started to rap.' Khan continues:

> What we didn't know was that our Cassio happens to be a fantastic rapper and a brilliant, very literary rapper. And David [Ajao], who played the person who is the highest military rank in Cyprus [Montano] –

obviously there's already a bit of an unsaid collision of status thing between Cassio and Montano – David could also rap. And they started rapping, they started battling with each other.

What started out as light-hearted, albeit drunken, mocking with a stanza from Montano about his parentage quickly devolved to race. Khan recalls:

> Cassio went there first, because it was a simple thing to do. But then David went to the shootings [in Ferguson, Missouri and elsewhere in America] that were going on and then David hit him with a rap about [that] and was very quick with it and had started to silence Cassio, who became more and more intimidated by the noise of the room that belonged to those people that were siding with Iago, the 'others' in the room. The room had suddenly become complicated in that way. Then David made a rap about Cassio being on Othello's leash. What we'd found was something very, very real in that.

In performance this improvization became a streamlined, three-stanza rap battle between Fortune-Lloyd's Cassio and David Ajao's Montano:

> CASSIO
>   This man became a solider, a tough choice, I'm sure.
>   'Cause it's rare to see a Black man on the right side of the law.
> MONTANO
>   This guy's a lieutenant, so we had better run.
>   'Cause we all know what happens when you give white people a gun.
> CASSIO
>   …
> MONTANO
>   This guy's a Florentine, he was a superstar before.
>   But now he's in the Cyprus wars, taking orders from a Moor.

The two men went toe-to-toe on that final line, until Cassio pushed Montano and the scripted brawl erupted. Through its subtle depiction of power structures, Khan's production held a mirror up to race relations, as the white officer lost his cool when confronted with the undeniable truth that he was inferior – at least in rank – to Othello, the Moor.

Joseph Marcell, King Lear, Shakespeare's Globe, 2013

After playing Brutus in *Julius Caesar* for John Dexter in 1988 (chapter 5), Joseph Marcell spent the early 1990s in Los Angeles in NBC's popular sitcom *The Fresh Prince of Bel-Air*, as the butler Geoffrey. Marcell continued working in classical theatre and in 1994 he directed a production of *Julius Caesar* in Los Angeles with a diverse company, including an African-American woman playing Mark Antony. Marcell explains:

> NBC at the time decided that, if I'm a classical actor, that I must be wasted not using my mind. So they set up a classical theatre workshop for me, they paid the insurance and everything, and the Screen Actors Guild gave it its blessing and it was for minority actors. So for three years every weekend at NBC in Burbank, actors would come in and we did a production of *Julius Caesar*, we did a production of *Antony and Cleopatra*, we did a production of *Richard III*. So they kept me going.

While Marcell has continued to act in both America and Britain, much of his Shakespeare work in the 2000s was with some of the most respected Shakespeare companies in the United States, rather than in Britain. Marcell says he goes where he is offered work, and Shakespeare was not on offer in Britain:

> The Shakespeare Theater in Washington, D.C. will call my American agents to find out if I'm available and they'll offer me something and say, 'Would you like to come?' and I'd say yes or no. Or I'll go to Oregon. I'll say yes or no. Whoever gives me the role and pays me is who I work for. I've been doing this nonsense for forty-two years and it is nice that what the Americans have afforded me – that Britain hasn't – is that the Americans are always curious to see if I'm available.

In 2005 Marcell's long-time collaborator, John Adams, invited him to play Claudius in *Hamlet* at the Haymarket Theatre, Basingstoke. He had not played a Shakespeare part in Britain since Sir Toby Belch at the Birmingham Rep in 1989. Marcell says he was attracted to Claudius through discussions with his director: 'John decided that what made Claudius special was that he was a high-class used-car salesman. A charmer of sorts – that's how he charmed Gertrude – and so I hadn't played that kind of role before.' In casting him, Adams also made a decision that Marcell describes as 'bold' because:

> It had been accepted that if you were going to have a non-white actor in such a production, it would be credible to have him play Polonius, but to have a non-white actor play Claudius with a white queen pushes [the boundaries] a little.

The title roles in the major tragedies, the gold standard of classical theatre, continue to be played primarily by white actors and Marcell had not played a title role in Britain since *Othello* in 1984. Comparing the Shakespeare careers of Joseph Marcell and three white peers, in terms of title roles played

TABLE 20 *Title roles played in British productions, by actor*

Joseph Marcell	Patrick Stewart	Simon Russell Beale	Ralph Fiennes
Othello (1984)	Henry V (1957)	Richard III (1992)	Henry VI (1988)
King Lear (2013)	King John (1970)	Hamlet (2000)	Troilus (1991)
–	Titus Andronicus (1981)	Macbeth (2005)	Hamlet (1995)
–	Henry IV (1982)	Timon of Athens (2012)	Richard II (2000)
–	Antony (2006)	King Lear (2014)	Richard III (2016)
–	Macbeth (2007)	Richard II (2018)	Antony (2018)

across their careers, is useful in illustrating the inequity. Table 20 shows the title roles played in Britain by Marcell, his RSC contemporary Patrick Stewart, and two white actors who began their careers in the 1980s, Simon Russell Beale and Ralph Fiennes.

These four performers have all had long and distinguished careers in classical theatre, but the discrepancy between the number of title roles played in Britain by Stewart, Beale and Fiennes and those played by Marcell is stark. Perhaps most striking, Patrick Stewart had already played two title roles by 1972, the year Marcell first joined the RSC. The three white actors have each played three times as many title roles in Britain as Marcell.

The serendipity of Marcell standing on the main stage at Shakespeare's Globe, having photos taken for an American magazine's 'Where are they now?' retrospective of *The Fresh Prince of Bel-Air*, led to Marcell's first title role in Britain in nearly thirty years:

> A crowd of Italian visitors to the Globe doing the tour were watching us and then they came down into the groundling spot of the auditorium and I thought it'd be interesting, let me see if I can do Lear carrying Cordelia. So I asked, 'Would you like to be in it?' and they said yes. So [one woman] came up and we did it, me walking forward and backwards and all sorts of things [carrying the woman]. Meantime Dominic's [Dromgoole, the Globe's artistic director] assistant had just come down to find out if I needed a cup of tea, so she saw this and told him. And at the end of the shoot he said, 'I heard about you carrying [a woman on stage], why?' And I said I was rehearsing for my Lear. 'Oh where do you want to do it?' I said, 'Well I don't want to do it at the RSC, I'd rather do it here.' He said, 'Are you serious?' 'Yeah, I'll do it here.' And that was it. Forgotten. Four months later I got this call: 'We want you to do King Lear with Bill Buckhurst directing.'

Bill Buckhurst's 2013 production was a touring version for the Globe's Discovery Space series. It was staged in both indoor and outdoor venues and, when revived the following year, toured internationally, including a run at the Folger Theater in Washington, D.C. 'You get to a certain age and that's the part you want to play', Marcell told Jonathan Croall (2015: 123). For Marcell, the key to the character is his absolute power:

> My King Lear was a king from the very first to the very last. There was no mistaking that he was the king. [That] means never having to hear the word 'No.' It's simply having your will, your way on everything. Everything. Never considering that there is an alternative. The only answer is, 'Yes, your majesty. Yes, my lord.' There is no other answer.

In voluntarily losing that power by giving up his kingdom to his daughters, he sees his world begin to fall apart. He has lost control of both his kingdom and his family. Marcell explains:

> That's where he begins to understand. At first he's totally confused by it. Because the force of his personality, his physical prowess is waning and he cannot understand it. And it is the gradual moving from a king to a man and he becomes a man. So that when he starts and talks about the poor people sitting out there, for the first time you actually hear that this man actually sees. 'Oh my god, you poor homeless people. What have I been doing?' He begins to understand, but he's still a king. But the man comes, too.

In casting Joseph Marcell, Bill Buckhurst nudged the mainstream into normalizing casting an African-Caribbean as King Lear. 'It's not the sort of role a non-white actor gets to play every day', Marcell said (Croall 2015: 123). Marcell's appearance as Lear was undoubtedly a breakthrough in integrated casting, but it was essentially a baby step towards greater equality. Buckhurt's production was a small-scale tour situated outside the Globe's main season. It played a few performances at the Globe itself, but the majority of the run took place away from its 'wooden O'. As of 2021, no performer of colour has played King Lear within a main stage season at the prestigious pinnacles of Shakespearean theatre: the Globe, the National Theatre or the RSC.

Shakespeare's histories, 2013–2015

Capitalizing on renewed interest in the Wars of the Roses generated by HBO's *Game of Thrones*, Shakespeare's Globe staged the *Henry VI* trilogy in 2013 with the white director Nick Bagnall at the helm. Part of the company's annual touring programme, the Globe's artistic director, Dominic

Dromgoole, felt the shows should visit towns where the battles depicted in Shakespeare's plays occurred. This decision also helped to generate headlines needed to bolster box office for these little-known plays. Dromgoole noted at the time: 'When you think of battlefields, you think of re-enactment and that's usually deemed slightly circumspect [*sic*], but the British are obsessed with our own history and that's a really interesting way that we engage with it' (*Guardian* 7 February 2013). This also turned out to be an exclusionary view of history, as Bagnall's fourteen-strong cast was all white.

By contrast, Michael Grandage's revival of *Henry V* at the Noel Coward pushed the boundaries of national identity. Instead of excluding performers of colour from Shakespeare's depictions of British history, Grandage cast Ashley Zhangazha to double as Chorus and Boy. At first glance, this may not seem significant, but the Chorus is the third largest role in *Henry V* and, as defined for this volume, one of the play's leading parts. Zhangazha was the first performer of colour to play the Chorus in Britain and as he recalls, the director's emphasis was on his relative youth:

> He was like 'What I want is for those moments of the Chorus talking to the audience to have energy, to have drive.' What Michael wanted was for the Chorus to come on and grab the audience. To really speak to the audience. And the way we aided that as well, was I was in modern dress, whereas everybody else was in period costume. So the Chorus was a direct link to now.

As the only character in modern dress, a Union Jack T-shirt and black jeans, Zhangazha's Chorus also represented contemporary England:

> I found something interesting in that about me as a young, Black man, because there's something quite patriotic about the Chorus. There was, on some level, some sort of subversion going on there as well. What do we expect to see with [the Chorus]? We expect to see, probably, an old white man talking about the glories of nationhood. But here was a young me, twenty-six at the time. A young, Black man coming on and saying, 'This is our country, this was a glorious time when this charismatic king defeated the French' and I was delivering those words. So I found that interesting.

By the time Trevor Nunn revived the *Henry VI* and *Richard III* tetralogy at the Rose Theatre, Kingston-upon-Thames in 2015, the entertainment industry was in the throes of its most comprehensive overhaul since the 1980s, in terms of race and gender. One crucial juncture came in the autumn of 2013, when Danny Lee Wynter saw ITV's 'Where Drama Lives' trailer. As he recounted, 'It featured not a single black, Asian or minority ethnic (BAME) actor. A discussion began with ITV's head of drama, Steve November, who had commissioned the trailer, and this gathered momentum to become the Act for Change project' (*Guardian* 7 July 2014). Act for Change quickly became a leading advocate for greater representation in the arts across all under-represented groups, including race, gender, class, sexual orientation and disability.

The Act for Change project was not a lone voice in the wilderness as calls for greater diversity gained momentum. The actor and comedian Lenny Henry and director Kwame Kwei-Armah posited the idea of using quotas to reverse the decline in representation that had occurred in the previous decade (*Screen Daily* 14 November 2013). The actors' union Equity also called for targets to be set to improve diversity, releasing a policy statement that laid out these objectives (*The Stage* 26 June 2015). The RSC came under scrutiny when it staged *The Orphan of Zhao*, a Chinese revenge tragedy, with a cast that included few British east Asians. This put a spolight on the lack of representation for east Asians both at the RSC and across the wider profession. Having emigrated to the United States by that time, David Oyelowo also related his experiences:

> I felt pushed out of the UK because of the glass ceiling I could feel my head bobbing against, having been given very genuine and real opportunities.... Things are worse now than they were when I was doing [the BBC drama series about MI5] *Spooks*, [or] when I was playing Henry VI – they just literally are. The opportunities that I was afforded are not there.
> (*The Stage* 29 September 2015)

When Trevor Nunn announced his *Wars of the Roses* in June 2015, the director described the production as 'very inclusive in a number of ways' (*The Stage* 11 June 2015). Nunn was talking about the actor–audience relationship in the Rose Theatre, however, not his performers; his cast of twenty-two was all white and while there had been no backlash against Bagnall's *Henry VI*s in 2013, reaction to Nunn's two years later was swift. Equity's Minority Ethnic Members' committee called Nunn's casting decision 'disappointing':

> The performance, as a cycle, of these plays together is a rare and special occurrence. To present this benchmark of British heritage in a way that effectively locks minorities out of the cultural picture (literally) flies in the face of the huge conversation taking place in British media at present.
> (*The Stage* 7 August 2015)

Trevor Nunn responded to the criticism from both Equity and Arts Council England, stating he had made an 'artistic decision' based on 'historical verisimilitude':

> The connections between the characters and hence the narrative of the plays, are extremely complex, and so everything possible must be done to

clarify for an audience who is related by birth to whom. Hence, I decided that, in this instance, these considerations should take precedence over my usual diversity inclinations.

(*Independent* 15 August 2015)

For Tanya Moodie, the RADA-trained Canadian of African-Caribbean descent, Nunn's intentionally all-white cast 'felt like a body blow.... Because he is reaffirming something that is a complete and utter fallacy. When you say the term "historical accuracy", in my head I hear "historical revisionism"' (*The Stage* 14 September 2015).

At the time of Nunn's production Tanya Moodie had recently finished playing Constance in *King John* in a co-production by the Royal and Derngate Theatres in Northampton and Shakespeare's Globe. Its white director James Dacre had cast three performers of colour in key roles: Moodie as Constance, alongside Joseph Marcell (Cardinal Pandulph) and Giles Terera (Austria). Of the three, Constance, as the third largest part in the play, was a leading role, but all were important developments in the history of integrated casting, as few, if any, performers of colour had yet played these characters in Britain.

Joseph Marcell decided to play Pandulph partly because it provided him with new opportunities:

> I'd never played the smarmy, self-confident operative before. A man who can see both sides, but has his directive and will do it, do what he's been told to do. And the way the man exercises his power. Pandulph has no insecurities. Just pure, naked, savouring power. And what I loved about him was he plays along and then he turns it and he, he's almost forensic in his kind of breaking down of other people's arguments. I've never played that kind of role before.

Tanya Moodie was similarly attracted to Constance's strength:

> What I like about playing her is that because she's so uncompromising in terms of what she wants and her objective because of her passion for her son. Also the reason why Constance is uncompromising is because Richard the Lionheart said that my son would be King. I love the fact that I can be in a place on stage with other people, many of whom have that same status and the power struggles are so sort of close together. So if I'm grappling, trying hard to get on top of somebody else on stage, they're actually very close to me in terms of status and power, and my sense of entitlement and superiority is so complete and so whole.

With Michael Grandage's *Henry V* and James Dacre's *King John*, performers of colour were finally playing substantial and complex parts in Shakespeare's histories, the genre that has traditionally been least representative. More than three decades after Hugh Quarshie had first played Hotspur (chapter 3), his casting was no longer the exception that proved the rule.

Paapa Essiedu, Hamlet, RSC, 2016

When Marcus Griffiths realized that two of his colleagues from the RSC's 2012 *Julius Caesar*, Cyril Nri and Theo Ogundipe, had, like Griffiths, auditioned for a production of *Hamlet* at the RSC, he believed *Hamlet* might be a repeat of *Julius Caesar*:

> We talked about it. Is this going to be what we think it's going to be? Like, basically getting the band back together from *Caesar*? Are we the new [Rolling] Stones of Black Shakespeare? Where they're just going to wheel us out every couple of years: 'We've got another Black play, there you go.' I didn't want [Godwin] to [set *Hamlet* in Africa] just because Paapa's Black. Do you know what I mean? Because it could easily be an English Black production with him and still work. It turns out it wasn't like that, but suspicions arose.

The white director Simon Godwin was crafting his production around his leading actor, Paapa Essiedu, which impressed Theo Ogundipe, who was 'struck' by the:

> idea of looking at Paapa's history, as a person, and using that to build [the production] around him. It was: let's take into account this person's being, not just their race, their ethnicity, their nationality, but their being, what has made them because [Paapa] didn't grow up in Ghana, but that is part of his [being] and I just thought that was really interesting.

While the production was built around Essiedu's Ghanian roots, the backgrounds of the entire cast contributed to the creation of the production's version of Denmark. Essiedu explains:

> It really did evolve because we were, because most of the cast weren't of African descent. There was definitely a portion of African-Caribbean descent. There were white actors. There were half-Filipino actors. There was a very global community that was created in there. I think we kind of experimented at one point with setting it in Ghana in 19-whatever and it just didn't feel right, didn't feel right for the company of actors that we had. Didn't feel right for me. It felt like we were placing something on top of the story in order to be clever or be seen on brand or whatever. And the challenge was to create something that felt organic, that felt organically bespoke to the play without it being a flourish that was put on top of it. And it took a long time for that to naturally evolve out of the rehearsal

room and we had to experiment with different things, accents, design elements, ideas.

Essiedu's heritage contributed to one aspect of the production, however: the supernatural element in *Hamlet*. Essideu explains:

> There's a different connection to the supernatural in Ghana to here [in Britain]. There's not the same scepticism. There's a far more visceral connection to the spiritual there and so I was talking a lot to people [in Ghana] about magic and about ancestors and how present that is in daily life. I relayed a lot of that to Simon. I think in many ways *Hamlet*'s a ghost story and it's so supernatural. If you really, really believe that Hamlet has seen the ghost of his father, you don't get into the thing of 'he's mad' or whatever. I felt that that was something that could be really rich in terms of the relocation of the story, in terms of unlocking that [so] that people don't think twice about the ghost.

Theo Ogundipe agrees that putting the play in a culture that acknowledges the power of spirits injects an urgency to Hamlet's encounters with his father's ghost: 'In Africa, spirits are important things. And dangerous things. And things that are believed by some; [while] some of us didn't believe.'

Ogundipe doubled Marcellus and Fortinbras in *Hamlet*, providing an opportunity to bring his understanding of the diverse nature of Africa into his characterizations. He was also the only member of the cast to adopt an African accent, which he used as Marcellus, while Fortinbras spoke in RP. He explains:

> Africa is so multidimensional. So you can have somebody from a village or a smaller town that may be educated in a different way, or less educated, than somebody else from somewhere else. Or just from a different class in that area. So I, personally, because of his occupation possibly, I felt [for] Marcellus it would be interesting if he was educated, but he was of a slightly different class. And therefore the received pronunciation accent that others had, he didn't quite have that. And I also decided that because I was playing Fortinbras as well, who, as a prince, would have had the best education. Even in Africa now princes, depending on how wealthy that royal family may be, are afforded a better education and afforded western education. So he was, as Hamlet was, sent away to Wittenberg, to Europe. So I knew that his position, his demeanour, would be slightly different. It was also to give a bit of juxtaposition or opposites for me to play [with, in terms of character].

Cyril Nri also thrived on working within the production's framework, equating Polonius with 'a civil servant' who suspects 'Claudius of not being fully clean. But he has to serve, he has to serve. And he will serve all the masters and he will serve them well. He has served the king before; he is going to serve this king.' In warning his daughter and instructing his son, Nri also found in Polonius parallels with 'a very, very west African father'. Nri drew on personal experience in Nigeria when crafting the private Polonius, including his recollection of serving kola nuts to the Biafran leader Ojukwu. In the 'Polonius Owusu family', as Nri called it:

> They have rituals in the same way many west African families [do]. She brings him the slippers. All that stuff. I did that. When I talk about me being a young kid serving Ojukwu kola nuts and whatever, that was a duty. I am the young, and I knew you had to do that. And that was about 'Dad's home! Oh, he's got people with him. I know I need to serve this; I need to do this because I'm pleasing dad.'

Cyril Nri's injection of Nigerian customs into his performance illustrates how Godwin's *Hamlet* created its Denmark by borrowing from the cast's individual heritages. Marcus Griffiths recalls, 'We were taking a lot from Ghanaian culture but we were also taking [from others], like Ewart [James Walters] played a Caribbean grave-digger and we were all speaking in English accents.' Born in Britain to Jamaican parents Griffiths, like Nri, was able to use his upbringing to play Laertes:

> We [Laertes and Ophelia] have grown up around the court, grown up around Hamlet. We've been educated abroad, at boarding school. So I think what we were creating was these children, not just with Hamlet but with these kids (Fortinbras, Hamlet, Laertes and Ophelia and Horatio), who are children of two worlds. They come with so much culture because of where they grew up, but they've also experienced another westernized kind of lifestyle, but have had to come home and deal with the politics that go on within their own community, but with a certain westernized mentality.

This Polonius Owusu family was incredibly close knit, as Nri observes:

> This is a man who loves his children and he's desperate to protect them. Desperate to protect them. I couldn't understand why, if he was sometimes played as this rather interfering, misogynistic dad, that his kids fall apart when he's gone. Why does his daughter go mad trying to work out what she does without this father figure? Why does his son go hell bent on revenge if he's this interfering booby who keeps telling him what to do?

This reading of the family helped Natalie Simpson to escape one of the pitfalls of playing Ophelia:

> I think traditionally Ophelia takes her father's advice to break up with Hamlet out of a patriarchal sense of duty. In our version, we wanted it to

be out of love for him, and her understanding that he truly has her best interests at heart. This was super useful to me in rooting her breakdown in a true sense of loss when she finds Polonius is dead, killed by the very man he warned her against. She has feelings of guilt, remorse and deep grief when he dies.

Grief was also a driving force for his Hamlet, as Paapa Essiedu explains:

> I think the very first thing that you've got to think about deeply, and feel deeply, is his recent grief. All of us either have had or will have a real proximity to grief in our life and – I have – and there is a hammer blow quality to it that changes you fundamentally. Everything [Hamlet] does, everything he says, all the masks that he puts on, how he relates to literally all the other characters in the play, be it his girlfriend, his uncle, his mum, Polonius, his friends. It all is connected to how he is processing the grief of the death of his father in a way that he was not prepared for.

The construction of a history for each character was important for the cast, each detailing how they had arrived at the point where the play begins. Paapa Essiedu talks about the importance of creating Hamlet's family's backstory with Tanya Moodie (Gertrude), Ewart James Walters (Hamlet's father) and Clarence Smith (Claudius):

> There's got to be a version before, that has basically led to this. So, is the marriage happy? is one question. And is the way that the marriage is presented to the son different to what the reality is? So there's an idea that Hamlet senior was much older than Gertrude. They had a kid and [Hamlet senior] was off not only fighting wars, but being a king. She was looking after the kid and we [Hamlet and Gertrude] had this very close, but very not healthy relationship, me and mum, which led to me being like, 'Well I need to get away from this whole thing, get away from this life and go to Wittenburg.' A recognizable, not particularly radical late-teen, late-adolescence, early-twenties rejection of what the parents are trying to make you into.

Creating this backstory for Hamlet's family was, Essiedu says:

> really important [in order] for that [past family dynamic] to be subverted. Those conventions [of a happy family before the play starts need] to be broken in terms of the mum being 'I don't understand why Hamlet's behaving like this. This is not the Hamlet that I know.' It's important that that's true. It *is* weird that I am behaving in this way. And [Hamlet] also has to be, 'It is mad that you're behaving like this because I know you, Mum, and you would never do that to my dad.'

In addition, Essiedu and Natalie Simpson created a backstory for the relationship between Hamlet and Ophelia, which helped to raise the stakes within the action of the play. Essiedu recalls:

> We [made] a decision that Ophelia was [the source of] a really important kind of sympathetic energy, understanding energy in the early part of the grief. In those first six weeks it's her that he's been talking to and crying with and intimately sharing how he feels.

Natalie Simpson concurs with Essiedu's assessment of the couple's closeness, adding:

> Our relationship was probably the most distant in our version of the play. Strangely enough, you don't ever see Hamlet and Ophelia happy together. You hear her speak of him fondly (before he scares her in her bedchamber), but their first on stage encounter is cold and violent. In our heads, they were very close, but it was a new relationship, and there hadn't been much time to get it off the ground before their parents intervened. Therefore, it made it easier for Ophelia to listen to her family's advice and leave him. But we also needed it to be clear that there were real, deep feelings there, which is why they argued so passionately when they were finally together. Ophelia is deeply hurt and confused by Hamlet's sudden change in behaviour to her, and this confirms her father's suspicions that he isn't right for her.

Paapa Essiedu speaks of a string of betrayals that Hamlet suffers during the course of the play, as Ophelia, Gertrude and his university friends, Rosencrantz and Guildenstern, all push him to an ever darker place. Hamlet's 'antic disposition' comes from that turmoil, mixed with his grief. Essiedu says Hamlet is '*pretending* to be mad' and he finds an outlet through art, inspired by Basquiat, in Godwin's production:

> Simon and I really wanted [Hamlet's] antic disposition to burst out from his mind. And for creativity to be an outlet. And how artists are given, like performance artists, for example, are given license to break every barrier of prudishness or social normity. So it's a different framework of judgement, which is actually freeing. It means that he can be as wild and be as mean and mercurial as he wants, as a kind of smokescreen to observe and to prove [Claudius' guilt], essentially. The Basquiat thing was really useful in terms of the anarchy of it.

The turning point in the play is Hamlet's unintended killing of Polonius. Essiedu explains:

> [Murdering Polonius] also has an impact on him. I don't think there's a cheapness to murder. He's not a murderer. He's not a killer, so having

FIGURE 10 *Paapa Essiedu (Hamlet) and Natalie Simpson (Ophelia)*. Hamlet, Royal Shakespeare Company, Stratford-upon-Avon, 2016. Photo by Donald Cooper/Alamy Stock Photo.

to drag that body off is again moving him into a different psychological place.

Polonius' death forces Claudius to act, banishing Hamlet and attempting to have his nephew killed. For Essiedu, Hamlet's eventual return to Denmark is poignant:

He comes back to Denmark as a different man. He's got a different philosophy. He's been changed. And it's like an extension of 'To be or not to be'. He's making his peace with the fact that he's going to die. He's going to try and enact his father's wish, but he knows that he's not going to survive it. He knows that. 'Let be.' Whatever happens will happen. And if I have to die, I'm going out doing what is important to me. That drives him towards the end of the play and again he has to kill a few more people, which is sad. A few more people have to die. But I think it's again sad that final speech when he's on the deathbed where he's like, fuck, what are people going to say about me? There's again another sense of what the hell was the point of all that? I've done all that. I'm going to die and people could just say whatever they want about me. So please, Horatio, make sure they don't just curse me the whole time. There's nothing I can do, I'm dead.

'It was a lack of faith'

Paapa Essiedu was the eighth performer of colour to play Hamlet in Britain since 1930 and the first African-Caribbean to play it at the RSC. The media attention lavished on Essiedu was reminiscent of that which greeted David Oyelowo sixteen years previously when he was cast as Henry VI. Both were young actors not long out of drama school, plucked from anonymity to play one of Shakespeare's title roles. While Essiedu endured no equivalent episode to that of an anonymous Oxford don opining that Oyelowo's casting left 'us' – presumably the British – open to ridicule (chapter 6), the 'hook' of the RSC's 'first Black Hamlet' was enticing for the press. There were, Essiedu recalls:

> a lot of the media interactions, bearing in mind this was my first real experience of dealing with media, doing interviews about myself. I had to field a lot of uninformed questions or very simple-minded questions, which I felt was quite disrespectful. I don't feel like anyone really prepared me for that. I don't think anyone at the RSC was particularly equipped for preparing for that either.

Showing how little has changed, the press in 2016 remained more interested in Essiedu's skin colour than his interpretation of Shakespeare's iconic part. The actor found that:

> frustrating, but it's frustrating because the world is frustrating. So I think we're living in naivety if we're expecting the media to suddenly just become completely woke. For me I try to be courageous in exposing it when someone asks me about it. If [a journalist is] asking me, 'How does it feel to be a Black actor playing this part?' I'm [replying,] 'You actually have to ask yourself why you're asking that question and you have to really, really deconstruct what you're trying to get. I know what you want me to say. You have to deconstruct why you're trying to elicit that from a twenty-five-year-old, quite inexperienced actor who's just trying to do his job.'

Simon Godwin's production of *Hamlet* also exposed other problematic aspects of the treatment of performers of colour in twenty-first century British Shakespeare.

Godwin's *Hamlet* had been cross-cast with productions of *Cymbeline* and *King Lear*. In April 2016, one month into the run of *Hamlet* in Stratford, the RSC announced *Cymbeline* and *Lear* would transfer to the Barbican in the autumn, but not *Hamlet*, along with two of the productions running in the Swan Theatre; the third, *Don Quixote*, later transferred to the West End. Officially the *Hamlet* cast were told the Barbican Centre had refused to allow the transfer of Paapa Essiedu's *Hamlet* because they did not want another production of the play so soon after Benedict Cumberbatch's 2015 appearance in the role there. Given the combination of *Hamlet*'s canonical status, *Cymbeline*'s relative unpopularity and the fact that a glut of white actors playing Hamlet simultaneously had never before been an issue, the reason given rings hollow. It was also box office poison, as critics savaged the RSC's 2016 *Cymbeline* while Paapa Essiedu's *Hamlet* became a five-star sell-out in Stratford. Reflecting on the lack of a West End transfer with the rest of the RSC's 2016 season, Essiedu notes:

> In terms of the Barbican thing, I think, if you asked anyone at the RSC, they'll put their hands up and say they fucked up, but again that was exactly the same thing I was just talking about. No one was expecting it to be good; no one was expecting me to be good. It was a lack of faith, basically.

Cyril Nri agrees:

> I think that was a lack of faith, personally. Because [the RSC] planned to take *Cymbeline*, which is a very difficult piece. [They] planned to take *Lear* [to the Barbican].

The way in which the RSC's revival of *Hamlet* in 2018 was announced was also problematic. In May 2017, the RSC revealed that Paapa Essiedu would return to play Hamlet in a revival of Simon Godwin's production. It was due to tour to several regional theatres and finish its run at the Hackney Empire in London. The RSC put out a press release, without having contacted the rest of the original cast. Cyril Nri had been in rehearsals at the National Theatre for Inua Ellams' play *Barbershop Chronicles* when he noticed several missed calls on his mobile phone. Nri takes up the story:

> The shock of getting all these calls during a day when Clarence [Smith, who played Claudius] is trying to get hold of me and various others. And finding out that the RSC have announced the tour of *Hamlet* without having informed the actors. So when Clarence gets hold of me and says, 'Did you know? Well, surely they would have told you, Cyril' I'm going, 'I don't know anything about it.' And then my agent coming through and saying, 'Oh they've come through and [apologized and made an offer]' and I'm going 'That's not good enough because, when you make these announcements...'. It was really at that point that the decision essentially was made [to not return to play Polonius] because of the arrogance and dismissal of the RSC.

Once again, the work of performers of colour was, at best, undervalued and, at worst, outright dismissed.

Black Theatre Live's *Hamlet* and Talawa's *King Lear*, 2016

While the RSC's 2016 production of *Hamlet* with Paapa Essiedu was one historic milestone in the integration of Shakespeare in Britain, other productions that year were equally important, including a second *Hamlet* and Talawa Theatre Company's production of *King Lear*. Black Theatre Live's *Hamlet* was the brainchild of Jeffery Kissoon, who originally developed it with the Lincoln Theatre in Columbus, Ohio. Although that partnership would not come to fruition, its legacy was visually imprinted on the production. The Lincoln is a landmark of African-American and jazz history and Kissoon had been struck by its auditorium decorated with Egyptian motifs and hieroglyphs, which became integral to his theme.

The Denmark of Kissoon's *Hamlet* was, as the production's education pack describes, 'a Black Empire of modern England'. This was signified in a set that used symbols of ancient Egypt, such as the Nubian Ankh, with contemporary British costumes. Kissoon's *Hamlet* melded Egyptian and English signifiers for a production that 'signalled an unbroken timeline between ancient Egypt and contemporary Britain' (Rogers 2018: 153). Kissoon describes the concept:

> We had to make a huge leap of imagination.... I just wanted to explore in our imagination, what – it's a big 'if', the magic 'if' – what would have happened, or what could it be like, if from the origin of time, the people who were there in the beginning up to 2016 today, there has been no other influence by any other invaders at all in this world. It's a Black world that has evolved all the way to 2016, untouched.
>
> (Kissoon 2016)

This 'if' was aurally and visually signalled through the use of a distorted version of *Jerusalem*, hieroglyphs, an ankh and the sound of drumbeats interspersed with church bells. Kissoon's premise attracted Patrick Miller to the production:

> I think they [Kissoon and his collaborator Mark Norfolk, who adapted the script] sold it to me really well. That the conceit was to assume that the Egyptian Nubian line hadn't been interfered with. So, therefore, this state could still exist now. It just happened to be called Denmark.

Jeffery Kissoon's production of *Hamlet* was also historic: the first production with a cast and crew comprising entirely practitioners of African-Caribbean heritage. Kissoon chose Raphael Sowole, who had been born in London to Nigerian parents, as Hamlet. Sowole became the ninth performer of colour in Britain to play the part since 1930 and, noting the dearth of Black Hamlets, he told the BBC: 'We are capable of doing it as well and we are interested in doing it. It's just a matter of opportunity, I think.' Playing Gertrude was also an important milestone because only Tanya Moodie had played the part in Britain before, opposite Paapa Essiedu at the RSC earlier in 2016. As Kissoon's Gertrude, Joy Elias-Rilwan, noted: 'I believe in showing Black women as women, not "stamp" prostitute, "stamp" maid. We're women. We have a pulse' (BBC News 14 September 2016).

Patrick Miller played Claudius, another character rarely portrayed by a performer of colour. Claudius is an authority figure and, when the play opens, king of Denmark; a man outwardly full of confidence, who has killed his brother and usurped his nephew, Hamlet. For Miller, Claudius was:

> somebody that I think somewhere in there believed he was doing the right thing to move the state on. I think there was love for Gertrude. Maybe [their affair] had been going on for quite a while anyway. And then, like a lot of those characters, once you get [power], you don't know what to do with it. And the guilt kicks in and that overrides everything. Most of his actions are not [those of a] twirly-thumbs, twirly-'tached [pantomime villain]. He's reacting to the immediate and with Hamlet he thinks: *I just need to get him out of the way because otherwise it's all going to fall apart.*

Jeffery Kissoon's *Hamlet* had been in gestation for three years but was staged shortly after the RSC's production with Paapa Essiedu had closed. Despite opening in Watford, near London, and touring to other venues in the capital's suburbs, the production only received two mainstream reviews, from *The Times* and *The Stage*. According to Black Theatre Live's white producer, Jonathan Kennedy, there had been 'several reviewers lined up' but 'when they knew the running time of the show and they had to get to Watford and then back to London, they pulled out' (qtd in Rogers 2018: 156). The proximity of the Palace Theatre, Watford, where the production opened, to central London – a fifty-minute drive via the M1 motorway or a twenty-minute train ride from Euston Station – shows the absurdity of this excuse and illustrates, once again, the continued undervaluing of the work of performers of colour.

Perhaps more disturbing than the press's lack of interest in covering the historic production were some audience members' stereotypical expectations for the African-Caribbean cast, as Patrick Miller recounts:

> There was a very friendly post-show Q&A one night after *Hamlet*, at Hexham [in Northumberland in the north of England]. We were being questioned over our authenticity because we didn't speak with what they thought were authentic accents: African, or something not English. I think they said it was beautifully spoken: 'It was all very clear. But we thought it would be more authentic if you'd used your accents.' The

really interesting thing about that authenticity conversation for me was that Hexham is close to where I was born and brought up, in Darlington, County Durham. So there was a double edge to it. I pointed this out when they were suggesting we use our own accents. There was a brief, uncomfortable silence. Then they moved on.

Michael Buffong finds the perception that performers of African-Caribbean descent are not British to be an endemic problem in productions of Shakespeare. 'Are you setting Shakespeare in an African country because, somehow, it's how you understand black actors doing Shakespeare?' the director asked rhetorically, when discussing his production of *King Lear* for Talawa (*The Stage* 28 March 2016). This apparent need for a dominant white theatre to portray its citizens of colour as foreigners prompted Buffong to set *King Lear* in ancient Britain. With a cast of performers predominantly from African-Caribbean backgrounds, Buffong's *Lear* reclaimed the Britishness that had been ceded by productions that use foreign locales to paint people of colour as foreigners.

For Rakie Ayola, part of the attraction of playing Goneril for Michael Buffong at Talawa in 2016 was this decision to set *King Lear* in Britain:

> I really loved it that Michael Buffong was interested in not removing his production of *King Lear* from the British Isles. I liked that he said, 'What if we're in Old Britain, ancient Britain and there just happen to be a lot of people who are Black. What happens then? Let's not feel the need to remove it, place it somewhere else in time or space.' And I loved that because, from my point of view, it meant that we weren't trying to create another world. And I liked being from here, because I am. So it suited me. It suited me a lot.

Crucially, the director also wanted to depict 'a black King in England in ancient time', as he told me in a 2017 interview. 'The black presence in this country goes back thousands of years', but that history is rarely shown on stage (qtd in Rogers 2018: 153).

Buffong's Lear was the veteran actor, Don Warrington, born in Trinidad and raised in Tyneside. *King Lear* was his first Shakespeare production since 1997, when he played Antonio in *The Merchant of Venice* at the Birmingham Rep. 'The idea of playing King Lear wasn't anywhere on my radar', Warrington said, adding, 'If there is such a thing as a classical theatre actor, I don't think that I have ever been one' (*The Stage* 8 April 2016). For an actor who was the first performer of colour to play Mark Antony in *Julius Caesar* (1979) and the aforementioned Antonio, his statement is instructive. That Warrington could not imagine playing Lear himself speaks to the continuing marginalization of performers of colour in British theatre from Shakespeare's title roles.

Alfred Enoch, Edgar, *King Lear*, Talawa, 2016

After the King of France in *King Lear*, Edmund is, at the time of writing, the role most frequently played by a performer of colour. The illegitimate son of the Duke of Gloucester, Edmund is the play's Machiavellian villain. He is both outsider and outlaw, two stereotypes that helps to explain why the vast majority of performers of colour to have played Edmund are of African-Caribbean descent. Edmund stands in contrast with the ostensible hero of the piece: his half-brother, the 'Legitimate Edgar' (1.2.16). Performers of colour play Edgar, who is neither outsider nor villain, far less often than Edmund. For his Talawa production in 2016, Michael Buffong chose an actor of mixed English and Brazilian heritage, Alfred Enoch, to play Edgar.

Edgar appears only three times in the first half of *King Lear* and Alfred Enoch became keenly aware of the two brothers' positions within the play, not only in terms of status but also their presence as the story unfolds. Enoch explains:

> The space [the brothers] occupy in the play mirrors themselves. Edmund comes in hard [at the beginning] as he's talking to the audience, and he sort of fades, literally, in the sort of space that he occupies. But when [Edmund's importance] fades [in the story], we get more of Edgar in the second half.

As the rightful heir to the Duke of Gloucester, Edgar's place in society is ostensibly secure. This makes the shock of his displacement by Edmund all the more jarring. For Enoch, Edgar begins the play in a place of privilege:

> I thought, here's someone who is incredibly privileged, who's benefiting [from that privilege], and Edmund's story is the opposite. Edmund's someone who has to graft to get everything that's his. So Edgar is easily supplanted because people who have privilege, people who have their advantages, don't need to come in a room and work hard to be seen, or top people, or hustle. So Edgar's complacent, because why would it be any other way? He knows he's going to inherit the land. He knows it's going to all go well for him. It was ever thus, as far as he [was concerned], his whole lifetime. So that's one of the reasons I don't think he perceives Edmund as a threat because what can possibly threaten his legitimacy? Nothing.

Edgar's status as the play's hero gradually unfolds and, for Enoch, the key to the character was found in the 'Poor Tom' sequence, arguably some of the most difficult scenes to stage effectively. The challenge was partly to adhere to the literal reading of Edgar's disguise as a practical means of escape: 'You can read this in such a way that he needs a practical disguise, he does it, he goes [mad] and then no one knows who he is.' But Enoch also wanted to find something more compelling in that narrative:

> I felt Poor Tom has to be the heart of Edgar and that has to be the thing that transforms him. And, actually, he needs to buy [the disguise] himself. He needs to not, I think, be fully in control and he has go there, for want of a better word, to motivate it, to make it work, to fill it. I mean there's so much detail, there's so much precision about Poor Tom's backstory about the serving man. The more I spent time with this, the more I thought this is, it was just very moving and felt very detailed and felt very full. And I think that was, in a way, the starting point, or the sort of main idea in a way: that Poor Tom has his own identity and it's through that Edgar, when he comes out, he comes out differently. He can take responsibility.

For Enoch living as Poor Tom pushes Edgar back into the world, towards the realization of his own personal responsibility:

> That's the transformation. That's the agent in a way that gives you the Edgar at the end, who takes responsibility, who has to fight for what's his because he's lost it. But I think it's more than just he loses and then he has to get it back. He's transformed. There's a taking of responsibility with the Gloucester sequence, with the avenging his father's death and the duel. He has to be practical. The whole thing transforms him, makes him a man of action as opposed to someone who's on the back foot, getting pushed around because he's not cognizant enough [to know] that this is a dangerous world.

Edgar's growth from privileged youth to potential king comes at the end of the play, after Lear had died and Kent uttered his intention to follow his King. Enoch's Edgar took command with a gesture, stopping Mark Springer's Albany from following Kent off stage. Having been through his trials as Poor Tom, Enoch's Edgar was ready to take on the full weight of responsibility for the kingdom.

Women of colour in Shakespeare, 2016–2018

Women of colour have been largely under-represented on the Shakespearean stage, but by 2016 the traditional gender landscape was changing. Women were taking ownership of Shakespeare by playing traditionally male parts (see Rogers 2020a), which also provided more opportunities for women of colour in classical theatre. Sheila Atim, an actress of Ugandan heritage, joined Phyllida Lloyd's all-female trilogy of Shakespeare plays for the

Donmar Warehouse for their 2016 revivals. One of Atim's parts in the Donmar trilogy was a stereotypical servant, Lucius in *Julius Caesar*, but her other two cast the actress against stereotype: Lady Percy in *Henry IV* and Ferdinand in *The Tempest*.

Phyllida Lloyd framed her productions in a women's prison, the premise being that the prisoners were rehearsing Shakespeare's plays. This meant that the actors played two characters: their Shakespeare parts and a female prisoner. Adding a layer of further complexity to the concept, the female prison characters were pretending to be men when performing Shakespeare. Atim thrived on this aspect of Lloyd's concept:

> I was really happy because of what Phyllida was doing with the progression of each prison character throughout the trilogy. I had a nice track of playing Lucius, then playing Lady Percy, then playing Ferdinand. So my prison character's being promoted, as it were, through each play.

Atim enjoyed playing Lucius, who, of her three parts:

> was the most fun in terms of just playing a young boy. But also being the tallest member of the company, you know, so having to adopt this really floppy, stupid physicality to off-set that I'm pushing six foot.

Lady Percy was a different challenge, particularly within the context of an all female company:

> Because [Lady Percy is] the woman left at home and left in the dark and then, left to pick up the shit, you know, of [a] husband [that's] dead; she's got a baby, now [her father-in-law] wants to go and avenge [his son's death]. That was quite sad, actually, in terms of exploring women's pain generally, where you're in an all female company. So, as Shelia, I'm empowered, [but] as the character I'm not. And as my prison character, I'm not [empowered] because I'm in gaol, performing this piece for one night only; there's all these layers of femininity.

Ferdinand, the young, male lover of *The Tempest*, was Atim's favourite of the three. The heir to the King of Naples, Ferdinand is shipwrecked on Prospero's island. Thinking he is the only survivor, he falls in love with Prospero's daughter, Miranda:

> I had a lot of fun with Ferdinand and I found it quite difficult. Ferdinand has a lot of magic done to him and, also, the whole thing is just quite mad. They're on this island and then Ferdinand is in love and [he thinks] his dad is dead [from] this shipwreck. He's going through a lot.

A Black woman as Ferdinand also highlights one major issue of representation that women of colour continue to face, as Atim observes:

> Let's look at whiteness for a minute, having a white woman at the centre of the romantic story is still easier for us than having a Black woman. Most of the time it is a Black man and a white woman [on screen, e.g. *Line of Duty* (Lennie James), *Luther* (Idris Elba)]. We can deal with that in a way that we cannot deal with Black women being in love. We can't handle Black women being in love. We can handle them being sexual objects, and I think, for whatever reason, we can handle Black men being in love, even if the Black man scares us. And God forbid we should have two Black people being in love.

Playing Ferdinand was liberating for Atim because his storyline is about falling in love: 'It's about showing a non-turbulent scenario by which a person of colour is having a nice time in a relationship. It doesn't happen often.'

While Sheila Atim revelled in the rarity of playing a character in a romantic relationship, Martina Laird explored power dynamics across multiple Shakespeare productions. She played Petruchio for Custom/Practice in 2016 at the Arts Theatre in London's Leicester Square. Director Rae McKen crafted a gender-flipped *Taming of the Shrew*, as Laird explains:

> What we were doing was imagining a world where women were in charge. So the male parts were played by women, but as women. The power roles were still the same – Petruchio was still the power role – but she's now a woman. The sexual braggadocio of the character is now in a woman.

The cast explored gendered physicality by working against social norms: the women became expansive while the men were forced to take up less space. Laird describes the exercise:

> What was great and really interesting was the women enjoyed it, walking around with a largesse of ownership, and the men absolutely hated it because now they were in a world where they were being reduced.

What she found in Petruchio was:

> a very different kind of female sexuality and a confidence and a way of actually standing on the earth that's very rooted. Petruchio is not held back by social mores. He's not held back by politeness or in any way going to reduce the character to fit into anything. Petruchio walks around creating their own world – and I'm saying 'their' trying to be gender neutral because that's the possibility here. It's not just Petruchio. Once the

father has been replaced by a mother, etc. etc., you have the conspiracy of gender; one is not alone: if I try it as a woman now to be Petruchio-like, I would stand out.

Martina Laird also played Junius Brutus, one of two tribunes, in Angus Jackson's 2017 production of *Coriolanus* at the RSC. In Shakespeare's Roman tragedy, Junius Brutus and Sicinius Veletus are the spokespeople for the plebeians in the Roman Senate. In Jackson's production, they were both played by women, Laird and the white actress Jackie Morrison. Laird describes them:

> One of the things I felt worked for me was that the tribunes are written as outsiders to this power structure. They clearly have more of a comfortable access to that world than the rest of the citizens, so they're somewhere between the citizens and patricians. But they are still outsiders.

The parallels between Shakespeare's tribunes and contemporary female politicians became apparent to Laird playing Junius Brutus:

> They are women in this male-dominant world; we get it. And there's a brilliant piece by Jess [Phillips] – the MP – who's written about that, about being shushed in the Houses of Parliament as a woman and the things that we have to deal with. And, sure enough, in our play, the tribunes are shushed. Literally, shushed. Menenius shushes them.

The necessity also for Laird to negotiate racial politics and stereotyping when deciding to take the *Coriolanus* job is revealing of contemporary attitudes, including her reasons for deciding to play Junius Brutus, a choice her director allowed her to make:

> I took the gig because the tribunes are an important part of the machinations of the play. I thought it was better for me to play Brutus because Sicinius talks more and pushes the point more. And I felt that, being a Black woman, that that would disappear into the angry Black woman stereotype. Because Sicinius considers less and gets in there and stirs and agitates directly and is in your face... It's about the argument and the face-off. And I was concerned that, if an RSC audience saw a Black woman of substantial size doing that, that's all that they would see. They would not see the argument.

Perhaps most revealing about the rapid advances in integrated casting since 2012 is that Martina Laird became the first woman of colour to play the Countess of Roussillon in *All's Well That Ends Well*. Caroline Byrne's production was staged in the Sam Wanamaker Playhouse, the studio theatre at Shakespeare's Globe. The play itself explores class and gender, with the Countess playing a pivotal part in their deconstruction. The Countess's status as widow, landowner and aristocrat is most pertinent here, as women of colour are frequently perceived differently. Martina Laird explains her experiences with others' perceptions:

> Mainly as a foreign Black person, and especially as a Caribbean, a West Indian, I think that people can manage to see you in the lesser-status parts, which is why the Countess thing was so interesting. They can see you as lesser status because they can't conceive class difference within the accent. So I think, with a West Indian accent, people will just accept it easily that you're either being funny or you're being of a lower status.

For these reasons, Martina Laird feels that 'getting cast as the Countess was interesting and a move forward'. With women of colour still underrepresented in a male-dominated industry, it was a rare opportunity for a woman of colour to play a mature, regal woman who was neither comedic nor of low status.

Josette Simon, Cleopatra, RSC, 2017

Josette Simon returned to the RSC in 2017 to play Cleopatra in Iqbal Khan's production of *Antony and Cleopatra*, eighteen years after her last Stratford appearance. She had been offered the part before:

> The thing about it was that Cleopatra has come up – popped up – in my career, many, many, many times. The first time was when I had just left Central and somebody wanted me to play Cleopatra. I can't even remember where it was, a regional theatre. Someone who wanted me to play Cleopatra based on exotica. It wasn't the play. The play is mature passion. You've got to build up to Cleopatra. And they are people who have lived a life, she and Antony. You can't play it when you're twenty, twenty-two, whatever it was. And [that offer] was only based on the fact of me being Black and young and someone thought it would be an exotic idea. So that was a load of rubbish.

Simon's Cleopatra was a complex, intelligent and powerful woman whose existence was not defined by her love affair with Mark Antony. Josette Simon asks:

> Who says you can't be an extraordinarily sexual creature and not be a political person? Yes, she has all these extraordinary qualities, as we know, but she's a fearsome politician. She could not have been a sexy

flibbertigibbet and run a country on her own. She inherited a country that was going through very difficult times and transformed it into this vibrant, wealthy, healthy economy. I remember saying to Iqbal in rehearsal once, 'I realize that she's stronger than Antony.' She is much, much more powerful than Antony. No question in my mind. Cleopatra is far more powerful than Antony. She doesn't botch her death.

Kim F. Hall observes that Cleopatra, Queen of Egypt, is a disruptive figure who competes for 'a legitimate place in the imperial text and provokes the possibility of alternative dynastic structures that are not purely European' (1995: 153). These struggles were at the heart of Iqbal Khan's production, as he explains:

The play is about: Where is the capital of the world going to be? Is it going to be Rome or Alexandria? If Antony [and Cleopatra] had won and the capital was Alexandria, things would be very different now. If the east was the belly button of the world, rather than Rome, things would look very, very different now. Those states, that story is a massive story.

Amber James, who played Charmian and understudied Cleopatra, recalls the importance to the production of not defining the Egyptian queen solely through a traditional male, sexualizing gaze:

We talked a lot about Cleopatra being a politician, not just a nymph, slut, any of those things. She's fucking clever. Really clever and understands the world. If she had won that battle, our world would look completely different now. Because it would have been, can you imagine? If the Egyptians had conquered the Romans? Fucking hell, we'd be run by Africans. It would be a totally different world and she could have done it.

Shakespeare's women are often silent at key moments, and exploring the reason for Cleopatra's gave Josette Simon the key to unlock her as a politician:

The other thing is that, when things start going wrong with Antony, he starts to crack. I said to Iqbal, 'Do you know what I feel about her? She doesn't crack. She calculates.' Even in the midst of disintegration and everything falling down, everything going wrong, she doesn't crumble. Her mind immediately calculates: what's the best way to deal with this? Always. Always. Always. There's not once in that play, when everything's going wrong does she fall to pieces. She pretends to, in front of Octavius Caesar, but she doesn't. She's already thinking. Those cogs are always at play. She's amazing. She's remarkable. She's the finest politician. And she doesn't always get the credit for that.

For Simon, Cleopatra's strength enabled the Queen to meet death on her own terms:

> The thing about the soothsayer and the asp and the figs is that this is Plan B. Plan A was to kill themselves if they were stormed by the soldiers. Her plan was to kill herself and, if that didn't work, the two hand-women would do it. [They] would either give her their knives or they would stab her. That was Plan A. That went wrong. They didn't execute that. So we're into plan B. And must not blow Plan B. She wants to die her way, [she's] not going to do a botched job like Antony. She's got to find a way to engineer her having the death that she wants. She's never going to go with Octavius. Ever. What she has to do is make him believe that she might. Not even for a second would she entertain going with [Octavius Caesar]. But she has to make him believe that she's crumbled. It's all awful; she's rather pathetic, tears, and he goes off feeling that he has conquered the great Cleopatra.

'They never asked me'

Josette Simon was the first woman of colour to appear in an RSC Shakespeare, as well as the first to play a leading Shakespearean role with the company (chapter 3). These are exceptional achievements, but there is also collective industry-wide failure in the fact that, thirty-five years after her RSC debut, Cleopatra was her first leading role in a Shakespearean *tragedy*, not just at the RSC but anywhere. Josette Simon's Shakespearean stage career – which has encompassed *Love's Labour's Lost*, *Measure for Measure*, *A Midsummer Night's Dream* (all RSC) and Kate in *Taming of the Shrew* (Haymarket, Leicester) – exemplifies how performers of colour have been largely segregated into Shakespeare's comedies (chapter 7). The rarity of a woman of colour playing a tragic lead at the RSC itself also makes Josette Simon's appearance as Cleopatra in 2017 both unusual and extremely important on an institutional level. Before Simon's Cleopatra, only one woman of colour had played a leading role in a Shakespearean tragedy at the RSC: Anneika Rose as Juliet in 2008, nearly ten years previously.

Perhaps the most revealing aspect of this collective failure to nurture women of colour in the profession is Simon's answer to a question I asked about the long gaps between her RSC seasons: 'Did they just never ask you back?' Josette Simon replied:

> You're the first person to say that. Obviously one thing that came up again and again [in interviews about Cleopatra] was 'Why has it been eighteen years?' Up until the last interview that I did, which I think it was six months ago or something, and I answered that 'Oh, I'd done a lot of theatre and I wanted to do more films and TV.' I had been doing a lot of

films and TV, but that's not the whole reason it took eighteen years to go back to the RSC. And I got up and I thought: *Why am I lying? Why am I lying about this?* This was a few months ago. It was twelve years between Isabella and Titania and eighteen years between Titania and Cleopatra because they never asked me. I was never asked. That's why. The only reason I was back at the RSC was because Iqbal Khan [asked me]. Otherwise it would still be longer. I still wouldn't be there. And this is the first time I've been completely up front about it. I don't know why I've not been before. I don't know why. I think it probably was because I was still there, finishing the London season, so I thought, I don't know. But I'm not lying about it anymore. The reason I hadn't been there for eighteen years is simply because I hadn't been asked to be there.

Sheila Atim, Emilia, *Othello*, Shakespeare's Globe, 2018

Sheila Atim played Emilia in Claire van Kampen's multiracial production of *Othello* at Shakespeare's Globe in 2018. Along with Atim and André Holland's Othello, van Kampen cast Aaron Pierre as Cassio and two actors of colour as Chorus, Ira Mandela Siobhan and Micah Loubon. Atim created a nuanced reading of Emilia, responding to the text and to an on-stage society that included several people of colour:

> My Emilia was Black because I'm Black. I think she's very aware of the racial dynamics at play. Even though it's not written like that because it wasn't written Black, but I had to bring that into it. I couldn't not. For me, it wasn't colourblind casting.

Relationships within Shakespeare's plays are often key to building character, and one of the most important for Emilia is with Othello's wife, Desdemona. For Atim, the dynamic between herself and the white actress Jess Warbeck (Desdemona) was formative. Although the text is peppered with references to Emilia addressing Desdemona as 'Madam' Atim says:

> We made it much less hierarchical. Partly because we were very similar in age – Jess Warbeck and I were only a year apart – and we wanted it to be like we were mates. I'm still her lady-in-waiting; I still get her ready for bed, do all the duties. But we wanted it to be clear that we have genuinely become friends.

Emilia's other important relationship in the play is with her husband, Iago. Atim's view was that 'Iago and Emilia's relationship was deteriorating.

It's been a long time since he's really shown her any affection.' Casting an African-Caribbean woman as Emilia opposite the character in Shakespeare most associated with racist behaviours produced what Sheila Atim describes as 'a subtle dynamic in the Emilia–Iago relationship':

> I thought about this a lot and it's very interesting how confused people get by that dynamic and therefore make all these excuses. 'Oh, well, it can't be about racism because they're married.' How many women in this world marry misogynists? And end up in horrendously abusive relationships and stay in them? I think Iago's racism is incredibly potent and most definitely has an impact on their relationship. I just don't know if either of them [is] aware of it or aware of what it is. They maybe wouldn't be able to say, 'It's this.' They wouldn't be able to put the finger on it, but it's definitely there and I think actually it's inflamed by Othello's presence and by Cassio's presence and these formidable Black men. I think it's made worse by that and the fact that Emilia gets on with them. I think that's – I think that ignites feelings that maybe were lying dormant for Iago, maybe were being suppressed.

Because the cast also included several performers of colour, Atim was able to explore Emilia's relationship with two African-Caribbean men – Othello and Cassio – in a multifaceted way. She explains:

> So for me Othello was somebody who I really didn't want to fail, I really didn't want him to fail because he's representing all of us, you know, in a way. So our necks are on the line and actually one of the more devastating aspects of the ending is not just that he's killed her best friend; it's that he ruined [things] for [himself] and for all of us. 'You've exposed all of us as barbarians, and we're not' and 'You were supposed to be the one who would turn that around, would turn that stereotype on its head and emancipate us from that stereotype, and now you haven't, because you've killed your wife on the bed'. And similarly for Cassio, it's like 'You started this brawl in this bar! We can't do that. We're not afforded that space to do that!'

Atim was able to use these attitudes in her last scene, when Emilia discovers Othello has murdered Desdemona:

> In that final scene, Emilia uses some quite derogatory terminology, which is different when it's coming from a Black person. And how do you rationalize that? Well, you rationalize that because she is saying, 'This is what you wanted; you've made yourself this thing that they have been calling us for generations and now you've done it.' It's not that she endorses those words, it's that she's using them to make a point. My Emilia, because she's Black, she's using them to make a point: 'This is

you now; this is what you've done by doing this.' I think this is what I'm saying: it adds layers to the commentary if you have other people of colour within that world because then it can really show the nuance of how racism operates within the society and how we feel about it, not just about how white people feel about it.

Working on a play that is predominantly about racism in a majority white space also presented challenges:

> The presence of more ethnic minorities [in a production or rehearsal room] does not mean the absence of racism. I think the productions that try and engage with that do it well if they fully go the whole way and discuss that, rather than just 'Oh, no, we've got some other actors in now to give them a chance to have a go.'

The performers of colour in the cast did much of their work on the production's potential to have a wider conversation about race and racism outside the rehearsal room, absent from white practitioners who were reluctant to discuss the implications of van Kampen's integrated casting. Atim explains:

> We didn't get to talk about it in the room as much as I would have liked, but I did get to talk to those individual actors. I did speak to André [Holland (Othello)]; I did speak to Aaron [Pierre (Cassio)]; I did speak to Ira [Mandela Siobhan (Chorus)]; just because, when you're on your tea break, you have these conversations. You're automatically going to do that work because I cannot be involved in a scene and remove the racial aspect from it.

Troilus and Cressida, RSC, 2018

In January 2018 the RSC announced that its season that autumn would include Gregory Doran's production of *Troilus and Cressida*. What captured headlines was the appearance, for the first time at the RSC, of what the press release calls a 'gender-balanced cast'. Women played half the roles in Shakespeare's play, including the actress of Ghanian heritage Adjoa Andoh as Ulysses. She was the first performer of African-Caribbean descent and only the second performer of colour to play Ulysses in Britain, the second-largest part in the play.

Adjoa Andoh was fascinated by the play, and how it begins in the middle of the Trojan war. She told Varsha Panjwani:

> It's not a climactic play. It's a play about the grind of war. And it's about the little incremental shifts in position that people take. And what happens

when you've been stuck somewhere for a long time, the personal rivalries that happened, the internecine stuff that happens.

(Andoh 2021)

To facilitate this sense of being in the midst of battle, Doran set his production in what Theo Ogundipe, who played Ajax, describes as a '*Mad Max* type of world':

> I just found that fascinating, because it made so much sense to me. I think that kind of dystopian future that we look at in film [is] mirrored to the decline of a supposed civilization. [It's] where we'll find ourselves when it all unravels through our own dismantling, atomic-bombing [of] each other.

Framing *Troilus and Cressida* through a science fiction lens enabled both the fifty-fifty gender split and its multiracial cast, as the genre is not confined by naturalistic or historical conventions.

Although the press fixated on women playing Shakespeare's men, Doran's *Troilus* replicated the wider state of contemporary integrated casting in Britain, in microcosm. The casting included a mix of ethnicities that had not been seen in a mainstream Shakespeare production since Roger Rees' *Julius Caesar* at the Bristol Old Vic in 1987 (chapter 3). The twenty-four-strong cast had eight performers of colour (33 per cent of the cast) from African-Caribbean, south Asian and east Asian heritages. This inclusivity also lays bare continuing under-representation in Shakespeare production, as the cast included only one performer each of east Asian, southeast Asian and south Asian heritages.

The ethnic breakdown of Doran's *Troilus* cast also mirrors the levels of representation across the industry. An Equity study of prime-time television scripted drama and comedy programming in 2018 found on-screen representation to be overwhelmingly white. Picturing representation as a pyramid with white performers at the top, there is a clear racial hierarchy apparent in descending order: White (82 per cent), African-Caribbeans (9 per cent), south Asians (7 per cent), east Asians (1 per cent) and Middle Eastern North African (MENA) (1 per cent) (Rogers 2020b). As with contemporary television programming, east Asian and MENA representation across British Shakespeare has remained almost non-existent. Gabby Wong's appearance as Andromache and Antenor in Doran's *Troilus* was, therefore, both a milestone for east Asian Shakespeareans and indicative of their place at the bottom of the representation pyramid. There were no performers from MENA backgrounds in Doran's cast.

Doran broke stereotypes in his casting several of his six performers of African-Caribbean descent, including Geoffrey Lumb as Paris, both warrior and lover of Helen of Troy; and Ewart James Walters' Trojan patriarch, Priam, whose moral compass compels him to object to his son's council's decision to keep Helen in Troy by walking off stage in silent protest (2.2).

Out of all Doran's casting against type, however, Adjoa Andoh's Ulysses, a character of vast intelligence whose arguments drive Shakespeare's narrative, was most prominent. Andoh describes her character to Varsha Panjwani:

> Ulysses, they talk about him being a wily fox. So when I think of Ulysses, I always think of that snouty cunning. So Ulysses is the wily fox who has to try and shift this situation, not with force of arms, but by playing the psychological game, which he does, but he does a lot of manipulation about who's the best warrior, who's in love with whom, who wants what, to shift things. So I really enjoyed the cunningness and the strategizing of Ulysses.
>
> (Andoh 2021)

Amber James played Cressida for Gregory Doran, a character that has come to be associated with words such as unfaithful, wanton, whore and, perhaps the one most aligned with stereotypes of women of colour, prostitute. When Doran asked James to play Cressida, she was unfamiliar with the play and unaware of this baggage associated with the character:

> I went on Amazon to buy my copy and the comments were like 'adulterous woman'. I was like: hang on a minute! Let me go back [to the script]. My first experience of the play wasn't that. And then I started to read up on it and I was going 'Oh, okay, people have seen this as she's just a betrayer. And she just is fickle.' And I didn't see it like that.

Neither did Doran; according to James, both viewed Shakespeare's Cressida as a victim of war, rather than the stereotypical whore.[3]

Doran's casting of Theo Ogundipe as Ajax was arguably the director's most problematic decision for *Troilus*. Although the Ajax of myth is, as Ogundipe notes, an honourable warrior, Shakespeare makes him 'a bit of an idiot'. Shakespeare's deconstruction of this Greek mythical character also conforms to the false stereotyping of African-Caribbeans as lacking in intelligence. This did not escape Ogundipe:

> It wasn't lost on me that I wasn't thought of as Achilles. That wasn't lost on me. And, ironically, I've auditioned for Achilles before for something else on screen and didn't get it. I also am of the opinion that it takes an intelligent person to really adequately play Ajax. And I was intrigued by that challenge. But it wasn't lost on me that the first thought wasn't Achilles; it was Ajax. That wasn't lost on me. But you know we're on a journey with this whole [integrated casting] journey, hence your book.

---

[3] For more on the performance history of Cressida and how performers and directors have broken these stereotypes, or conformed to them, see Rogers (2013).

Ogundipe also felt that he was cast as Ajax because he had worked both at the RSC and with Doran before:

> I know that Greg knew I had comedic capability, so I don't think it was a personal dig in the sense that he didn't think I couldn't play Achilles or whatever. I just think he thought: *This is perfect for you because I've seen you do this kind of thing before. I've worked with you a few times now, I know you'd be perfect doing this.*

In pushing racial and gender boundaries, Gregory Doran's *Troilus and Cressida* reflected the state of integrated casting in 2018. Although it pushed boundaries in casting Andoh, in its casting breakdown via race and adherence to persistent stereotypes, it also conformed to the status quo. With all its complexities, however, the production illustrates how far integrated casting has come since 1966, while highlighting that there are many challenges remaining before British Shakespeare attains true equity.

Coda – 2019 ... and beyond?

In 2019 Shakespeare's Globe embarked on a year-long exploration of the history plays, beginning with *Richard II* co-directed by Adjoa Andoh and Lynette Linton. You may remember Table 18 (chapter 7, page 169), which illustrates the first time a performer of colour played the six largest parts in the play. It is worth turning back to view it now because three of those first castings occurred at the Globe with this 2019 production: Richard II (Adjoa Andoh), Duke of York (Shobna Gulati) and Northumberland (Indra Ové).

When *Richard II* began its run, Britain was about to take the unknown fork in its historical road, known colloquially as Brexit. Conversations about nationhood and who belongs to the group known as 'British' felt, in multiple ways, as if the country had returned to 1966. Then, Alf Garnett, played by the white actor Warren Mitchell, was the irascible central figure of Johnny Speight's popular BBC television comedy, *Till Death Us Do Part*.[4] Alf Garnett was a highly vocal opponent of the social change overtaking Britain in the 1960s. While Garnett's verbal repertoire included homophobic and sexist rants, it was his loudly espoused anti-immigrant views and his persistent use of racist epithets that are most pertinent here. While Alf Garnett was conceived as a character who would, as Speight asserted, 'make people

---

[4] The prolific American television producer, Norman Lear, bought the rights for *Till Death Us Do Part* and based the hit CBS comedy *All in the Family* on the British show. Alf Garnett was changed from a working-class man from the East End of London to a working-class man from New York City's Queens borough, Archie Bunker, played by Carroll O'Connor. The basic character had not changed as Archie Bunker also espoused racist and sexist views, but with an American accent.

realise how silly [racism] is' (qtd in Schaffer 2010: 461), the character also validated the opinions he expressed. In 2019 one real-life Alf Garnett, Nigel Farage, stoker of Brexit and espouser of anti-immigrant rhetoric, continued to advocate for an immigrant-less future, using coded language to hearken back to a, frankly, fictitious image of an England (for it *is* mainly England this conversation revolves around) populated only by white people.

The Adjoa Andoh-Lynette Linton *Richard II* was a statement of ownership, not only of Shakespeare but of Britain in 2019. Andoh remembers her meeting with the Globe's artistic director, the white performer Michelle Terry, in which she laid out her concept:

> And I said [to Terry]: 'Right, we're in the middle of this conversation about who is part of this nation, what it means to be a part of this nation [Brexit]. And I want to shake that conversation up. And the way I want to do it is I want to have a cast of all women of colour. And I want those women of colour to be women from every part of the globe that Britain colonized, because people from this island went somewhere else uninvited, did something there, made huge profits from their activities, and we've ended up having a relationship with this country.' And having a relationship is a very nice way of putting it, I suppose.
>
> (Andoh 2021)

Richard II was yet another historic Shakespeare production: the first with an all women of colour cast, including women from African, Caribbean, south Asian and east Asian heritages. Later that season, the Globe continued its history cycle and installed another woman of colour, Sarah Amankwah, as an English king: Henry V. She was the second person of colour to play the part in a major production in Britain, nearly twenty years after Adrian Lester's ground-breaking performance at the National Theatre. Six months later, these conversations around nationhood, identity and who owns Shakespeare stalled as the coronavirus pandemic hit Britain.

The progress that had been made in the further integration of British Shakespeare since 2012 now seems uncertain. As theatres have gradually re-opened, there have been indications that providing opportunities to performers of colour remains important to many decision makers. The season that re-opened Shakespeare's Globe in the summer of 2021 included a production of *Romeo and Juliet* directed by a woman of colour, Ola Ince, who cast Rebekah Murrell and Alfred Enoch as Juliet and her Romeo. It was, as Sheila Atim observes earlier in this chapter, that rare depiction of 'two Black people being in love'. At the RSC, Roy Alexander Weise's production of *Much Ado*, set to open in Stratford in February 2022, was announced in October 2021. It is another pairing of two African-Caribbeans playing leading characters in love: Akiya Henry and Michael Balogun as Beatrice and Benedick. Cush Jumbo also debuted as Hamlet in September 2021 – the first woman of colour and only the tenth performer of colour to play the part in Britain since 1930 – in a long-awaited production at the Young Vic that had been postponed due to the pandemic from July 2020. These seem to be the exception as the majority of Shakespeares staged in 2021 use the same, tired tropes in casting performers of colour: stereotypes, sidekicks, minor characters.

Few lessons seem to have been learned by theatres in the wake of George Floyd's murder in Minneapolis in May 2020, even though racial injustice has loomed large in wider socio-political conversations. For example, the white actor Ian McKellen led a company as Hamlet at the Theatre Royal, Windsor, whose racial diversity relied on stereotypes (Laertes) or was to be found in the play's minor characters (Marcellus, Guildenstern, Player Queen). The cast of ten at the Watermill Theatre for its *As You Like It* was 40 per cent minority ethnic, but only one was a lead part, Celia. With Celia's status as Rosalind's sidekick, it is hard to argue she has agency within much of the story. The RSC's *Comedy of Errors* also places its minority ethnic actors in either minor roles or parts, like Luciana, outside of what Cyril Nri describes as the 'intellectual kernel' of the piece.

The RSC compounds the marginalization of its performers of colour in *Comedy* with stereotypes in performance, most egregiously by costuming a British actor of African-Caribbean descent in African robes and having him speak with an African accent. This type of othering is common in contemporary television drama, which frequently segregates performers of colour in parts requiring them to play a foreigner (Rogers 2020b), but the practice's continued presence on television – and on the Shakespearean stage – reinforces the belief that people of colour are not British. This approach is also less dramatically interesting and has become as cliché as casting a performer of colour as Caliban in *The Tempest* or the Witches in *Macbeth*. As Patrick Miller observes:

> We're constantly being pushed back into a small box and that happens still in theatre. As you say, specifically casting people as slaves or whatever because that's the easiest thing to do. I think we were talking about it last night, but when Black actors are in productions, 'Oh do it with an African accent because that'd be more interesting and it'll place it.' Yes it does [place it], but I can do a Geordie accent, I can do Australian. And there are Geordies and Australians that happen to be this hue as well. So why not do that? That's as interesting. So the frame is quite small still, even now.

The narrow reference points – stereotypes – used in the casting and the audition process have been revealed, in a survey recently published by the Sir Lenny Henry Centre for Media Diversity, to be one of the most egregious sites of institutional racism in the industry (Rogers 2021b). Directors and those involved in casting are in desperate need of education and self-reflection, never more so than in the current moment as racial justice continues to dominate the headlines: 'Why is Laertes often played by African-Caribbean men? Is it because of the stereotypes of violence that, of all the other roles in *Hamlet*, I am casting Laertes this way?' or 'Why do I want this young, British actor of African-Caribbean descent to speak Shakespeare in a foreign accent?'

The productions of 2021 described above are redolent of diversity policies that are implemented without reflection: 'box-ticking'. Julie Spencer, currently the Interim Principal and Director of the School of Acting at ArtsEd, is one of a handful of people of colour in decision-making positions in the industry. She wants to see more 'gate openers' implementing real change. For Spencer, it's about empowering students – *all* students, regardless of gender, class, ethnicity – to tell their own stories and to own Shakespeare:

> It's not easy. It's hard work, but if people [in power] aren't telling the stories that you want to tell, then we can equip them [students], get them ready. So a lot of the work here that I'm writing is about putting in those professional practices sessions: this how you'd set up a company, who you'd speak to, what are the ten things that you need to set up telling your own story? Actor training can no longer be about the voice, but on top of that we've got to nurture desires to tell the stories they want to tell. Who you are, your archetype, whatever you are, whatever your casting is, that's very important, but also the fact is – and I feel that very strongly about working class actors and women and people of colour – is that they're not going to tell your story. They're [the decision makers] not interested. And why would you want them to tell your story? Why would you want a white middle-aged man to tell your story? [Your story is] equally as valid. You can tell your own stories. We can. That's how it's moving.

REFERENCES

All references to the works of Shakespeare are to the Arden Complete Works of Shakespeare. Where productions have cut or changed speeches, I have retained Arden's line numbering for the entire speech, but have quoted the promptbook or archive video directly.

All newspaper articles are cited parenthetically rather than listed in the References section.

Works cited

Akala. *Natives: Race and Class in the Ruins of Empire*. London: Two Roads, 2019.

Allam, Roger. 'The Duke in *Measure for Measure*', in *Players of Shakespeare 3: Further essays in Shakespearian performance by players with the Royal Shakespeare Company*. Eds. Russell Jackson and Robert Smallwood. Cambridge: Cambridge University Press, 1993.

Andoh, Adjoa. Interview with Varsha Panjwani. Women and Shakespeare podcast. 23 April 2021.

Bate, Jonathan and Eric Rasmussen, eds. *The RSC Shakespeare Complete Works*. New York: The Modern Library, 2007.

Beaton, Norman. *Beaton But Unbowed: An Autobiography*. London: Methuen, 1986.

Beauman, Sally. *The Royal Shakespeare Company: A History of Ten Decades*. Oxford: Oxford University Press, 1982.

Berkowitz, Gerald. '*King Lear*'. *Shakespeare Bulletin* 12 (3) (Summer 1994).

Billington, Michael. 'Mr. Robert Lowell on T.S. Eliot and the Theatre', in *Robert Lowell: Interviews and Memoirs*, ed. Jeffrey Meyers. Ann Arbor, MI: The University of Michigan Press, 1988.

Bourne, Stephen. *Black in the British Frame: The Black Experience in British Film and Television*. Second edition. London and New York: Continuum, 2001.

Brokaw, Katherine Steele. 'Ariel's liberty', *Shakespeare Bulletin* 26 (1) (Spring 2008).

Carpenter, Sandy and Alby James. 'Black and British Temba Theatre Forges the Mainstream: An Interview with Alby James'. *TDR* 34 (1) (Spring 1990).

Chakrabarti, Lolita. *Red Velvet*. London: Methuen Drama, 2012.

Chambers, Colin. *Black and Asian Theatre in Britain: A History*. London and New York: Routledge, 2011.

Cochrane, Claire. *The Birmingham Rep: A City's Theatre, 1962–2002*. Birmingham: Sir Barry Jackson Trust, 2003.

Cooke, Dominic. '*Pericles* in Performance: The RSC and Beyond', in *Pericles*, ed. Jonathan Bate and Eric Rasmussen. Basingstoke: Palgrave Macmillan, 2012.

Cooke, Lez. *British Television Drama: A History*. Second edition. London: British Film Institute Publishing, 2003.

Croall, Jonathan. *Performing King Lear: Gielgud to Russell Beale*. London: Bloomsbury Arden Shakespeare, 2015.

Croll, Doña. Interview with Varsha Panjwani. Women and Shakespeare podcast. 23 May 2020.

Dasgupta, Rana. *Capital: A Portrait of Twenty-first Century Delhi*. Edinburgh: Canongate Books, 2014.

DiBattista, Maria. *Fast-Talking Dames*. New Haven, CT and London: Yale University Press, 2001.

Duberman, Martin Bauml. *Paul Robeson*. London: The Bodley Head, 1989.

Eddo-Lodge, Reni. *Why I'm No Longer Talking to White People About Race*. London: Bloomsbury, 2018.

Equality and Human Rights Commission. *How Fair is Britain?: Equality, Human Rights and Good Relations in 2010*. 2011.

Evans, Nicholas M. 'Ira Aldridge: Shakespeare and Minstrelsy', in *Ira Aldridge: The African Roscius*, ed. Bernth Lindfors. Rochester, NY: Rochester University Press, 2007.

Eyre, Richard. 'On Directing *Richard III*', in *Le Tyran: Shakespeare Contre Richard III*. Eds. Dominique Goy-Blanquet and Richard Marienstras. Amiens: C.E.R.L.A. Amiens-Charles V, 1990.

Fenwick, Henry. 'The Production', in *BBC TV Shakespeare: Othello*. London: British Broadcasting Corporation, 1981.

Findlater, Richard, ed. *At the Royal Court: 25 Years of the English Stage Company*. London: Amber Lane Press, 1981.

Gaskill, William. *A Sense of Direction: Life at the Royal Court*. London and Boston, MA: Faber and Faber, 1988.

Goldberg, Susan. 'For Decades, Our Coverage Was Racist. To Rise Above Our Past, We Must Acknowledge It'. *National Geographic*. April 2018.

Gould, Michael. *The Biafran War: The Struggle for Modern Nigeria*. London and New York, NY: I.B. Tauris, 2013.

Griffiths, Trevor R. '"This Island's Mine": Caliban and Colonialism', in *The Yearbook of English Studies*, vol. 13, Colonial and Imperial Themes Special Number (1983).

Hall, Kim F. *Things of Darkness: Economies of Race and Gender in Early Modern England*. Ithaca, NY and London: Cornell University Press, 1995.

Hall, Kim F. '*Othello* and the Problem of Blackness', in *A Companion to Shakespeare's Works*, vol. 1. Eds. Richard Dutton and Jean E. Howard. Oxford: Blackwell, 2003.

Hall, Stuart. 'From Scarman to Stephen Lawrence', *History Workshop Journal* 48 (Autumn 1999).

Hartmann, Paul and Charles Husband. *Racism and the Mass Media*. London: Davis-Poynter, 1974.

Hibbard, George. 'Introduction', in *Love's Labour's Lost*. Oxford: Clarendon Press, 1990.

Hill, Errol. *Shakespeare in Sable: A History of Black Shakespearean Actors*. Amherst, MA: The University of Massachusetts Press, 1984.

Hingorani, Dominic. 'Tara Arts and Tamasha: Producing Asian Performance – Two Approaches', in *Alternatives Within the Mainstream: British Black and Asian Theatres*. Ed. Dimple Godiwala. Newcastle: Cambridge Scholars Press, 2006.

Hingorani, Dominic. 'Ethnicity and actor training: A British Asian actor prepares'. *South Asian Popular Culture* 7 (3) (2009).

Holden, Anthony. *Olivier*. London: Weidenfeld and Nicolson, 1988.

Holland, Peter. 'Shakespeare Performances in England, 1993–94', in *Shakespeare Survey 48*. Cambridge: Cambridge University Press, 1996.

Howard, Tony. '"My Travail's History": Perspectives on the Roads to *Othello*, Stratford-upon-Avon 1959'. *Shakespeare Bulletin* 28 (1) (Spring 2010).

Husband, Charles, ed. *White Media and Black Britain: A Critical Look at the Role of the Media in Race Relations Today*. London: Arrow Books, 1975.

Hytner, Nicholas. *Balancing Acts: Behind the Scenes at the National Theatre*. London: Jonathan Cape, 2017.

Igweonu, Kene. 'Talawa', in *British Theatre Companies, 1980–1994*. Ed. Graham Saunders. London: Bloomsbury, 2015.

Johnson, James Weldon. *Black Manhattan*. New York, NY: Atheneum, 1968 [1930].

Jones, James Earl. *Othello*. London: Faber and Faber, 2003.

Joseph, Paterson. *Julius Caesar and Me*. London: Methuen Drama, 2018.

Joshua, Harris and Tina Wallace. *To Ride the Storm: The 1980 Bristol 'Riot' and the State*. London: Heinemann Educational Books, 1983.

Kamaralli, Anna. 'Writing about motive: Isabella, the Duke and moral authority', in *Shakespeare Survey 58*. Cambridge: Cambridge University Press, 2005.

Kingsley, Ben. 'Othello', in *Players of Shakespeare 2*. Eds. Russell Jackson and Robert Smallwood. Cambridge: Cambridge University Press, 1988.

Kirwan, Peter. *Shakespeare in the Theatre: Cheek By Jowl*. London: The Arden Shakespeare, 2019.

Kissoon, Jeffery. 'Jeffery Kissoon discusses his all-black Hamlet'. *Theatre Voice* podcast. 31 October 2016.

Knox, Simone. 'Representations of British Chinese Identities and British Television Drama: Mapping the Field'. *Journal of British Cinema and Television* 16 (2) (2019).

Lindfors, Bernth, '"Mislike Me Not For My Complexion…": Ira Aldridge in Whiteface'. *African American Review* 33 (2) (Summer 1999).

Lindfors, Bernth. *Ira Aldridge: The Early Years, 1807–1833*. Rochester, NY: University of Rochester Press, 2011.

Lindfors, Bernth. *The Theatrical Career of Samuel Morgan Smith*. Trenton, NJ: Africa World Press, 2018.

Little, Ruth and Emily McLaughlin. *The Royal Court Theatre: Inside Out*. London: Oberon Books, 2007.

Makonnen, Atesede. '"Our Blackamoor or Negro Othello": Rejecting the Affective Power of Blackness'. *European Romantic Review* 29 (3) (2018).

Miller, Jonathan. *Subsequent Performances*. London and Boston, MA: Faber and Faber, 1986.

Newton, Darrell M. M. *Paving the Empire Road: BBC Television and Black Britons*. Manchester: Manchester University Press, 2011.

O'Hara, Helen. *Women vs. Hollywood: The Fall and Rise of Women in Film*. London: Robinson, 2021.

Olivier, Laurence. *On Acting*. London: Weidenfeld and Nicolson, 1986.
Oyelowo, David. *Henry VI, part I*. London: Faber and Faber, 2003.
Pines, Jim, ed. *Black and White in Colour: Black People in British Television Since 1936*. London: BFI Publishing, 1992.
Potter, Lois. *Othello*. Shakespeare in Performance. Manchester and New York, NY: Manchester University Press, 2002.
Quarshie, Hugh. *Second Thoughts About Othello*. Chipping Campden: Clouds Hill Printers, 1999.
Quarshie, Hugh. 'Is Othello a racist play?'. RSC. 9 August 2015.
Rogers, Jami. '*Twelfth Night*'. *Cahiers Elisabethains* 67 (1) (May 2005).
Rogers, Jami. 'The "Fascism and Its Consequences" Season: Richard Eyre's *Richard III* and Its Historical Moment'. *Shakespeare Bulletin* 30 (2) (Summer 2012).
Rogers, Jami. 'The Shakespearean Glass Ceiling: the State of Colorblind Casting in Contemporary British Theatre'. *Shakespeare Bulletin* 31 (3) (Fall 2013).
Rogers, Jami. 'Cressida in twenty-first century performance'. *Shakespeare: the Journal of the British Shakespeare Association* 10 (1) (2014).
Rogers, Jami. 'David Thacker and Bill Alexander: Mainstream directors and the development of multicultural Shakespeare', in *Shakespeare, Race and Performance: The Diverse Bard*, ed. Delia Jarrett-Macaulay. London: Routledge, 2016.
Rogers, Jami. 'Talawa and Black Theatre Live: "Creating the Ira Aldridges That Are Remembered": Live Theatre Broadcast and the Historical Record'. *Shakespeare and the 'Live' Broadcast Experience*, Eds. Pascale Aebischer, Susanne Greenhalgh and Laurie L. Osborne. London: Bloomsbury Arden Shakespeare, 2018.
Rogers, Jami. 'Women Playing Shakespeare's Men: Achieving Equality on the Twenty-first Century British Stage', in *The Palgrave Handbook of the History of Women on Stage*. Eds. Jan Sewell and Clare Smout. London: Palgrave, 2020. [2020a]
Rogers, Jami. *Diversity in Peak Broadcast Scripted Television: 2018: A report commissioned by Equity's Race Equality Committee*. London: Equity, 2020. [2020b]
Rogers, Jami. 'The British Black and Asian Shakespeare Performance Database: Reclaiming Theatre History', in *Shakespeare and Digital Pedagogy: Case Studies and Strategies*. Eds. Diana Henderson and Kyle Sebastian Vitale. London: Bloomsbury Arden Shakespeare, 2021. [2021a]
Rogers, Jami. 'Race Between the Lines: Actors' Experience of Race and Racism in Britain's Audition and Casting Process and On Set'. Birmingham: Sir Lenny Henry Centre for Media Diversity, 2021. [2021b]
Rokison-Woodall, Abigail. *Shakespeare in the Theatre: Nicholas Hytner*. London: Bloomsbury Arden Shakespeare, 2017.
Rosenthal, Daniel. *The National Theatre Story*. London: Oberon Books, 2013.
Ross, Karen. *Black and White Media: Black Images in Popular Film and Television*. Cambridge: Polity Press, 1996.
Sanders, Norman, 'Introduction', in *Othello*. Cambridge: Cambridge University Press, 1984.
Schafer, Elizabeth. *Ms-Directing Shakespeare: Women Direct Shakespeare*. London: The Women's Press, 1998.

Schaffer, Gavin. '*Till Death Us Do Part* and the BBC: Racial Politics and the British Working Classes 1965-75'. *Journal of Contemporary History* 45 (2) (April 2010).
Shirley, Frances A. *Shakespeare in Production: Troilus and Cressida*. Cambridge: Cambridge University Press, 2005.
Smallwood, Robert. 'Shakespeare Performances in England, 1998'. *Shakespeare Survey 52*. Cambridge: Cambridge University Press, 1999.
Solomon, Alisa. '"Look at History": An Interview with Zakes Mokae'. *Theater* 14 (1) (1982).
Thompson, Ayanna. 'Practicing a Theory/Theorizing a Practice: An Introduction to Shakespearean Colorblind Casting', in *Colorblind Shakespeare: New Perspectives on Race and Performance*. Ed. Ayanna Thompson. New York, NY and London: Routledge, 2006.
Thompson, Ayanna. 'To Notice or Not To Notice: Shakespeare, Black Actors, and Performance Reviews'. *Borrowers and Lenders: The Journal of Shakespeare and Appropriation* 4 (1) (2008).
Thompson, Ayanna. *Passing Strange: Shakespeare, Race and Contemporary America*. Oxford: Oxford University Press, 2011.
Thompson, Ayanna. 'Introduction', in *Othello*. London: Bloomsbury Arden Shakespeare, 2016.
Thompson, Ayanna. 'In conversation with Dawn Monique Williams', in *Shakespeare, Race and Performance: The Diverse Bard*. Ed. Delia Jarrett-Macauley. London: Routledge, 2017.
Van Dijk, Teun A. *Racism and the Press*. London and New York, NY: Routledge, 1991.
Vaughan, Virginia Mason and Alden T. Vaughan. 'Introduction', in *The Tempest*. Revised edition. London: Bloomsbury Arden Shakespeare, 2011.
Woudhuysen, Henry. 'Introduction', in *Love's Labour's Lost*. London: Bloomsbury Arden Shakespeare, 2014.
Yin, Winifred. *A Nightmare for a Century?: 'Two Gents' at Stratford*. Unpublished MPhil thesis. Birmingham: University of Birmingham, 1992.

Interviews with author

Atim, Sheila. 15 April 2019.
Ayola, Rakie. 11 February 2018 and 19 April 2019.
Bailey, Nicholas. 29 October 2019.
Bazely, Paul. 16 October 2019.
Bishop, Jeanmarie. 1 May 2018.
Chakrabarti, Lolita. 23 March 2018.
Dastor, Sam. 10 January 2020.
Enoch, Alfred. 8 February 2019.
Essiedu, Paapa. 24 August 2019.
Fearon, Ray. 7 December 2019.
Garven, Jamie. 1 May 2020.
Ghir, Kulvinder. 14 April 2018.
Griffiths, Marcus. 20 September 2017.

James, Amber. 15 August 2019.
Joseph, Paterson. 23 April 2020.
Khan, Iqbal. 7 October 2019.
Laird, Martina. 8 December 2017 and 4 January 2020.
Lester, Adrian. 23 November 2018.
Longmore, Wyllie. 1 February 2019.
Marcell, Joseph. 23 March 2018.
Miller, Patrick. 19 May 2019.
Nri, Cyril. 8 June 2018.
Ogundipe, Theo. 11 October 2017 and 5 October 2019.
Robinson, Patrick. 13 January 2020.
Rubin, Leon. 14 January 2019.
Sheen, Lucy. 26 August 2018.
Simon, Josette. 25 February 2019.
Simpson, Natalie. 25 September 2020.
Spencer, Julie. 15 April 2019.
Thacker, David. 16 March 2019.
Thomas, Ben. 6 May 2019.
Tyson, Cathy. 19 June 2019.
Verma, Jatinder. 20 May 2019.
Walker, Rudolph. 22 August 2019.
Watts, Graham. 5 November 2019.
Yip, David. 29 April 2019.
York, Daniel. 26 October 2018.
Zhangazha, Ashley. 23 August 2019.

Multicultural Shakespeare project interviews

Akinbode, Akintayo. Interview with author. 24 July 2015.
Alexander, Bill. Interview with Tony Howard. 28 May 2014.
Dumezweni, Noma. Interview with author. 24 September 2015.
James, Alby. Interview with Tony Howard. 4 July 2014.
Moodie, Tanya. Interview with author. 26 June 2015.
Msamati, Lucian. Interview with author. 9 July 2015.

INDEX

Aaron Davis Hall, Harlem 115
accents 13, 16, 21, 31, 46, 51, 84,
  90–1, 129, 159, 161, 166, 177,
  190, 191, 198–9, 205, 215, 216
Act For Change Project 187
actor training 13, 21, 22, 41, 76, 216
Adams, John 4, 5, 43, 116, 117, 119,
  183
Adams, Robert 7, 11, 12
Admirable Crichton, The 54
Ajao, David 181, 182
Akinbode, Akintayo 181
Akuwudike, Jude 148
Albany Empire 79, 80
Aldridge, Amanda Ira 8, 32
Aldridge, Ira 1–2, 3, 4, 5, 6, 7, 8, 12,
  15, 22, 46, 87, 139*n*
Alexander, Bill 60, 116, 117, 119, 129,
  130, 137, 138
Alexander, Roy 56, 82
All God's Chillun Got Wings 7
all white casts, *see* casting
Allam, Roger 73
Almeida Theatre 169, 173
Amankwah, Sarah 144*n*, 214
Andoh, Adjoa 144*n*, 169, 171, 176,
  210–1, 212, 213, 214, 216
Angadi, Darien 41
Ansorge, Peter 101
Angels in America 102
apartheid 34, 37
Armatrading, Tony 66, 67, 117
Aron, Pal 117, 137
Arts Council 5, 13, 76, 112, 187
Arts Theatre, London 203
Ashcroft, Peggy 8, 31
Attenborough, Michael 121, 124, 131
Attenborough, Richard 34, 62
Atim, Sheila 201, 202, 203, 208–10,
  214

audience, reactions to casting 6, 48, 63,
  67–8, 77–8, 80, 99–100, 106,
  107, 136, 138, 145
audition 15, 22, 27, 42, 43, 53, 58, 65,
  95, 97, 107, 112, 123–4, 125,
  129–30, 159, 160, 161, 168,
  189, 212, 215
Ayola, Rakie 3, 106–7, 108, 109, 111,
  117, 118, 119, 127, 129–30,
  131, 134, 137, 138, 199

Bahl, Ankur 173, 174
Bailey, Nicholas 124–6, 151
Bandele, Biyi 130, 132
Baptiste, Thomas 42, 43
Barber, Paul 71
Barbican Centre 52, 195–6
Barton, John 67, 172
Basquiat 193
Bassett, Linda 157
Batz, Michael 65
Bazely, Paul 112–4, 135, 159, 160–2
BBC 8, 12, 16, 20, 21, 23, 39, 40, 42,
  43, 49, 52, 61, 63, 65, 76, 93,
  97, 102, 126, 127, 160, 167,
  169*n*, 187, 198, 213
  BBC Television Shakespeare 39, 40
  dispute with Equity about casting
  Othello 39, 40, 42
Beadle-Blair, Rikki 138
Beale, Simon Russell 146, 184
Bean, Sean 68, 69
Beaton, Norman 27–30, 33, 34, 35, 42,
  47, 49, 51, 87, 94, 97, 101, 113,
  146, 151, 158
Behn, Aphra 1, 66, 67, 130, 132
Benito Cereno 27, 28
Bennett-Warner, Pippa 168, 169
Beresford, Stephen 160–2
Berry, Cicely (Cis) 68

Bhatt, Yogesh 86
Bhattacharjee, Paul 160, 161
Biafran War 28, 172, 175, 191
Birmingham Repertory Theatre 109, 116–20, 129, 130, 137–8, 183, 199
Black and White Minstrel Show, The 20, 39
'Black actor' 4, 5, 11, 12, 13, 39, 40, 42, 46, 47, 48, 51, 52, 54, 82, 96, 107, 117, 131, 136, 142, 149, 156, 163, 170, 171, 195
'Black canon' 33, 50, 53, 63, 64, 65, 93, 109, 111, 131, 145, 155
Black Macbeth, The 24, 31–2, 33, 80, 90
'Black part' 1, 38, 49, 50, 51, 52, 53, 56, 59, 64, 67, 78, 119, 151, 156, 165
'Black production' 82, 157, 189
Black Star 5
Black Theatre Live 197–9
blackface *see also* 'black up' 20, 39
'black up' 8, 19, 20, 33, 39, 46, 47, 64, 127
Blood Knot, The 25, 34
Bogdanov, Michael 128
Bovell, Brian 55, 56
Boyd, Michael 43, 44, 45, 46, 129, 130, 142, 144, 148, 173, 174
Boyle, Danny 98, 100
Branagh, Kenneth 59, 154, 155
Brewster, Yvonne 21, 35, 81, 83, 84, 87, 88, 90, 91
Brexit 17, 214
Brideshead Revisited 114
Bridewell Theatre, London 128
Bristol Old Vic Theatre 16, 44, 75–8, 107, 127, 173, 211
Bristol Old Vic Theatre School 53, 63, 142
British Black and Asian Shakespeare Performance Database 2, 3, 21, 154
British Empire 32, 46, 110*n*, 136
British Union of Fascists 114
Broadway 13, 15, 50, 52
'Bronze Age of *Othello*' 62
Brook, Peter 139, 140, 141, 142
Browne, Maurice 8

Bruce, Angela 56, 64
Buckhurst, Bill 184, 185
Buffini, Fiona 164, 169
Buffong, Michael 116, 199, 200
Burford, Priyanga 65
Bushell-Mingo, Josette 119, 163–4
Byrne, Caroline 204

Caesar, Burt 57
Caird, John 99
calypso 15, 16, 27
Carne, Rosalind
casting 6, 40, 41, 51, 52, 61, 74, 100, 107, 116, 117–8, 136–7, 147–8, 163
    actors' experiences of racism in 6, 51, 61, 103, 145, 151
    all white cast 66, 94, 110, 113, 132, 152, 163, 186, 187, 188
    see also characters, Shakespeare's
    colourblind 99, 107, 114, 115, 137–8, 157, 158, 208
    colour-conscious 137
    cross-cast 60, 132–3, 134, 137, 195
    cross-cultural 157–9, 162, 174
    directors and 38, 42, 60, 75, 86–7, 94, 95–6, 98, 99, 107, 116, 117–8, 123–4, 147–8
    'firsts' 9, 12, 13, 22, 24, 28, 31, 33, 37, 41, 42, 43, 46, 52, 53, 55, 56, 58, 60, 61, 63, 64, 65, 66, 69, 70, 76, 77, 78, 83, 84, 85, 87, 97, 98, 101, 102, 106, 113, 115, 117, 123, 124, 126, 128, 131, 132, 133, 136, 142, 144, 145, 146, 163, 169, 171, 173, 174, 180, 186, 195, 197, 199, 204, 207, 210, 213, 214
    gender-flipped 86–7
    inherited roles 39, 53, 95
    integrated 2, 10, 13, 17, 24, 27, 33, 37, 41, 43, 50, 51, 55, 57, 61, 66, 70, 74, 76, 81, 82, 94, 95, 119, 121, 122, 126, 141, 148, 151, 152, 156, 157, 158, 163, 168, 169, 179, 185, 188, 204, 210, 211, 212, 213
    integration 1, 6, 16, 19, 49, 90, 96, 119, 127, 151, 152, 197, 214

occupational segregation 156
resistance to integrated casting 55, 59–60, 68, 168
Central School of Speech and Drama 58, 91, 205
Chakrabarti, Lolita 5, 6, 88, 91, 113
Chance, Carlton 79
Channana, Raghaav 161
characters, Shakespeare's
  All's Well That Ends Well
    Countess of Roussillon 204–5
  Antony and Cleopatra
    Alexas 41
    Antony 22, 70, 71, 75, 95, 99, 139, 184
    Charmian 145, 206
    Cleopatra 68, 75, 78, 83, 84, 85, 128, 129, 131, 132, 205–7, 208
    Decretas 142
    Eros 83
    Iras 58
    Octavius Caesar 84
  As You Like It
    Celia 215
    Rosalind 101, 102–6, 111, 127, 128, 129
  Coriolanus
    Coriolanus 128, 139
    Junius Brutus 204
    Sicinius Veletus 204
    Tullus Aufidius 142
  Comedy of Errors, The
    Amelia 174
    Luciana 215
    Officer 174
  Cymbeline
    Iachimo 56
    Posthumus 56
  Hamlet
    Claudius 9, 183, 192, 198
    Fortinbras 107, 190, 191
    Gertrude 183, 192, 193, 198
    Guildenstern 215
    Hamlet 7, 8, 13, 39, 61, 70, 111, 112, 128, 138–42, 148, 155, 156, 157, 170, 184, 190, 192–4, 195, 197, 214, 215
    Laertes 94, 102, 111, 125, 137, 191, 215, 216
    Lucianus 107n
    Marcellus 102n, 190, 215
    Ophelia 130, 137, 191, 192, 193
    Player Queen 215
    Polonius 138, 141, 183, 190–1, 192, 193, 194, 196
    Rosencrantz 102n, 193
  Henry IV
    Henry IV 8, 9, 184
    Hotspur 52, 63, 99, 189
    Lady Percy 202
    Lord Hastings 52
    Sir Richard Vernon 52
  Henry V
    Boy 186
    Captain Jamy 148
    Chorus 186
    Henry V 113, 144n, 146–8, 184, 214
    Hostess 148
    Montjoy 148
    Queen Isabel 148
  Henry VI
    Duke of Gloucester 143n
    Duke of York 143n
    Earl of Warwick 143n
    Edward IV 143n
    Henry VI 142–4, 148, 184, 187, 195
    Joan la Pucelle 143n
    Talbot 143n
  Julius Caesar
    Brutus 78, 95, 119, 171, 173, 182
    Caius Ligarius 171
    Calphurnia 77
    Cassius 77, 171, 172–3, 173n
    Julius Caesar 77, 78, 171
    Lucius 38, 53, 54, 65, 171, 202
    Mark Antony 76, 107n, 156, 171, 183, 199
    Octavius Caesar 77
    Pindarus 53, 54, 63, 64
    Portia 77, 78, 171
    Soothsayer 113, 176
  King John
    Austria 188
    Constance 188
    King John 184

Melun 95
Pandulph 188
King Lear
  Albany 89
  Cordelia 88
  Duke of Burgundy 125–6
  Duke of Gloucester 88, 89
  Edgar 123, 200–1
  Edmund 87, 111, 113, 200
  Fool 89, 113
  Goneril 88, 199
  Kent 90, 111
  King Lear 1, 5, 8, 10, 11, 22, 35, 39, 70, 87, 88, 111, 139, 156, 157, 184–5, 199
  King of France 98, 99–100, 111, 125, 168, 200
  Oswald 98, 99
Love's Labour's Lost
  Berowne 9, 10, 59, 122
  Boyet 43
  Dumaine 98
  Longaville 123
  Rosaline 59–61, 74
Macbeth
  Banquo 32, 54, 55, 64, 66, 67, 68, 77, 99, 154
  Bloody Sergeant 66
  Lennox 41, 102*n*
  Macbeth 1, 7, 8, 31, 33, 34, 39, 70, 112, 116, 119, 126, 139, 154, 156, 157, 184
  Macduff 54, 55
  Malcolm 31, 32, 54, 55, 56, 115
  Ross 54, 55, 116
  Scottish Doctor 66
  Seyton 66, 79, 115, 153, 154
  Witch 19, 24–7, 29, 31, 33, 34, 37, 41, 58, 64, 130–1, 215
Measure for Measure
  Angelo 35, 51, 71–2, 87, 113
  Claudio 71, 73–4
  Duke 51, 71, 73–4, 113
  Isabella 51, 71–5, 99, 113, 128, 130, 131, 134, 208
  Juliet 107*n*
  Lucio 51, 113
  Mistress Overdone 165

Merchant of Venice, The
  Antonio 14*n*, 108, 199
  Duke 106–7
  Launcelot Gobbo, also Young Gobbo 49, 77
  Lorenzo 107, 145
  Nerissa 59, 63, 64, 82, 108, 109
  Portia 12, 20, 106–9, 111, 128, 129
  Prince of Morocco 12, 14, 49, 64, 74, 107–8, 111, 123, 145, 168
  Shylock 1, 6, 7, 8, 10, 12, 106–8, 111, 117
  Solanio 27, 106
Merry Wives of Windsor, The
  Fenton 38, 102
Midsummer Night's Dream, A
  Demetrius 101
  Egeus 113
  First Fairy 50
  Helena 49, 56, 64, 129
  Hermia 49, 64, 113
  Hippolyta 64, 107*n*, 113
  Lysander 64, 101, 102
  Moth 113
  Oberon 50, 51, 64, 113, 131
  Puck 43, 50, 51, 64, 65, 77, 101
  Theseus 56, 64, 113
  Titania 50, 51, 64, 107*n*, 131–2, 208
Much Ado About Nothing
  Beatrice 60, 78, 174, 176, 214
  Benedick 60, 155, 214
  Claudio 38, 94
  Conrade 41, 94, 155
  Don Pedro 9, 79, 154–5
  Hero 178
  Leonato 176
  Margaret 58
Othello
  Bianca 109, 165–7
  Cassio 165–7, 180–2, 208, 209, 210
  Desdemona 8, 20, 43, 126, 166, 179–80, 208, 209
  Emilia 180, 208–210
  Iago 8, 10, 11, 126, 165, 166, 178–9, 180–2, 208–9

INDEX

Lodovico 179
Montano 180, 181–2
Othello 1, 4, 6, 7, 8, 9, 10, 11,
   12, 13, 14, 15, 16, 19, 20,
   23–4, 27, 32, 37, 39, 40, 41,
   42, 43, 44, 45, 46, 47, 48, 49,
   51, 55, 56, 62, 63, 64, 70, 95,
   97, 98, 102, 111, 113, 117,
   119, 122, 123, 126, 127, 131,
   132, 138, 139, 144, 145, 148,
   156, 157, 166, 178, 179, 180,
   181, 182, 183, 184, 208, 209
Roderigo 38
Pericles
Gower 15, 95–6, 122, 158
Marina 123, 158
Pericles 158
Richard II
Aumerle 169
Bolingbroke 8, 9, 169
Duke of York 169, 213
Exton 38
Groom 169
John of Gaunt 169
Mowbray 169
Northumberland 169, 213
Queen Isabel 169
Richard II 144n, 169, 184, 213
Richard III
Catesby 95
Duchess of York 114
Edward IV 114, 143n
First Murderer 113
Lord Lovel 113
Marquess of Dorset 113
Richard III 1, 7, 68, 113, 184
Tyrrell 113
Romeo and Juliet
Friar Laurence 80
Juliet 78, 80, 82, 83, 115, 119,
   145, 151, 207, 214
Mercutio 122, 124, 145
Paris 79
Potpan 37
Romeo 37n, 56, 68–9, 70, 79,
   82, 97, 101, 119, 122, 124,
   131, 139, 145, 214
Tybalt 66, 67, 68, 122
Taming of the Shrew, The

Kate 131, 207
Petruchio 203–4
Tempest, The
Antonio 57, 117
Ariel 27, 28, 29, 30, 33, 35, 51,
   57, 87, 93, 94, 107n, 111,
   117, 118, 119, 129, 133
Caliban 28, 29, 30, 33, 44, 57,
   63, 75, 93, 94, 111, 117, 118,
   215
Ceres 28, 93
Ferdinand 57, 102, 123, 174,
   202, 203
Iris 28, 93
Juno 28, 93, 174
Miranda 57, 78, 102n, 107n,
   117, 119, 174, 202
Prospero 22, 28, 30, 33, 56, 57,
   111, 117, 118, 119, 133
Timon of Athens
Alcibiades 134
Apemantus 134
Philotus 173
Poet 134
Timon 184
Titus Andronicus
Aaron 1, 49, 52, 63, 119
Titus Andronicus 139, 184
Troilus and Cressida
Achilles 87, 212–3
Ajax 211–3
Andromache 98, 100, 211
Cressida 87, 100–1, 212
Diomed 86
Hector 87, 135
Helen of Troy 86, 211
Paris 135, 211
Patroclus 98, 100
Priam 135, 211
Thersites 86
Troilus 101, 124n, 135, 144, 184
Ulysses 87, 210, 212
Twelfth Night
Antonio 110
Curio 53, 109, 110, 173, 174
Fabian 38, 109, 110
Feste 109, 110, 160–2
Malvolio 9, 109, 110, 160
Orsino 102, 109, 110, 137, 160

228   INDEX

Olivia 109, 110, 111, 161
Maria 109, 110, 111, 174
Sebastian 109, 110, 137, 161
Sir Andrew Aguecheek 110, 160, 161, 162
Sir Toby Belch 109, 110, 116, 183
Valentine 109, 110
Viola 109, 110, 137, 160
Two Gentlemen of Verona, The
　Julia 164–5
　Lucetta 163–5
　Outlaw 52
　Silvia 41, 164*n*
　Sir Eglamour 41
　Speed 38, 39, 43, 50, 163
　Valentine 39, 163
Winter's Tale, The
　Antigonus 158
　Autolycus 65
　Camillo 157, 158
　Cleomenes 52
　Dion 158
　Dorcas 66
　Florizel 101, 102, 125
　Hermione 65, 77, 157
　Leontes 9, 65, 157
　Paulina 56, 157
Charles Doran Shakespeare Company 8
Cheek By Jowl 102–6, 174
Chekov, Anton 159, 160, 161
Chester Gateway Theatre 63
Chinese Detective, The 76
Churchill, Caryl 159
Civil Rights Movement 28, 39
Clarke, Sharon D. 80
Clauzel, Nigel 122
'closed shop' 34, 42, 47, 146
Coard, Bernard 141
Coe, Peter 24, 31–2, 33, 80, 90
colonial past, Britain's *see also* imperialism 28–9, 32, 57, 85, 90, 93–4, 118
colour bar 7, 11, 13
colourblind, *see* casting
colour-conscious, *see* casting
Coleridge, Samuel Taylor 62
Company (Donmar Warehouse 1995) 136–7

conflict, *see* stereotypes
Connaught Theatre, Worthing 27
Connor, Edric 15, 96
Contact Theatre, Manchester 70–1, 75
Cooke, Dominic 157–9
Coventry Theatre 1, 2
Cox, Brian 113
Croft, Michael 63
Croll, Doña 82–3, 85, 91, 127–8
Cooke, Winston 102
critics, *see also* reviews, racism in 9, 14, 25–6, 30, 31, 32, 47–8, 55, 61, 74–5, 82, 90–1, 99, 106, 127, 138, 144, 145, 161, 196
　Agate, James 9
　Barber, John 30, 31, 46, 61
　Bayley, Clare 128
　Berkowitz, Gerald 90, 91
　Billington, Michael 28, 65, 84, 93, 117, 127, 148, 149
　Boycott, Rosie 166–7
　Coveney, Michael 46, 106
　Evans, Gareth Lloyd 16
　Gore-Langton, Robert 144
　Gross, John 161
　Holland, Peter 90–1
　Hoyle, Martin 54–5, 63
　Hurran, Kenneth 99
　Husband, Stuart 156
　Kingston, Jeremy 74, 129, 144
　Levin, Bernard 14
　Lewis, Peter 26, 30
　Lister, David 148
　Marcus, Frank 32
　Nightingale, Benedict 141
　Norris, Fred 138
　Osborne, Charles 99
　Peter, John 74, 126
　Shorter, Eric 64, 78
　Shulman, Milton 26, 27, 30, 144
　Smallwood, Robert 129
　Spencer, Charles 127, 157
　Thornber, Robin 75
　Trewin, J. C. 11, 14, 55
　Wallace, Pat 14
　Wardle, Irving 31, 91
　Woddis, Carole 127
cross-casting, *see* casting

cross-cultural productions 16, 31–2, 51–2, 144–6, 157–62
Crucible, The 49
Cry Freedom 34
cultural appropriation 15, 16, 33, 51, 90
Cumberbatch, Benedict 196
Cusack, Sinead 153
Custom/Practice 203

Dacre, James 188
Dalton, Timothy 52
Daniels, Ron 50, 57, 171
Dastor, Sam 113, 132, 133–4, 169
Davies, Howard 58
de Jersey, Peter 102, 135, 142
de la Tour, Frances 130
de Molina, Tirso 98, 100
de Souza, Edward 113
Dear, Nick 98, 100
Debayo, Jumoke 19, 25, 26, 37
Deep Are the Roots 13
Deer, Evroy 88
Derby Playhouse 107n
Desmond's 101
Dexter, Felix 65
Dexter, John 95, 182
Dhiendra 77
Diamond, Jeff 91
Dickens, Charles 54, 62
Dixon, Anthony 102n
Doll's House, A 84
Domingo, Anni 56
Donmar Warehouse 136–7, 156, 168, 169, 202
Donnellan, Declan 102–6
Don Quixote 195
Doran, Gregory 130, 132, 134, 171, 172, 174–5, 210–3
Drake, Fabia 62
Dromgoole, Dominic 184, 186
Dubhey, Neha 161
Dumezweni, Noma 129, 130–1
Dunlop, Frank 41

East is East 160
education, *see also* actor training 22, 141, 181, 190
Ejiofor, Chiwetel 156, 165, 167

Elba, Idris 203
Elias-Rilwan, Joy 198
Eliot, T. S. 124, 132
Elliott, Marianne 155
Emmanuel, Alphonsia 57, 128
Emperor Jones, The 7
Empire Road 43, 44
English Shakespeare Company 94, 128
Enoch, Alfred 173, 200–1, 214
Equality and Human Rights Commission 155
Equity 39–42, 43, 50, 61, 63, 66, 97, 121, 126, 187, 211
    dispute with the BBC over casting *Othello* 39–42
    television diversity study 40, 211
Espejel, Inigo 81
Essiedu, Paapa 189–90, 192–4, 195, 196, 197, 198
Euba, Femi 19, 25, 26, 37
Everyman Theatre, Liverpool 56, 123, 128, 131
exoticism *see* stereotypes
Eyre, Richard 112–5, 125–6, 159
Eziashi, Maynard 158

Family Reunion, The 132
Farr, David 173
Fearon, Ray 70, 98, 101, 102, 111, 122–4, 125, 131, 132, 154, 172
Feast, Michael 124
Fiennes, Ralph 101, 144, 184
Flannery, Peter 95
Fleetwood, Kate 157
Flesh to a Tiger 24
Folger Theater, Washington, D.C. 185
football 16, 23, 41, 152
Forbes Robertson prize (RADA) 133
Fortune-Lloyd, Jacob 180–2
Fresh Prince of Bel-Air, The 182
Fugard, Athol 25, 34, 62

Game of Thrones 185
Gandhi 62
Gardnier, Kenneth 106, 110n, 111
Garven, Jamie 106–9, 111, 145
Gaskill, William 24–5, 29, 33, 34
genres, *see* Shakespeare, William: Comedies, Histories, Tragedies

George, Jenni 50, 66, 67
Ghaggar, Gurdip Singh 80
Ghir, Kulvinder 79–80, 160, 161
Gielgud, John 10, 21, 31, 124, 126
glass ceiling 3, 24, 37, 52, 83, 93, 97, 120, 129, 131, 149, 151, 154, 155, 173, 187
Godwin, Simon 189, 191, 193, 195, 196
Golden Girls 59, 60
Goldberg, Whoopi 126
Goold, Rupert 168, 169
Gordon, Trevor 66, 67
Grandage, Michael 165–6, 167, 168, 169, 186, 188
Grant, Cy 15–6, 42
Great Expectations 54
Griffiths, Marcus 171, 175, 189, 191
Guildhall School of Music and Drama 167, 170, 171
Gulati, Shobna 169, 213
Guinness, Alec 24, 31
Guthrie, Tyrone 9, 12, 136

Hackney Empire, London 196
Hale, John 15–6
Hall, Nell 28
Hall, Peter 37n, 94, 112–3, 156
Hammond, Mona 31, 81, 89, 91
Hampstead Theatre 25, 44
Hands, Terry 61–2, 81, 96, 98, 123
Harewood, David 71, 82, 91, 111, 126–7
Harlem Globetrotters 40
Haroun and the Sea of Stories 133, 159–60
Harris, Yvette 51, 113
Harrison, John 50, 65, 133
Haworth Shakespeare Company 115–6, 154
Haymarket Theatre, Basingstoke 145, 183
Haymarket Theatre, Leicester 56, 64, 75, 207
Heath, Gordon 13, 42
Heath, Marcus 106
Henriques, Pauline 163
Henry, Lenny 187
Hicks, Greg 69
Hill, Errol 13, 133

Hingorani, Dominic 112–4
His Dark Materials 151
Hoare, David 84
Holder, Ginny 117, 119
Holder, Ram John 77–8, 116
Holland, André 208, 210
Hollander, Tom 104n
Holm, Ian 125
Holman, Clare 164
Hopkins, Anthony 39
Hunt, Marsha 113
Hutson, Martin 137
Hytner, Nicholas 71–5, 98, 99, 146–8, 173, 179–80
Hyu, Paul Courtenay 107, 145

Ibsen, Henrik 84, 159
Igawa, Togo 66, 67
Ijinle Theatre Company 25
immigrant 17, 19, 21, 27, 30, 52, 89, 90, 124, 141, 166, 213–4
immigration 14, 16, 19, 20, 23, 26, 27
imperialism 8, 26, 28, 180, 206
Indigo 74
inherited roles, *see* casting
integrated casting, *see* casting
institutional racism 7, 13, 17, 97, 158, 207, 215
'intellectual kernel' 33, 93–4, 158, 215
Irons, Jeremy 67
Irvine, Adrian 125
Israel, Solomon 174
ITV 20, 114, 186
Iwuji, Chuk 144n

Jackson, Angus 204
Jackson, Barry 166
Jacobs, Kemi-Bo 65
Jacobs, Olu 113
Jaffrey, Raza 160
James, Alby 52, 81–2, 91, 163
James, Amber 206, 212
James, Emrys 171–2
James, Lennie 203
James, Oscar 37, 54, 58, 61, 80, 135
Jeeves and Wooster 20, 114
Jefferson, Thomas 62
Jeremiah, Ivanno 175
John, Errol 13, 14, 16, 22, 24, 42, 46, 145

Johnson, Caroline 66, 67, 116
Johnson, James Weldon 4
Jones, James Earl 39, 40, 42, 49, 50, 97, 126
Joseph, Paterson 3, 69, 98–101, 102*n*, 124*n*, 144, 151, 171, 177

Kae-Kazim, Hakeem 63, 74, 113, 116
Kalipha, Stefan 51, 56, 113
Kani, John 175
Kant, Immanuel 62
Karim, Scott 180
Kean, Edmund 4, 62
Kennedy, Jonathan 198
Khan, Iqbal 175–7, 180–2, 205–6, 208
Kiendl, Teddy 79–80
King, Rowena 98
King, Shelley 86
Kingsley, Ben 2, 37, 58, 61–3, 98, 138
Kissoon, Jeffery 31, 32, 55, 63, 71, 78, 111, 113, 117, 119, 171, 197–8
Kitt, Eartha 84–5
Kumalo, Alton 37–9, 41, 42, 43, 53, 54, 58, 59, 61, 80, 97, 163, 173
Kushner, Tony 102
Kwei-Armah, Kwame 2, 187
Kyle, Barry 59–60

Laird, Martina 165–7, 203–5
Lamb, Charles 62
largest roles *see also* leading roles 10*n*, 28, 51, 55, 56, 63, 67, 95, 119, 143, 153, 155, 157, 169, 186, 188, 210
Larmour, Brigid 70, 75
Last Days of Don Juan, The 98, 100
Latchmere Theatre 83
Lawrence, Stephen 17
Lawson, Samantha 151
Laye, Dilys 69
leading roles *see also* largest roles 8, 9, 10, 20–1, 23, 40, 42, 48, 51, 55–7, 58, 69, 70, 81, 82, 83, 87, 95, 109, 113, 115, 116, 117, 120, 123, 124, 127, 128, 129, 131, 144, 151, 153, 154, 157, 158, 172, 174, 186, 188, 207, 214, 215
  definition 10*n*, 143*n*, 153, 186

League of Coloured Peoples 12
Leeds Playhouse 50, 65, 75, 133
Lesser, Anton 157
Lester, Adrian 2, 5–6, 101–6, 111, 126, 136–42, 144*n*, 146–9, 179–80, 214
Library Theatre, Manchester 22, 125
Lickorish, Vicky 64
Life and Adventures of Nicholas Nickleby, The 62
Lim, Bronwyn Mei 145
Lindo, Delroy 126
Linton, Lynette 213, 214, 216
Lion and the Jewel, The 25
Littlewood, Joan 43
Liverpool Playhouse 160
Livesey, Roger 33
Llewellyn, Suzette 110
Lloyd, Phyllida 201, 202
Lockhart, Calvin 63
Loh, Daniel York 63, 77, 107*n*, 145–6
London 2012 Olympics 17, 173
London Academy of Music and Dramatic Art (LAMDA) 22, 65, 66, 69, 125, 142, 153, 163
London Actors Theatre Company 115
London Bubble 129
Longmore, Wyllie 3, 5, 21–2, 27, 55, 70, 75, 95
Loubon, Micah 208
Love Thy Neighbour 44
Lumb, Geoffrey 211
Lyon, Julian 107*n*
Lyric Theatre, Hammersmith 43, 45

McCabe, Richard 117, 134
McFarlane, Cassie 50
McFarlane, Colin 63
McGregor, Ewan 166, 167
McKellen, Ian 113, 125, 159, 215
McKen, Rae 203
McNamara, Desmond 115
Macowan, Michael 9
Mahoney, Louis 37, 58, 61, 121, 124
maids, *see* stereotypes
Malik, Art 54, 56
Malvern Festival Theatre 19, 23, 24, 27, 37, 178
Mannoni, Octave 28, 30

Marcell, Joseph 4–5, 39, 42–3, 45–6, 50, 54, 56, 63, 95, 97, 116, 182–6, 188
Martin, Shereen 160
Marlowe, Christopher 123
Marshall, Herbert 5
Master Harold … and the Boys 34
Matshikiza, John 54, 116
Mendes, Sam 98, 100–1, 126–7, 136, 137
Mephisto 165
Mercury, Freddie 78
Mercury Theatre, Colchester 63
Mermaid Theatre 24, 27–30
Messina, Cedric 39, 40, 41
Mirren, Helen 37
Miller, Jonathan 20, 24, 27–30, 33–4, 51, 56–7, 77, 87, 93–4
Miller, Patrick 102*n*, 115–6, 198, 199, 215
Mirodan, Vladimir 122
Mistry, Rohinton 133
Moby Dick 124
Mokae, Zakes 19, 25, 34–5, 37
Mona Lisa 165
monkey, *see* stereotypes
Monroe, Carmen 81
Moodie, Tanya 127, 188, 192, 198
Moon on a Rainbow Shawl 14, 24
Mosley, Oswald 114
Mountview Theatre Club 22
Moving Theatre 145, 173*n*
Moyheddin, Zia 37*n*
Msamati, Lucian 157, 158, 180–1
Mu-Lan Theatre Company 144–6
Murder in the Cathedral 53, 124
Murphy, Gerard 67
Mydell, Joseph 66, 67, 157–8, 169

Nathanial, Miriam 28
National Front 16, 55
National Geographic 32
national identity 84, 90–1, 114–5, 118, 136, 143–4, 146, 148, 159, 186, 198–9, 213, 214
National Student Drama Festival 53, 142
National Theatre 10, 35, 39, 51, 67, 78, 87, 90, 94, 95, 101, 102, 112–5, 119–20, 122, 125–7, 133, 134–6, 143, 146–8, 154, 158, 159–60, 162, 167, 173, 178, 179–80, 185, 196, 214
National Youth Theatre 63, 74, 113, 125
NBC 182–3
Negro Arts Theatre 12
Neil, Aaron 137
Newman, Paul 126
Nevada Shakespeare Company 34
Niles, Sarah 9
Noble, Adrian 94–5, 131, 134, 153
Noble, Cecilia 102*n*, 148, 174
Noel Coward Theatre 186
Norfolk, Mark 197
Northcott Theatre, Exeter 43
Northern Broadsides 31
Northumberland Theatre Company 110*n*
Nottingham Playhouse 102
November, Steve 186
Nunn, Trevor 50, 52, 81, 97, 134–6, 186, 187–8
Nri, Cyril 33, 53–4, 83–4, 93–5, 97, 101, 142, 158, 171–3, 175–8, 189, 190–1, 196, 215

occupational segregation, *see* casting
Octagon Theatre, Bolton 5
Odeke, Anne 65
Odyssey, The 96
Ogundipe, Theo 176, 189, 190, 211, 212–3
Ogura, Toshie 107*n*
Okonedo, Sophie 163, 169*n*
Old Vic Theatre 9, 10, 12, 14, 84, 93–4, 112, 124, 133, 145
Olivier, Laurence 15, 16, 19–20, 21, 22, 31, 39, 90, 124, 125, 133, 146
Omere, Ivy 128–9
Oroonoko 1, 130, 132–3
Orphan of Zhao, The 187
Osoba, Tony 41
Osuagwu, Abraham 113
'other', *see* stereotypes
'othering', *see* stereotypes
Out of Joint 154

outsider, *see* stereotypes
Ové, Indra 113, 169, 213
Oxford Stage Company 102, 118, 123
Oyelowo, David 132, 142–4, 148–9, 187

Paines Plough 4–5, 43
Palace Theatre, Newark-on-Trent 8
Palace Theatre, Watford 198
Parish, Diane 88, 91, 118
Patarot, Hélène 145
Patel, Bhasker 115–6
performers of colour *and*
  depiction as foreigners 16, 84, 159, 162, 177, 199, 215, 216
  erasure 2, 3, 4, 6, 11, 76
  exclusion 10, 12, 13, 14, 15, 16, 20–1, 30, 31, 32, 33, 38, 39, 40, 42, 46, 51, 52, 66, 70, 74, 76, 78, 84, 91, 94, 97, 103, 111, 114, 122–3, 132, 138, 144, 151, 152, 153, 156, 158, 186
  limitations placed by society 6, 82, 156–7, 167
  marginalization of 2, 22, 67, 159, 199, 215
  opportunity, lack of *or* limited 13, 14, 22, 27, 30, 34, 35, 38, 39, 40, 44, 51, 54, 76, 80, 109, 120, 128, 129, 145, 158, 167, 187, 198
  racism, experience of 68, 75, 78, 82, 99–100, 103, 122, 158, 168
  underestimation of the abilities of 127, 141–2, 177–8, 196
Phillips, Anthony 110
Phoebus Cart 107*n*
Phoenix Theatre, Leicester 16
Pierre, Aaron 208, 210
Pimlott, Steven 124, 130
Plantagenets, The 95
Plouviez, Peter 39, 40
Porter, David 43
postcolonial 28–9, 32, 57
Pownall, David 4, 5
Powell, Enoch 16
Pride and Prejudice 22
Primary Colors 126
prostitute, *see* stereotypes

Pryce, Jonathan 69, 153
Public Theater, New York City 39

Quarshie, Hugh 52–3, 54, 56, 63, 66–8, 74, 81, 97, 99, 124, 125, 156, 178–9, 189
Queen 78

race relations 19, 56, 75, 182
Race Relations Act (1965) 19
racism 3, 6, 7, 8, 13, 15, 16–7, 20, 25–7, 28, 33, 34, 58, 61, 62–3, 68, 74, 75, 78, 80, 82, 99–100, 103, 108, 117, 122, 126–7, 138, 143–4, 145, 158, 165, 168–9, 178, 179, 209–10, 213–4
  and attitudes to integrated casting 58, 59, 60, 68, 74, 75, 138, 143–4, 145, 168
  in Britain 3, 6, 13, 15, 16–7, 19, 28, 143, 213–4
  critics and 8, 14, 16, 25–7, 55, 61, 74, 75, 78, 90–1, 99, 126–7, 144
  institutional racism 7, 13, 17, 58, 97, 111, 158, 207, 215
Ramsay, Alasdair 145
Rayne, Stephen 115, 116
received pronunciation (RP), *see also* accents 21, 31, 32, 84, 90–1, 177, 190
Reckord, Lloyd 24
Red Velvet 5–6
Redgrave, Vanessa 68, 71
Rees, Roger 37–8, 41, 57, 59, 75–8, 80, 173*n*, 211
Resnick 160
reviews, racism in 8, 14, 16, 25–7, 55, 74, 75, 78, 90–1, 99, 126–7
Richardson, Ralph 8, 21
Richardson, Tony 15
Richmond, Doyle 42, 54, 102
Ridley, John 23–4
Rigby, Terence 159
Riverside Studios 107*n*
Robeson, Paul 7–8, 12, 13, 15, 32, 42, 46, 178
Robinson, Patrick 65–70, 94, 97, 101, 116, 124*n*, 153–5
Romans, The 50

Rose, Anneika 207
Rose, Jason 54
Rose Bruford College of Speech and Drama 21–2, 37, 91, 122, 131
Rose Theatre, Kingston 186, 187
Ross, Dorothy 28
Ross, Ricco 56–7
Roundhouse Theatre 24, 31–2
Rover, The 66–7
Royal and Derngate Theatres, Northampton 188
Royal Academy of Dramatic Art (RADA) 6, 13, 82, 91, 101, 127, 133, 168, 188
Royal Court Theatre 19, 24–7, 44, 81, 122
Royal Court Writers' Group 24
Royal Exchange Theatre, Manchester 5, 53–4, 56, 75, 82, 102, 123, 125
Royal Hunt of the Sun, The 134
Royal Shakespeare Company (RSC) 37–9, 46, 50, 52–4, 57, 58–63, 65–70, 71–5, 76, 78, 80, 81–2, 93, 94–6, 97–101, 102, 113, 115, 116, 119–20, 121–4, 125, 126, 128, 129–34, 136, 142–4, 148, 153–5, 156, 157–9, 163–5, 170, 171–8, 180–2, 184, 185, 187, 189–196, 198, 204, 205–8, 210–3, 214, 215
Royalty Theatre, London 1
RP, *see* received pronunciation
Rubin, Leon 75–6, 77
Rudman, Michael 51, 84, 90, 158, 159
Rushdie, Salman 133, 159

Saba, Sirine 132
Saddler, Howard 173*n*
Sapani, Danny 111
Savoy Theatre, London 8, 32, 178
School For Scandal, The 116, 123
Scott, Margaretta 12
Scofield, Paul 39, 51, 127
Section 28
Sergeant Musgrave's Dance 49
Seth, Roshan 113
servants, *see* stereotypes
Shaffer, Peter 134

Shakespeare and Company, Lenox, Massachusetts 50
Shakespeare Memorial Theatre 4, 11, 15, 87*n*, 169
Shakespeare Theater, Washington, D.C. 183
Shakespeare, William
  All's Well That Ends Well 204–5
  Antony and Cleopatra 15, 22, 41, 58, 70–1, 75, 82–5, 112, 128–9, 130, 131, 142, 145, 152, 183, 205–8
  As You Like It 101, 102–6, 112, 113, 127, 128, 129, 152, 215
  see also characters, Shakespeare's
  Comedies 38, 52, 101, 109, 153, 207
  Comedy of Errors, The 15–16, 98, 174, 215
  Coriolanus 39, 96, 112, 142, 204
  Cymbeline 54, 56, 94, 113, 195–6
  Hamlet 9, 43, 57, 59, 61, 102*n*, 107*n*, 111, 112, 115, 125, 130, 137, 138–42, 148, 152–3, 155, 183, 189–94, 195–6, 197–8, 216
  Henry IV 8, 52, 202
  Henry V 59, 146–8, 186, 188
  Henry VI 95, 142–4, 148, 185–7
  Histories 38, 52, 53, 94–5, 144, 148, 153, 169, 185–9, 213–4
  Julius Caesar 17, 38, 53, 54, 64, 65, 74, 75–8, 80, 100, 107*n*, 113, 125, 171–5, 177–8, 182, 183, 189, 199, 202, 211
  King John 95, 154, 155, 184, 188
  King Lear 11, 50, 79, 87–90, 98, 111, 113, 123, 125–6, 155, 168–9, 182–5, 195, 197, 199–201
  Love's Labour's Lost 9, 10, 43, 59–61, 98, 112, 122, 123, 128, 207
  Macbeth 19, 24–7, 29, 31–2, 34, 37, 41, 54–5, 56, 58, 64, 66, 67, 68, 77, 79, 80, 90, 102*n*, 109, 112, 115–6, 119, 130, 152, 153–5, 215
  Measure for Measure 14, 35, 51–2, 56, 67, 71–5, 77, 84, 87, 90,

107n, 113, 128, 129–30, 134, 158, 165, 207
Merchant of Venice, The 7, 8, 12, 14, 15, 27, 49, 59, 64, 74, 77, 82–3, 106–9, 111, 112, 123–4, 129, 145, 168–9, 199
Merry Wives of Windsor, The 38, 102
Midsummer Night's Dream, A 43, 49, 50–1, 52, 56, 64, 66, 77, 101, 102, 107n, 109, 113, 129, 131–2, 152, 207
Much Ado About Nothing 9, 17, 38, 41, 58, 60, 79, 94, 98, 112, 113, 154–5, 174–5, 177, 178, 214
Othello, see also characters, Shakespeare's: Othello 11, 14, 19, 20, 22, 23–4, 37, 38, 39, 40, 42–8, 49, 51, 54, 56, 61–3, 64, 95, 97–8, 102, 109, 112, 117, 119, 126–7, 131, 146, 156–7, 165–7, 178–82, 208–10
Pericles 15, 95–6, 122, 123, 157–9
Richard II 8, 10, 38, 66, 98, 112, 144n, 169, 184, 213–4, 216
Richard III 1, 27, 59, 95, 112–5, 159, 183, 184, 186
Romeo and Juliet 37, 38, 41, 56, 66, 67, 68–70, 79–80, 81–2, 97, 109, 119, 121–2, 124, 131, 144–6, 152–3, 156, 214
Taming of the Shrew 203–4, 207
Tempest, The 22, 24, 27–30, 33, 35, 51, 56–7, 58, 75–6, 87, 93–4, 102, 107n, 109, 111, 112, 113, 117–20, 123, 128, 129, 133, 138, 152, 174, 202, 215
Timon of Athens 131, 132, 133–4, 173
Titus Andronicus 1, 49, 52, 119
Troilus and Cressida 39, 77, 85–7, 91, 98, 100–1, 134–6, 210–3
Twelfth Night 9, 38, 53, 102, 109–11, 116–7, 137, 152, 160–2, 173–4
Two Gentlemen of Verona 38, 39, 41, 43, 50, 52, 163–5, 169
Two Noble Kinsman, The 67

Winter's Tale, The 9, 52, 56, 65, 66, 77, 94, 102, 112, 113, 125, 157–9
Tragedies 23, 38, 39, 139, 152–3, 155–7, 183, 207
Shakespeare's Globe 10, 65, 78, 144n, 154, 169, 171, 173, 184–5, 188, 205, 208–10, 213–4
Sharma, Madhav 80
Sheen, Lucy 21–2, 77–8, 107n
Shelley, David 129
Sher, Antony 68, 130, 146
Sherlock Holmes 50
Sherman Theatre, Cardiff 106–9, 129
Shodeinde, Shope 65, 77
Show Boat 8
Shylock X 27
Sibtain, Joplin 122, 180
sidekick, *see* stereotypes
Simon, Josette 57, 58–61, 71–5, 106, 122, 127, 131–2, 205–8
Simpson, Natalie 191–2, 193
Sinden, Donald 39
Singer 95
Singhateh, Faz 137, 148
Siobhan, Ira Mandela 208, 210
Siva, Rohan 148
Skriker, The 159
Slaughter City 96
slavery 1, 20, 62, 76, 130, 132
slave 27–8, 33, 62, 63, 74, 215
Slowe, Georgia 82
Smith, Clarence 98, 99–100, 168, 192, 196
Smith, Samuel Morgan 7, 12, 46, 139n
Society for Theatre Research 122
Sofaer, Abraham 7, 8–11, 12, 87n, 169
Sondheim, Stephen 136
Sowole, Raphael 197–8
Soyinka, Wole 24–5
Speight, Johnny 213
Speak of Me as I Am: a Conversation with Ira Aldridge 5
Spencer, Julie 83, 98–101, 115, 216
Spender, Stephen 95
Springer, Mark 135, 148
St. George's Theatre 169
Statements After An Arrest 62
Steele, Janet 79

stereotypes 13, 15, 23, 27, 28–9, 31, 32, 33, 34, 38, 39, 41, 42, 47, 53, 54, 55, 56, 60, 64, 65, 82, 83, 93, 94, 100, 101, 112, 113, 131, 135–6, 141–2, 145, 149, 154, 163, 164–7, 174, 179, 180, 200, 204, 209, 211, 212, 213, 215, 216
- 'angry black' *see also* aggressive 47, 82, 204
- aggressive 82
- casting against stereotype 54, 56, 65, 100, 101, 106–7, 142–3, 202, 211
- conflict 134, 157
- criminals 55, 101, 142
- 'exotic' *or* exoticism 27, 32, 33, 55, 64, 65, 125, 175, 205
- 'feisty' 166, 167
- intelligence 23, 47, 141, 212
- maids 59, 60, 65, 82–3, 163–5, 198
- messengers 15, 38
- monkey 165, 168
- 'native' 28, 30, 32, 33
- 'noble savage' 32, 135
- 'other' 20, 25n, 51, 64, 91, 119, 125, 162
- 'othering' 51, 136, 215
- outlaw 52, 200
- outsider 103, 113, 155, 178, 200
- primitive 8, 29, 32, 50, 179
- prostitute 65, 109, 165, 167, 198, 212
- savage 29, 32, 33, 135, 179, 209
- servants 13, 15, 22, 30, 38–9, 41, 50, 52, 53–4, 58, 60, 63, 83, 94, 97, 99, 109, 110, 111, 124, 163–5, 171, 174, 178, 202
- sidekick 155, 215
- slave 27–8, 33, 63, 215
- subservience 29, 33, 39, 53, 55, 56, 111, 205
- supernatural 25, 33
- token 155
- violence 27, 113, 143, 216
- witch *or* witchcraft 19, 25, 29, 31, 32, 33, 41, 58, 64, 131, 151, 215

Stewart, Patrick 52, 184
Stock, Mildred 5
Stokes, Simon 115
Straker, Peter 51, 77, 113, 173n
Such A Long Journey 133
'suitable roles' *see also* 'Black part' 21, 23, 24, 29, 39, 41, 49, 51, 52, 61, 65, 78, 96
Supple, Tim 133–4
Syal, Meera 174
Sylvester, Suzan 123
Sylvestre, Cleo 41

Talawa Theatre Company 80, 81, 82–85, 87–91, 197, 199–201
Tales from Ovid 133
Tamburlaine 123
Tara Arts 5, 80–1, 85–7, 91, 148
Taste of Honey, A 21, 22, 49
Temba Theatre Company 80, 81–2, 91, 163
Terera, Giles 188
Terry, Michelle 214
Thacker, David 30, 44, 46–7, 54–5, 95–6, 97, 122, 123, 129, 134, 163, 164
Thatcher, Margaret 44, 102
Theatr Clwyd, Mold 113
theatre criticism, *see* reviews, racism in
Theatre Royal, Gravesend 7
Theatre Royal, Stratford East 102
Theatre Severn, Shrewsbury 154
Theatre Workshop 43
Thomas, Ben 84, 87–8, 90, 91, 111
Thomas, Heidi 74
Thomas, Trevor 113
Till Death Us Do Part 213
Tobias and the Angel 41
Toomey, Patrick 104n, 106
token, *see* stereotypes
training, *see* actor training
Trials of Brother Jero, The 25
Tricycle Theatre 3, 5
Trotter, Stewart 43
Tull, Walter 23
Tynan, Kenneth 13
Tyson, Cathy 57, 109, 128–9, 165

Uhiara, Ony 158
understudy 52, 68–70, 97, 101, 124, 130, 131, 136, 144, 164*n*
United! 23

van Kampen, Claire 208, 210
Varla, Zubin 119
Verma, Jatinder 80, 85–7, 148–9
verse speaking 10, 12, 13, 14, 15, 16, 27, 31, 32, 41, 46, 47, 63, 74, 78, 84, 96, 113, 122, 129, 139, 141, 145, 172, 177
violence *see* stereotypes
Visnevski, Andrew 56
Volpone 132

Walcott, Derek 96, 123
Walford, Glen 56–7
Walker, Rudolph 20–1, 22–4, 27–8, 29–30, 37, 42–4, 46–8, 49, 51–2, 54, 55, 56, 63, 75–6, 93, 95–6, 97, 122, 134, 158, 178
Wallace, Naomi 96
Walter, Harriet 130
Walters, Ewart James 50, 171, 191, 192, 211
Warbeck, Jess 208
Warner, Deborah 94, 95, 113
Warrington, Don 56, 199
Washington, Denzel 155
Watts, Graham 68, 69
Webber, David 90, 91, 111
Welsh College of Music and Drama 106
West, Timothy 77

'whiting up' *see* whiteface
White, Willard 97–8, 131*n*
whiteface 1, 5, 6, 13, 22, 68, 86
whiteness 62, 114–5, 135, 137, 140, 157, 158, 203
Whyman, Erica 65
Wieth, Mogens 14
Wilkinson, Tom 160
William Poel Prize 122
Wilson, Snoo 58
Wilson, T-Bone 55
Wirthner, Naomi 131
Wolfit, Donald 8, 11, 88
women of colour 64, 65, 81, 83, 94, 109, 127–31, 165, 201–5, 207, 212, 214
Wong, Denise 107*n*
Wong, Gabby 211
World Shakespeare Festival (WSF) 173, 174
Woyzek 78
Wrede, Caspar 14
Wringer, Leo 50, 65, 77, 95, 111
Wyndham's Theatre 13

Yip, David 41–2, 76, 77, 107*n*, 144
Yorick Theatre Company 56
York, Susannah 115
Young Vic Theatre 2, 41–2, 44, 46–8, 54–5, 56, 63, 76, 77, 82, 107*n*, 215
Yugoslavia, civil war 85–6

Zengeni, Brigid 164–5
Zhangazha, Ashley 167–8, 169–70, 186

www.ingramcontent.com/pod-product-compliance
Lightning Source LLC
Chambersburg PA
CBHW050350230426
43663CB00010B/2069